Teac.

VOICES of FREEDOM

English and Civics for U.S. Citizenship

FOURTH EDITION

Bill Bliss

WITHDRAWN FROM
SAN DIEGO COUNTY LIBRARY

PEARSON
Longman

*Dedicated to Benjamin and Flora Bliss, Nathan and Sophia Bliss, and
Nat and Betty Meister.*

The cooperation of U.S. Citizenship and Immigration Services,
Washington District Office, Fairfax, Virginia, is gratefully acknowledged.

Voices of Freedom: English and Civics for U.S. Citizenship, Teacher's Guide Fourth Edition

Copyright © 2010, 2002, 1994, 1989 by Prentice Hall Regents
Pearson Education, Inc.
All rights reserved.
No part of this publication may be reproduced, stored in a retrieval system, or transmitted in any
form or by any means, electronic, mechanical, photocopying, recording, or other without the prior
permission of the publisher.

Pearson Education, 10 Bank Street, White Plains, NY 10606

Editorial director: Pam Fishman
Vice president, director of design and production: Rhea Banker
Director of electronic production: Aliza Greenblatt
Manager of electronic production services: Warren Fischbach
Director of manufacturing: Patrice Fraccio
Senior manufacturing buyer: Dave Dickey
Prepress buyer: Ray Keating
Marketing director: Oliva Fernandez
Production editor: Diane Cipollone
Assistant editor: Katherine Keyes
Development editor/Photo coordinator: Mary Perrotta Rich
Senior digital layout specialist: Wendy Wolf
Text and cover design: Wendy Wolf

Photo Credits
Cover: Shutterstock and Getty Images, Inc./Purestock.
Illustrations: Richard E. Hill

ISBN 0-13-813159-7
ISBN 978-0-13-813159-3

Pearson Longman on the Web
PearsonLongman.com offers online resources for teachers and students. Access our Companion
Websites, our online catalog, and our local offices around the world.

Visit us at pearsonlongman.com.

Printed in the United States of America
9 10 – V092 – 14

CONTENTS

TO THE TEACHER   v

A   Personal Information ★ Identification Cards ★ Alphabet ★ Numbers   2

B   Personal Information ★ Months of the Year ★ Dates   16

1   Maps & Geography ★ States & Capitals
★ Famous U.S. Landmarks ★ U.S. Territories   26

2   The Flag   38

3   Branches of Government   46

4   The Senate ★ The House of Representatives ★ The President
★ The President's Cabinet ★ The Supreme Court   56

5   Types of Government & Economy ★ The Rule of Law
★ Federal & State Government ★ Public Officials
★ The Constitution ★ The Bill of Rights   74

6   Native Americans ★ Christopher Columbus ★ Discovery ★ Colonization   88

7   The Revolutionary War ★ The Declaration of Independence   100

8   The Constitution ★ The 13 Original States ★ The Federalist Papers
★ Benjamin Franklin ★ Branches of Government
★ The Bill of Rights ★ George Washington   116

9   The War of 1812 ★ The National Anthem ★ Expansion ★ Wars in the 1800s
★ The Civil War ★ Abraham Lincoln ★ Amendments   134

10   Industrial Revolution ★ Labor Movement ★ Immigration
★ 20th-Century History ★ Civil Rights Movement ★ September 11, 2001   150

11   National Holidays ★ U.S. Presidents   166

12   Citizens' Rights ★ Citizens' Responsibilities
★ Participating in Our Democracy ★ The Oath of Allegiance   176

APPENDIX   190

WORKSHEETS   191
Writing Practice   193
Reading Practice   207
Civics Practice   221
Interview Practice   233
Worksheets Answer Key   279

TEACHER'S RESOURCES   283
Needs Assessments: Pictorial & Checklist   285
Pre/Post Assessment Forms A & B   289
Pre/Post Assessment Answer Key   293
Student Name List Mask   295
Project Activity Observation Checklist   296
Performance-Based Assessment Records   297
Technology Enrichment   311

TO THE TEACHER

Welcome to the fourth edition of *Voices of Freedom*! The new full-color edition prepares students for the civics and English requirements of the new U.S. citizenship test and features activities designed to promote civic participation. The text also serves as a basic course for students in EL/Civics programs. It is designed for students at low-beginning, beginning, and low-intermediate levels whose limited language skills prevent them from using standard civics materials.

The text simultaneously develops students' civics knowledge and basic English skills. It introduces the required government and history topics through a research-based sequence of lessons that integrate a carefully controlled progression of grammar and vocabulary. This fourth edition includes many features specifically designed to prepare students for the new citizenship test and to promote active participation in class and in the community:

- Students practice the 100 official civics test questions throughout the text.
- Interview dialogs and civics test dialogs prepare students to communicate successfully during their appointment at the U.S. Citizenship and Immigration Services (USCIS) office.
- Unit tests include the required civics questions and the specific reading and writing test formats used in the citizenship exam.
- A new illustrated test-preparation section in the appendix walks students through the step-by-step procedures they will follow and the types of questions they will answer during their appointment at the USCIS office.
- Audio CDs included with the student text contain all readings, dialogs, the 100 civics questions, and listening comprehension activities.
- Civic participation activities include projects, issue discussions, and "online field trips" that enrich learning, promote student teamwork, and meet EL/Civics program goals.

In addition to the civics curriculum, *Voices of Freedom* prepares students to handle the give-and-take of interview questions about information on the N-400 citizenship application form since this is the basis for the USCIS officer's assessment of English language ability. This preparation includes critically important functional interview skills—communication strategies such as asking for repetition, asking for clarification, checking understanding, hesitating, and correcting.

Throughout the text, students also have many opportunities to share information about their native countries. In this way, *Voices of Freedom* aims to give respect and attention to each student's country,

history, and culture as the student learns about the government, history, and civic life of the United States.

INSTRUCTIONAL FORMATS AND ACTIVITIES

Voices of Freedom lessons contain the following types of activities:

Vocabulary Previews: Picture dictionary lessons at the beginning of each unit introduce key vocabulary in a clear, easy-to-use format.

Readings: Basic information about government, history, and civics is introduced through short readings that are accompanied by one or more photographs. The readings are designed for high readability by low-level students. They are printed in large-size type, each sentence appears on a separate line, and there is very generous spacing between lines and between paragraphs.

Interview Dialogs and Civics Test Dialogs: Conversation practice activities provide students with authentic examples of the communication that occurs between a USCIS officer and a citizenship applicant during the interview. These dialogs cover a wide range of topics, including personal identification, personal information about background and family, and question-and-answer exchanges about government, history, and civics. The interview dialogs provide crucial practice since an applicant's English speaking ability is assessed through the normal course of the interview.

Check-Up Exercises: Workbook-style activities provide intensive skills practice in grammar, vocabulary, reading, and writing. Students need little or no teacher instruction or supervision to do these activities, so they are appropriate as homework or for use in class.

Civics Checks: The 100 official civics test questions are presented throughout the text in a chart format that enables students to easily practice alone or with a partner. Since many questions have multiple acceptable answers, students can choose to practice a single answer or to become familiar with alternative answers to a question.

Listening Exercises: Many units contain a listening activity, most of which require students to listen carefully for questions that sound the same or might otherwise be easily confused. Students learn to listen closely to avoid mistakes they might make during an interview due to their misunderstanding of a USCIS officer's question. All listening exercises are included on the Audio CDs. For the teacher, scripts for the listening exercises appear at the back of the textbook and in the Teacher's Guide.

"Questions & Answers" Activities: Unique lessons offer students important practice with the multiple ways a question might be posed by a USCIS officer. Students first study various ways that a particular question might be worded, and then they practice asking and answering questions with other students. In this way, students will not only know the answers, they will also "know the questions."

Review Lessons: At the end of many units, students do one or more review exercises. These serve to review the content of the unit and to cumulatively review content introduced earlier. Two unique formats for review activities are the "Information Exchange," in which students interview each other and record information collected during the interviews, and the "Talking Time Line," in which students match events with their dates, write the events on a time line, and then practice asking and answering questions based on the information.

Unit Tests: An assessment at the end of each unit evaluates student achievement of the learning objectives while developing the specific test-taking skills required for success during the English and civics exam. Each test contains the following: the official civics questions and answers that relate to a unit's content; a vocabulary activity in which students complete civics facts with words from the USCIS writing vocabulary list; and a reading and writing section where students read the types of questions and write from dictation the types of sentences that appear in the USCIS test. (Note: There are no multiple-choice items on the unit tests because that test-item format isn't used in the new citizenship exam.)

Unit Summaries: Lists of key unit vocabulary, grammar structures, and functional expressions appear at the end of each unit and serve as a convenient resource for review.

Civics Enrichment Activities: Activities at the end of each unit promote students' active participation in class and in the civic life of the community.

CIVIC PARTICIPATION ACTIVITIES bring civics instruction alive by involving students in local government through visits to city hall and representatives' offices, attendance at local government or school board meetings, and classroom visits by local officials.

PROJECT ACTIVITIES enable students to work together in teams or as a class to decorate bulletin boards with civics content, create local maps, simulate an Election Day in class, or have a Thanksgiving celebration.

COMMUNITY ISSUES DISCUSSIONS encourage students to apply civics content to their own lives, to identify issues and problems related to their well-being in the community, and to brainstorm solutions.

DEBATES organize students into teams, each team taking one side of an issue and arguing positions in front of the class.

INTERNET ACTIVITIES use online resources to take virtual field trips to historic places, to visit the websites of government officials, and to do simple web-browsing tasks to find information.

The expanded Appendix provides several valuable resources:

On the Day of Your USCIS Interview, a helpful information section, reminds students about what they should bring to their appointment and offers practice checking in at the USCIS office.

The **English Speaking Test Prep** section prepares students to communicate successfully during all phases of their citizenship interview and exam—very important since the USCIS officer will evaluate the student's English speaking ability during the course of the interview. This section helps students practice how to greet the officer, how to engage in small talk while walking to the interview room, and how to provide or verify personal information that appears on the citizenship application. Students also learn how to ask for repetition and how to ask the officer to paraphrase a question they don't understand. This section also provides important practice with the challenging "Part 10" questions on the application form—the "Have you ever" questions that include difficult vocabulary and ask about sensitive subject matter such as criminal background, failure to pay taxes, and other issues that can jeopardize an application for citizenship.

Reading and Writing Test Prep sections provide the official vocabulary lists for the USCIS reading and writing tests. USCIS does not provide sample sentences for the tests, but these pages offer students practice with possible test sentences that appear in the textbook lessons.

The **100 Civics Test Questions** appear in a convenient chart format for easy review. The official USCIS English and Spanish versions of these questions and answers are presented side by side. Other language translations are available at www.uscis.gov.

The appendix also includes a comprehensive **Index** and a **Correlation Key** that provides a convenient reference for integrating the civics curriculum with lessons in English language programs including *Side by Side Plus*, *Word by Word*, and *Foundations*.

LOW BEGINNING-LEVEL STUDENTS

For students who are low-level beginners, the first two preparatory units of *Voices of Freedom* provide a basic foundation in English communication and literacy. The units introduce or review the alphabet, numbers, and basic vocabulary and expressions through the context of personal identification skills, in a sequence that is appropriate for low beginners. The easy exercise formats are designed to give these students a feeling of immediate success and momentum in their study of English and Civics. Students who already have some basic understanding of English can skip these preparatory units and begin their studies with Unit 1.

TEACHER'S GUIDE LESSON INSTRUCTIONS

Each teacher's guide unit opens with a convenient two-page overview that provides a listing of each lesson, its instructional objectives, and its location in the student text and in the teacher's guide. The overview also contains the key vocabulary, grammar, and functional expressions in the unit, the corresponding reproducible worksheets and audio program tracks, and the related practice available in other textbook programs (*Foundations*, *Side by Side*, *Side by Side Plus*, *Word by Word*, *Word by Word Basic*, *ExpressWays*, and *Access*).

For each lesson, the teacher's guide offers suggestions for previewing the lesson content, step-by-step teaching instructions, an answer key, and expansion activities. For each reading passage, extensive reading comprehension questions are provided. For each dialog lesson, strategies are offered to create dynamic interactive conversation practice in class, and explanations highlight the important functional interview skills that students practice in the dialogs in order to assure they are prepared for their interview with the USCIS officer.

WORKSHEETS

The *Voices of Freedom* worksheets included in this teacher's guide are fully coordinated with the units in the student book and with the English Test practice sections in the appendix. They are designed to offer valuable supplemental practice in class or at home.

Writing Practice worksheets offer students fundamental practice tracing and copying letters, numbers, words, and sentences. The worksheets for preparatory Units A and B provide students with practice writing the alphabet, numbers, months, and dates. The worksheets for Units 1–12 include all the words on the official USCIS writing vocabulary list. Even if students already have basic writing skills, they may benefit from this practice in order to assure that their formation of letters and their writing of words and sentences is legible and accurate. Lower-level students will find it helpful to complete a unit's tracing and copying practice before taking the unit test in the student book, which requires students to write sentences from dictation as on the USCIS exam.

Reading Practice worksheets provide a unique combination of reading and writing practice that prepares students for the reading portion of the USCIS exam. The first section of each worksheet contains columns of words that appear on the official USCIS reading vocabulary list. Students should practice reading these words aloud. The second section of each worksheet consists of sentences with blanks, which students complete by filling in the correct words from a choice-box. All the words students write are included on the official USCIS writing vocabulary list. And all the sentences that students complete in the worksheets for Units 1–12 are plausible sentences that might occur in the reading portion of the USCIS exam. Therefore, after students fill in the sentences, they should practice reading the sentences aloud.

Civics Practice worksheets offer practice with all the USCIS civics test content, including principles of American democracy, the system of government, rights and responsibilities, U.S. history, geography, national symbols, and holidays.

Interview Practice worksheets include a variety of resources that support the English Test practice sections on pages 213–225 of the student book. The specific pages and sections are indicated at the bottom of each worksheet.

Flash Cards provide 100 picture cards and accompanying word/sentence cards that highlight key vocabulary related to the USCIS interview. These include the actions involved in arriving at the office, checking in, being sworn in, and presenting identification. They also include the most important words and concepts related to the officer's questions concerning the applicant's Form N-400, including eligibility for citizenship, residence, family, employment, time outside the United States, and the very challenging "Part 10" questions—the "Have you ever . . ." questions that contain particularly difficult vocabulary about criminal offenses, beliefs, attachment to the Constitution, and other topics. Suggestions for use of the Flash Cards appear on pages 191–192 of this teacher's guide.

Matching Activities offer students practice matching pictures and words/sentences, practice matching questions that have the same meaning (in order to recognize different ways the USCIS officer might ask a question), and practice matching questions and answers.

TEACHER'S RESOURCES

The final section of this teacher's guide offers tools for effective instruction, assessment, and documentation of student progress.

Needs Assessment forms are designed to help programs and teachers gather input from students about their needs and interests in order to guide the development of instruction. A Pictorial Version provides a simple illustrated format for low-beginning-level students. Students can check the pictures and draw their own to indicate their curriculum preferences. A Checklist Version offers a more detailed list of topics for high-beginning-level and intermediate-level students with some reading ability.

Pre/Post Assessments can be used to evaluate students' prior knowledge and skills before instruction as well as to assess their achievement of learning objectives and readiness for the USCIS exam at the end of the course. Two Pre/Post Assessments are provided. In each assessment, Part A contains sixteen of the 100 official USCIS civics questions. Part B contains questions about the student's Form N-400 information that typically occur during the USCIS interview and serve as the basis for the officer's evaluation of English verbal skills. If time and resources allow for one-to-one administration of the assessment, evaluate each student individually as the student answers the questions in Parts A and B orally. Alternatively, students can write answers to the questions. Part C requires a brief one-to-one administration to evaluate the student's ability to read the sentences aloud. Part D can be a whole-class dictation. Suggestions for use of the Pre/Post Assessments appear on pages 283–284 of this teacher's guide.

Performance-Based Assessment Records are tools for evaluating and documenting student participation and performance in each unit's Civics Enrichment activities, which are designed to promote students' active participation in class and in the civic life of the community. Scoring rubrics guide the alternative assessment of these projects, issues discussions, community tasks, field trips, and Internet activities. The Student Name List Mask provides a convenient way to make a list of students' names and then affix it to each of the Assessment Record forms. The Project Activity Observation Checklist provides an assessment tool for evaluating students as they participate in all phases of a project and develop skills in leadership, teamwork, and communicating information—key workplace skills identified by the Secretary's Commission on Achieving Necessary Skills (SCANS).

A **Technology Enrichment** section provides a list of websites for Internet activities that expand upon the topics in each unit.

TEACHING TECHNIQUES

Voices of Freedom has been designed for ease-of-use for the teacher as well as the students. Teachers should feel encouraged to use the text's activities in the way that is most appropriate for their teaching styles and the needs and learning styles of their students.

Three of the central learning devices in the text are the readings, the Civics Check question-and-answer charts, and the dialogs (the Interview and Civics Test conversations). For these three types of activities, teachers may want to use or adapt the following suggestions:

Readings

1. Have students talk about the photograph and/ or their own experiences in order to establish a context, or schema, for what they are about to read.

2. Have students read silently. (If you wish, you may read the passage aloud or play the audio program as they read silently.)

3. Ask students a simple question about each line of the reading. For low beginners, ask the questions in the sequence of the reading. For higher-level students, you might want to ask the questions out of sequence.

4. Ask students if they don't understand any vocabulary. Have students help define any unfamiliar words.

5. Do a choral repetition of the reading, line by line. (This is not reading practice, but rather is speaking practice—appropriate since most of the reading content in *Voices of Freedom* is the basis for the conversation practice that follows.)

6. **Class Circle Reading:** Have students read the passage as a class with different students reading each line in turn. You can assign who will read in a variety of ways: by seating patterns, by calling on students, or by letting students take turns spontaneously.

7. **Pair Practice:** Have students work in pairs, reading the passage to each other paragraph by paragraph, for further speaking practice. Circulate around the room, checking students' reading and pronunciation, and focus attention on students who need more assistance.

8. When comprehension questions about a reading appear in the "Check-Up" exercises that follow, have students first write their answers and then practice in pairs asking and answering these questions aloud.

Civics Check Question & Answer Charts

The chart format for presentation of the 100 official civics test questions enables students to easily practice in class, with a study partner outside of class, or alone. In class, students can practice the questions and answers in a variety of ways:

PAIR PRACTICE: Have students work in pairs, taking turns asking and answering the questions.

LINE PRACTICE: Have students stand in two lines facing each other. Each pair of facing students should take turns asking and answering a question. After sufficient time for this practice, say "Move," and have one line of students move down one position while the other line remains in place. (The student at the end of the line moves to the beginning of the line.) In this way, new pairs are created and students practice with another partner. Continue until students have practiced all the questions.

"ROUND ROBIN": Have students circulate around the room and ask each other the questions. Students should move on to another person after they have taken turns asking and answering a question.

This classroom practice will prepare students to extend learning outside of class by working with a study partner. Students can also practice alone, reading the questions in the left column while covering the answers in the right column and then checking their answers. (Note: Since many questions have multiple acceptable answers, you might encourage low beginners to consistently practice a single answer to a question, while higher-level students can practice the multiple answers.)

Interview Dialogs and Civics Test Dialogs

1. Set the scene. Have students look at the photograph and decide who the people are. You might simply mention in a word or two what they are talking about, such as "the person's address" or "the flag."

2. Have students listen to the dialog with their books closed. Present the dialog yourself (taking both roles), present it with the help of another student, have two students present it to the rest of the class, or play the audio. (If a dialog line has a blank and an answer-choice box, use the first answer to complete the line. The audio always contains the first answer.)

3. Choral Repetition: Have students repeat each line of the dialog in unison after you. (Books still closed.)

4. Have students open their books and look at the dialog. Ask if there are any questions about vocabulary.

5. Choral Conversation Practice:

   a. Divide the class into two groups (two halves or by rows). Have Group 1 say Speaker A's lines in unison, and have Group 2 say Speaker B's lines. Then reverse.

      and/or

   b. Say Speaker A's lines and have the entire class say Speaker B's lines in unison. Then reverse.

6. Call on one or two pairs of students to present the dialog.

7. Pair Practice: Have students practice the dialog in pairs, taking turns being Speaker A and Speaker B. Encourage students to look at each other during the practice rather than "burying" their heads in the books. This will help their spoken language sound more authentic and conversational.

   (You can pair students in different ways. You can pair students of similar ability together and thereby focus your attention on those pairs of students who require more attention. Or you can pair weaker students with stronger ones so that your more capable students have the opportunity to consolidate their skills while providing help to others in the class.)

8. New Dialogs: In Units A and B, the Interview dialogs are followed by "skeletal" dialogs with blank lines. Have students insert their own information and practice new conversations.

(Note: In Units 1–12, many Civics Test dialogs have blank lines and answer-choice boxes since many questions have multiple acceptable answers. You might encourage low beginners to consistently practice the first answer to a question, while higher-level students can practice the multiple answers. The audio always contains the first answer.)

A FINAL WORD: THE GOAL OF CIVICS EDUCATION

A century ago, the goal of citizenship education in so-called "Americanization" classes was to indoctrinate students with U.S. civics information in a way that often discredited their native countries and cultures. It was as though students had to renounce their backgrounds and heritages in order to acquire knowledge about their new country. Now we aspire to a nobler effort: to offer students the language skills and civics knowledge they need to attain citizenship, to live full and productive lives, and to participate fully in the civic life of their communities and the country, and to do so through an educational program that recognizes and respects the diversity of cultures, histories, and experiences that our students bring to our classrooms . . . and the nation.

Bill Bliss

LESSONS & UNIT ACTIVITIES	OBJECTIVES	STUDENT TEXT	TEACHER'S GUIDE
Vocabulary Preview	Identifying information on a permanent resident card and social security card	1	3
Permanent Resident Card	Identifying parts of a name; Filling out a form with name information	2–3	4–5
Interview: Could You Spell That, Please?	The alphabet; Giving name information to the USCIS officer; Spelling aloud one's name; Listening for name spelling; Filling out a form with name information	4–5	6–7
Numbers	Numbers 0–9; Identifying A-number, social security number, telephone number; Filling out a form with name and number information	6–7	8–9
My Address	Numbers 10–90; Giving address information; Reading addresses; Listening for address information	8–9	10–11
Interview: What's Your File Number?	Giving A-number, telephone number, and address information to the USCIS officer; Filling out a form with name, address, and numerical information	10–11	12
Civics Enrichment	Discussing forms of personal identification; Project: Making a list of emergency telephone numbers; Discussing difficulties using emergency services in the community	12	13
On the Day of Your USCIS Interview*	Identifying what to bring to the USCIS interview; Arriving at the USCIS office; Checking in	213	14
The English Test (Speaking)*	Greeting the USCIS officer; Walking to the office; Swearing in; Presenting identification	214–215	15

* These interview preparation lessons are in the Appendix for students' convenience. They can be introduced in this unit and then reviewed along with the other interview preparation lessons as students get ready for their appointment at USCIS. (If you prefer, you can do these lessons later in the course if that is more appropriate for the timing of your students' interviews.) Interview Practice worksheets accompany these lessons.

UNIT RESOURCES

Worksheets:
Unit A Writing Practice
Unit A Reading Practice
Interview Practice Worksheets 1–6

Audio Program:
CD 1: Tracks 2–12

RELATED PRACTICE

Foundations: Unit 1
Word by Word Basic: pages 2–7, 34, 40–41, 240–241
Word by Word: pages 1–3, 15, 18, 160
Side by Side / Side by Side Plus: Book 1, Units 1, 2
Side by Side Interactive CD-ROM / Side by Side TV: Level 1A, Segments 1–3
ExpressWays: Book 1, Unit 1
Access: Units 1, 2

KEY VOCABULARY

PERSONAL INFORMATION

address
apartment number
area code
avenue
city
country
county
e-mail address
family name
file number
first name
full name
given name
home address
last name
middle name
name
number
phone number
social security number
state
street
surname
telephone number
zip code

IDENTIFICATION CARDS

A-number
card
permanent resident card
social security card
USCIS A-number
USCIS file number

IMMIGRATION STATUS

citizen
citizenship
permanent resident

ACTIONS

apply
spell
want (to)
write

OTHER WORDS

a
am
and
capital letters
daytime
evening
for
from
I
include
including
is
my
of
please
that
the
this
United States of America
what
work
yes
your

NUMBERS

0   zero (oh)
1   one
2   two
3   three
4   four
5   five
6   six
7   seven
8   eight
9   nine
10 ten
11 eleven
12 twelve
13 thirteen
14 fourteen
15 fifteen
16 sixteen
17 seventeen
18 eighteen
19 nineteen
20 twenty
30 thirty
40 forty
50 fifty
60 sixty
70 seventy
80 eighty
90 ninety

GRAMMAR

TO BE

My name **is** Carlos Rivera.
I**'m** a permanent resident.

WH-QUESTIONS

What's your family name?

FUNCTIONAL EXPRESSIONS

CLARIFYING

Could you spell that, please?
You mean . . . ?

TEXT PAGE 1 VOCABULARY PREVIEW

You may want to introduce these words before beginning the unit, or you may choose to wait until they first occur in a specific lesson. If you choose to introduce them at this point, here are some suggestions:

1. Have students look at the permanent resident card and the social security card on text page 1 and identify the words they already know.

2. Present the vocabulary. Say each word and have the class repeat it chorally and individually. Check students' understanding and pronunciation of the words.

3. Practice the vocabulary as a class, in pairs, or in small groups. Have students cover the word list and look at the permanent resident card and the social security card. Practice the words in the following ways:

   • Say a word and have students tell the number of that word on the illustration.
   • Give the number of an item in an illustration and have students say the word.

TEXT PAGES 2–3 PERMANENT RESIDENT CARD

FOCUS

TOPICS

Personal information
Permanent resident card

GRAMMAR

To Be

My name **is** Carlos Rivera.
I'm a permanent resident.

NEW VOCABULARY

a	middle name
applying	my
citizen	name
citizenship	last name
family name	permanent resident
first name	permanent resident card
full name	surname
for	the
given name	this
I	United States of America
I'm	want
is	

GETTING READY

1. **Introduce name, first name, middle name, and last name.**

   a. Write your first, middle, and last name on the board.

   b. Point to your name and say, "My full name is _____."

   c. Point to your first name and say, "My first name is _____."

   d. Point to your middle name and say, "My middle name is _____."

   e. Point to your last name and say, "My last name is _____."

   f. Ask individual students:

      "What's your first name?"
      "What's your middle name?"
      "What's your last name?"
      "What's your full name?"

   g. For higher-level students, you can also introduce the synonyms for *last name* (*family name* and *surname*) and the synonym for *first name* (*given name*). Then ask more questions using these terms.

2. **Introduce the following forms of the verb To Be.**

   am   **I'm** a permanent resident.

   is   My name **is** Carlos Rivera.

PREVIEWING THE READING

Have students talk about the title and the photograph to establish the context of the passage.

Ask some or all of the following questions:

   Where is he? (He's at the USCIS office. / He's at the office of U.S. Citizenship and Immigration Services.)
   Why? (He's applying for citizenship.)
   Where is he from? (Have students guess.)
   Is he happy? nervous? Why?
   What's this card? (A permanent resident card.)
   What's the name on the card? (Carlos M. Rivera.)
   What's the mark on the right? (A fingerprint.)
   Do you have a permanent resident card? (Have students show their cards.)
   Point to your name on the card.

READING THE PASSAGE

1. Have students read the passage silently. (If you wish, you may read the passage aloud or play the audio program as students read along silently.)

2. **Check reading comprehension:** Ask students a question about each line of the passage. For beginning-level students, ask these questions in the order below so that the questions follow the sequence of the passage. For higher-level students, ask the questions in random order.

   What's his name?
   What is he?
   What is this card?

   What's his last name?
   What's his first name?
   What's his middle name?
   What's his full name?

   What's he applying for?
   What does he want to be?

3. Ask students if they have any questions about the passage; check understanding of vocabulary.

4. **Choral Repetition:** Read aloud each line of the passage and have students repeat.

5. **Class Circle Reading:** Have students read the passage aloud as a class, with different students reading each line. (You can assign each line to a particular student or by seating patterns, or by letting students take turns spontaneously. In large classes, have a different group or row of students read each line.)

4 ★ UNIT A

6. **Pair Practice:** Have students work in pairs, reading the passage to each other, section by section. Circulate around the room and check students' reading and pronunciation, focusing more attention on students who need more assistance.

EXPANSION

Introducing Oneself

Have students walk around the class introducing themselves to each other. Participate in the activity yourself to encourage students to feel comfortable.

CHECK-UP

VOCABULARY CHECK

1. name
2. last
3. first
4. citizen
5. card
6. citizenship

GRAMMAR CHECK

1. is
2. I'm
3. My
4. I'm
5. be

WRITING: *What's Your Name?*

Have students print their first, middle, and last names on the blank lines for Exercises 1–3 and in the boxes for Exercise 4. Low-beginning-level students may need to copy this information from a model. Point out to students that *last name*, *family name*, and *surname* are synonymous, and so are *first name* and *given name*.

FOCUS

TOPICS

The alphabet
Personal information

GRAMMAR

WH-Questions

What's your family name?

To Be

What**'s** your first name?

FUNCTIONAL INTERVIEW SKILL

Reporting personal information

NEW VOCABULARY

and
please
spell
that
what
your
Could you spell that, please?

GETTING READY

Introduce the alphabet.

a. Use flash cards or write the letter A on the board. Have students repeat, "A."

b. Next to A, use the flash card B or write the letter B. Have students repeat, "A, B."

c. Continue with the letters C, D, and E.

d. Next, point to these letters at random. Have students say the letters.

e. Continue the above steps with groups of five or six letters at a time until you have completed the alphabet.

f. Have the class repeat the alphabet.

PRACTICING THE MODEL DIALOG

1. **Setting the Scene:** Have students look at the photograph and determine who is talking: a USCIS officer and an applicant for citizenship. Establish the context: "The USCIS officer is asking questions about the applicant's name."

2. **Listening:** With books closed, have students listen to the dialog—presented by you, by a pair of students, or on the audio program.

3. **Choral Repetition:** With books still closed, model each line and have the whole class repeat in unison.

4. **Reading:** With books open, have students follow along as two students present the model dialog. Ask students if they have any questions and check understanding of vocabulary.

5. **Choral Conversation Practice:** Divide the class in half. Have Group 1 ask the questions and Group 2 give the answers; then reverse. (Or: You ask the questions and have the whole class answer in unison; then reverse.)

6. Call on one or two pairs of students to present the model dialog.

PRACTICING NEW DIALOGS

1. Call on one or two pairs of students to present new dialogs, using the skeletal dialog as a guide and filling in the blanks with the appropriate information.

2. **Pair Practice:** Have students practice making new dialogs in pairs, taking turns being the USCIS officer and the applicant.

3. Call on one or two more pairs of students to present their new dialogs to the class.

EXPANSION

"Alphabet Soup" Game

a. Write the 26 letters of the alphabet randomly on the board, or use flash cards.

b. Divide the class into teams.

c. Point to a letter or show a flash card. The first player on Team 1 says the letter. The team gets a point for a correct answer.

d. Show a different letter to the first player on Team 2. If the answer is incorrect, show the same letter to the second player on Team 1 or the first player on Team 3.

e. The team with the most correct answers wins.

CHECK-UP
ALPHABET PRACTICE

1. A, E, M, N
   NAME

2. A, C, D, R
   CARD

3. A, L, S, T
   LAST

4. A, F, I, L, M, Y
   FAMILY

LISTENING

Have students complete the exercises as you play the audio program or read the following:

Listen and circle the correct answer.

1. A. What's your family name?
   B. Martinez.
   A. Could you spell that, please?
   B. M-A-R-T-I-N-E-Z.

2. A. What's your last name?
   B. Garza.
   A. Could you spell that, please?
   B. G-A-R-Z-A.

3. A. What's your surname?
   B. Ly.
   A. Could you spell that, please?
   B. L-Y.

4. A. What's your last name?
   B. Moreno.
   A. How do you spell that?
   B. M-O-R-E-N-O.

5. A. What's your family name?
   B. Wong.
   A. How do you spell that?
   B. W-O-N-G.

6. A. What's your surname?
   B. Mansour.
   A. Could you spell that, please?
   B. M-A-N-S-O-U-R.

ANSWERS

1. Martinez
2. Garza
3. Ly
4. Moreno
5. Wong
6. Mansour

WRITING: *Fill Out the Form*

This exercise offers students practice with a simulated section of the N-400 Application for Naturalization form. Have students write their own names as requested. Low-beginning-level students may need to copy this information from a model.

FOCUS

TOPICS

Numbers 0–9
Identification cards
A-number, Social security number, Telephone
number

GRAMMAR

To Be

My A-number **is** A-92475816.

NEW VOCABULARY

number	zero (oh)	five
A-number	one	six
social security card	two	seven
social security number	three	eight
telephone number	four	nine

GETTING READY

Teach the numbers 0–9.

a. Write 0 on the board. Say "zero" and have students repeat.

b. Next to 0 write 1. Say "one" and have students repeat.

c. Point to 0 and 1 on the board as you say "zero, one" and have students repeat.

d. Introduce the numbers 2, 3, and 4, using steps b and c.

e. Point to these numbers at random and have the class say them.

f. Continue the above steps with the numbers 5–9.

g. Have the class count from 0 to 9.

h. Have individual students count from 0 to 9.

PREVIEWING THE READING

Have students talk about the title and the illustrations to establish the context of the passage. Ask some or all of the following questions:

What are these cards? (permanent resident card/ social security card.)
Do *you* have a permanent resident card? (Have students show their cards.)
What's this number? (Point to the A-number.)
Point to *your* A-number on *your* card.
What's *your* A-number?

Do *you* have a social security card? (Have students show their cards.)
What's this number? (Point to the social security number.)
Point to *your* social security number on *your* card.
What's *your* social security number?

(Point to the third illustration on the page.)
What's this? (A telephone number/a telephone listing.)
Where is it? (In a telephone book.)
Do *you* have a telephone?
What's *your* telephone number?

READING THE PASSAGE

1. Have students read the passage silently. (If you wish, you may read the passage aloud or play the audio program as students read along silently.)

2. **Check reading comprehension:** Ask students a question about each line of the passage. For beginning-level students, ask these questions in the order below so that the questions follow the sequence of the passage. For higher-level students, ask the questions in random order.

   What's this card?
   What's his A-number?

   What's this card?
   What's his social security number?

   What kind of number is this?
   What's his telephone number?

3. Ask students if they have any questions about the passage; check understanding of vocabulary.

4. **Choral Repetition:** Read aloud each line of the passage and have students repeat.

5. **Class Circle Reading:** Have students read the passage aloud as a class, with different students reading each line. (You can assign each line to a particular student or by seating patterns, or by letting students take turns spontaneously. In large classes, have a different group or row of students read each line.)

6. **Pair Practice:** Have students work in pairs, reading the passage to each other, section by section. Circulate around the room and check students' reading and pronunciation, focusing more attention on students who need more assistance.

EXPANSION

1. Number Clapping

   a. Clap your hands or tap on the desk. Have students respond by saying the number of claps.

   b. Have a student clap or tap. Have the other students respond.

2. Interviews

   a. On the board, write:

> last name
> first name
> telephone number
> social security number

   b. Ask, "What's your last name?" Have a student answer.

   c. Ask, "Could you spell that, please?" Write the name on the board as the student spells it.

   d. Continue with first name, using steps b and c.

   e. Ask, "What's your telephone number?" Write the number.

   f. Ask, "What's your social security number?" Write the number.

   g. In pairs, have students ask for and write the information about each other.

CHECK-UP

MATCHING

1. c
2. d
3. b
4. a

ANSWER THESE QUESTIONS

New Vocabulary: area code, home telephone number, include, phone number, work

Have students answer the questions with their own information. Low-beginning-level students may need to copy this information from a model.

(Note: An A-number can have seven, eight, or nine digits, depending on when it was issued by USCIS. Students with seven-digit numbers need to put two zero [0] numbers before their A-number when they fill out USCIS forms. Students with eight-digit numbers need to put one zero [0] number before the A-number. For example, Carlos Rivera, the person on text page 6, would write his A-number as A-092475816.)

WRITING: *Fill Out the Form*

New Vocabulary: daytime phone number, evening phone number

This exercise offers students practice with a simulated section of the N-400 Application for Naturalization form. Have students provide the information as requested on the form. Low-beginning-level students may need to copy the information from a model. Make sure students write in capital letters.

FOCUS

TOPICS

Numbers 10–90
Giving address and apartment number
Giving city, state, and zip code

GRAMMAR

To Be

My address **is** 80 Stanley Avenue.

NEW VOCABULARY

address
apartment
avenue
city
of
state
the
United States of America
zip code

ten
eleven
twelve
thirteen
fourteen
fifteen
sixteen
seventeen
eighteen
nineteen

twenty
thirty
forty
fifty
sixty
seventy
eighty
ninety

GETTING READY

1. **Teach the numbers 10–100.**

   a. Review the numbers 0–9.

   b. Write 10 on the board. Say "ten" and have students repeat.

   c. Next to 10 write 11. Say "eleven" and have students repeat.

   d. Point to 10 and 11 on the board as you say "ten, eleven" and have students repeat.

   e. Introduce the numbers 12–19, using steps c and d.

   f. Erase the board and have individual students count from 0 to 19.

   g. Write 20 on the board. Say "twenty" and have students repeat.

   h. Write 21–29 on the board. Count from 21 to 29 and have students repeat number by number.

   i. Have individual students count from 0 to 29.

   j. Write 30 on the board. Say "thirty" and have students repeat.

   k. Write 40, say "forty," and have students repeat.

   l. Point to 30 and 40 as you say "thirty, forty" and have students repeat.

   m. Continue through 100, using steps k and l.

   n. Write numbers randomly on the board. Have the class read them. Then have individual students read them. For example, "36, 43, 51, 27, 89."

2. **Introduce addresses.**

   Write a local address on the board and point out each part. For example, "This is the building number. This is the street number." Do this for city, state, and zip code.

PREVIEWING THE READING

Have students talk about the title and the photograph to establish the context of the passage. Ask some or all of the following questions:

Where is he? (Inside the USCIS office.)
Why? (He's applying for citizenship.)
What is he saying/thinking? (Students guess.)
What do you see on the left? (The American flag.)
What do you see behind him? (A banner.)
What is on the banner? (The Pledge of Allegiance.)
(With higher-level students, you might want to practice the Pledge of Allegiance on page 42 of the student text.)

READING THE PASSAGE

1. Have students read the passage silently. (If you wish, you may read the passage aloud or play the audio program as students read along silently.)

2. **Check reading comprehension:** Ask students a question about each line of the passage. For beginning-level students, ask these questions in

the order below so that the questions follow the sequence of the passage. For higher-level students, ask the questions in random order.

> What's his address?
> What's his apartment number?
> What's the name of his city?
> What's the name of his state?
> Where is California?
> What's his zip code?

3. Ask students if they have any questions about the passage; check understanding of vocabulary.

4. **Choral Repetition:** Read aloud each line of the passage and have students repeat.

5. **Class Circle Reading:** Have students read the passage aloud as a class, with different students reading each line. (You can assign each line to a particular student or by seating patterns, or by letting students take turns spontaneously. In large classes, have a different group or row of students read each line.)

6. **Pair Practice:** Have students work in pairs, reading the passage to each other section by section. Circulate around the room and check students' reading and pronunciation, focusing more attention on students who need more assistance.

YOUR INFORMATION

Have students practice completing the sentences with their personal information.

EXPANSION

1. Interviews

a. Write on the board:

> last name
> first name
> address

b. Ask, "What's your last name?" Have a student answer.

c. Ask, "Could you spell that, please?" Write the name on the board as the student spells it.

d. Continue with first name.

e. Ask, "What's your address?" Write the address.

f. In pairs, have students ask for and write the information about each other.

2. Reading Maps

Using a map of the United States showing cities and states, have students identify cities and states where they have visited or lived.

3. Addressing Envelopes

Have students address envelopes to relatives or friends who live in another city or state. (Students can take these envelopes home to use for mailing letters to the addressees.)

CHECK-UP
MATCHING

1. d
2. f
3. e
4. a
5. c
6. b

READING ADDRESSES

New Vocabulary: street

Have students practice reading addresses. Note that there are two ways to say a three-digit building number. Four-digit building numbers are said as two separate two-digit numbers.

LISTENING

Have students complete the exercises as you play the audio program or read the following:

Listen and circle the number you hear.

1. My address is thirty Main Street.
2. My address is thirteen Spring Street.
3. My address is fifty Stanley Avenue.
4. My address is forty-six fifteen Donaldson Street.
5. My address is eighteen thirty-nine Parkman Avenue.
6. My address is eight forty-two Conway Avenue.

ANSWERS

1. 30
2. 13
3. 50
4. 4615
5. 1839
6. 842

FOCUS

TOPIC

Giving personal information

GRAMMAR

To Be

What's your USCIS file number?

WH-Questions

What's your address?

FUNCTIONAL INTERVIEW SKILLS

Reporting personal information
Asking for clarification

NEW VOCABULARY

including
USCIS file number
yes
You mean . . . ?

PRACTICING THE MODEL DIALOG

1. **Setting the Scene:** Have students look at the photograph and determine who is talking: a USCIS officer and a citizenship applicant. Establish the context: "The USCIS officer is asking the applicant for information."

2. **Listening:** With books closed, have students listen to the dialog—presented by you, by a pair of students, or on the audio program.

3. **Choral Repetition:** With books still closed, model each line and have the whole class repeat in unison.

4. **Reading:** With books open, have students follow along as two students present the model dialog. Ask students if they have any questions and check understanding of vocabulary.

5. **Choral Conversation Practice:** Divide the class in half. Have Group 1 ask the questions and Group 2 give the answers; then reverse. (Or: You ask the questions and have the whole class answer in unison; then reverse.)

6. Call on one or two pairs of students to present the model dialog.

PRACTICING NEW DIALOGS

1. Call on one or two pairs of students to present new dialogs, using the skeletal dialog as a guide and filling in the blanks with the appropriate information.

2. **Pair Practice:** Have students practice making new dialogs in pairs, taking turns being the USCIS officer and the applicant.

3. Call on one or two pairs of students to present their new dialogs to the class.

CHECK-UP

QUESTIONS AND ANSWERS

1. Have the entire class practice saying the questions. Then as a class activity, have different students ask other students one of the questions. Continue this way until all students have asked and answered a question.

2. Have students interview each other in pairs, taking turns asking and answering the questions.

WRITING: *Fill Out the Form*

Have students practice writing the complete information requested on this simulated section of the N-400 Application for Naturalization form.

TEXT PAGE 12

CIVICS ENRICHMENT

> ### PERFORMANCE-BASED ASSESSMENT
> These civics enrichment activities are designed to promote students' active participation in class and in the civic life of the community—through projects, issues discussions, community tasks, field trips, and Internet activities. Reproducible performance-based assessment forms for use in evaluating and documenting student participation in these activities are included in the Teacher's Resources section.

CIVIC PARTICIPATION

Have students discuss other forms of personal identification besides permanent resident cards and social security cards—driver's licenses, passports, state identification cards, school identification cards, and other documents. Have them discuss the kinds of identification they have, why forms of personal identification are important, and where they get them.

PROJECT

In this project, students make a list of emergency telephone numbers for their community. They need to find out the information, create a list (or perhaps a more attractive brochure page with pictures or icons of the emergencies), make copies, and distribute them to all students so that they can be posted near the telephone in each student's home. Have students take responsibility for all aspects of this project. Have them identify the particular tasks involved in the project, who will accomplish each task, what resources are needed, and what form the final product will take. Use the project as a basis for building students' skills in leadership, teamwork, and acquiring, evaluating, and communicating information—key SCANS* skills useful for success in the workplace.

COMMUNITY ISSUES

Problem-Posing Discussion: Have students discuss whether it is difficult to use emergency services in their community, and have them discuss any reasons for this. (Students commonly describe long waiting times for the arrival of emergency personnel in their neighborhoods, the uncertainty of when it is appropriate to dial 911 and when it isn't considered necessary, and their concern about the expense of emergency ambulance services. From the viewpoint of emergency services personnel, some students and their families misuse ambulance services by calling them in situations that are not life-threatening, while other students may not think to use emergency services in situations that require them.) Have students identify key issues and problems and share ideas about how to solve them.

UNIT SUMMARY

KEY VOCABULARY

Have students review the lists of words they have learned in this unit. Encourage students to get a small notebook where they can write down vocabulary that is new for them.

GRAMMAR

Have students review the sentence-examples of grammar in this unit. For enrichment, have higher-level students look for more examples of this grammar in the unit and write additional sentences.

FUNCTIONAL EXPRESSIONS

Have students review the functional expressions and find where they occur in this unit. For enrichment, have students make up new conversations that use these functional expressions and present them to the class.

UNIT REVIEW WORKSHEETS

Unit A Writing Practice
Unit A Reading Practice

*Secretary's Commission on Achieving Necessary Skills

FOCUS

TOPICS

What to bring to the USCIS interview
Arriving at the USCIS office
Checking in

FUNCTIONAL INTERVIEW SKILLS

Following instructions
Giving name

NEW VOCABULARY

administratively close your case
alien registration card
appointment
appointment letter
bag
citizenship
conveyor belt
document
driver's license
interview
listen for your name
meet
metal detector
metal object
officer
passport
passport-size photograph
permanent resident card
reentry permit
reopen your case
reschedule
security checkpoint
state identification card
take a seat
tray
USCIS office
waiting area

Explain to students that while they study civics and language skills, they will also prepare for their interview at the USCIS office. These interview preparation lessons are in the Appendix for students' convenience. Students will practice one or more of these lessons in each unit. Later, as they prepare for their appointment at USCIS, they can review this entire Appendix section to get ready for their interview. (If you prefer, you can do these lessons later in the course if that is more appropriate for the timing of your students' interviews.)

WHAT TO BRING

As a class, have students read aloud the checklist of what to bring to the interview. Have them read the instructions in the "Important" section. Check their understanding of the vocabulary and the instructions.

ROLE PLAY: *Arriving at the USCIS Office; Checking In*

Have students practice the dialogs in pairs, taking turns being the USCIS officer and the applicant. Then have pairs of students present dialogs to the class.

WORKSHEETS

Interview Practice Worksheets 1–2

FOCUS

TOPICS

Greeting the USCIS officer
Walking to the office
Swearing in
Presenting your identification

FUNCTIONAL INTERVIEW SKILLS

Greeting people
Engaging in small talk
Following instructions
Responding to requests for identification

KEY VOCABULARY

GREETING THE USCIS OFFICER

conduct your interview	Nice meeting you, too.
I'm _____.	Okay.
Nice to meet you.	Please follow me.

SMALL TALK ABOUT TRANSPORTATION

bring/brought me by car	take/took the bus
drive/drove	take/took the subway
get here	traffic
how long	trouble parking
on time	walk

SMALL TALK ABOUT WEATHER

cloudy	It stopped *raining*.
cold	It's *sunny* now.
cool	outside
hot	raining
I don't like it.	sunny
I like it.	warm
Is it still *raining*?	weather

SMALL TALK ABOUT WHO ACCOMPANIED YOU

anyone	friend
by myself	husband
come	wife

SMALL TALK ABOUT PREPARING FOR THE INTERVIEW

class	prepare
English	study
go to a school	teacher's name
how many days a week	U.S. history and
interview	government
nervous	

SWEARING IN

do you understand	remain standing
file	sit down
have a seat	solemnly affirm
information	solemnly swear
lie	stand
please be seated	statements
promise	take a seat
raise your right hand	tell the truth

PRESENTING IDENTIFICATION

alien registration card	most recent
current	passport
driver's license	passport-size photograph
expired	permanent resident card
forms of identification	state identification card
identification	

INTRODUCING THE ENGLISH TEST PRACTICE

As a class, have students read the direction lines that accompany these first four procedures that occur during their USCIS interview. Emphasize that the English test might begin in the waiting area when the USCIS officer calls the student's name. As the student and the USCIS officer walk from the waiting area to the office where the interview will occur, it is common for the officer to engage the student in simple "small talk" conversation on topics such as the weather or how the student arrived at the office. This gives students the opportunity to make a good first impression by showing that they have sufficient language skills to discuss these topics. It is also important that students practice the language involved in standing up to be sworn in for the interview and in presenting their identification documents to the USCIS officer. These are basic language tasks that are essential for a successful interview.

ROLE PLAY

Have students work in pairs and role-play the entire sequence of action in these dialogs: the officer greeting the applicant in the waiting area, the officer and the applicant walking to the interview room while engaging in small talk, the officer swearing in the applicant, and the applicant presenting identification to the officer. Have students take turns being the USCIS officer and the applicant. Then have pairs of students present their role plays to the class.

WORKSHEETS

Interview Practice Worksheets 3–6

UNIT

PERSONAL INFORMATION   DATES
MONTHS OF THE YEAR

LESSONS & UNIT ACTIVITIES	OBJECTIVES	STUDENT TEXT	TEACHER'S GUIDE
Vocabulary Preview	Identifying months of the year; Reading a date	13	17
I Was Born in Monterrey	Giving information about name, city, state, place of birth, and family to the USCIS officer; Filling out a form with information about date of birth and country of birth; Identifying terms for family members; Sharing family photographs with the class	14–15	18
Interview: What's Your Place of Birth?	Giving information about place of birth, native country, and geographical information; Recognizing different ways a question may be asked; Listening for correct information requested about date and place of birth	16–17	19
Interview: What's Your Date of Birth?	Giving information about date of birth; Asking for repetition; Checking understanding; Identifying months of the year; Recognizing different ways a question may be asked; Marking dates of events on a calendar	18–19	20–21
Interview: Are You Still Living at 86 Central Avenue?	Verifying address information; Correcting information	20	22
Interview: Let Me Verify Some Information	Verifying information about name, nationality, and date of birth; Giving date that permanent residence status was received; Correcting information; Recognizing different ways a question may be asked; Filling out a form with personal information	21–22	23
Review	Asking and answering questions about name, nationality, place of birth, date of birth, address, telephone number	23	24
Civics Enrichment	Touring the school and introducing self to school personnel; Project: Writing a paragraph about nationality, country of birth, and city or town where born; Project: Making a class calendar of student birthdays, U.S. holidays, native country holidays, and other special dates	24	24
The English Test (Speaking)*	Identifying requirements of the English Speaking Test; Asking for repetition; Showing confidence and pride during the interview; Giving information about name, other names used, or the desire to change name; Giving information about eligibility for citizenship	216–217	25

* This interview preparation lesson is in the Appendix for students' convenience. It can be introduced in this unit and then reviewed along with the other interview preparation lessons as students get ready for their appointment at USCIS. If you prefer, you can do these lessons later in the course if that is more appropriate for the timing of your students' interviews. Interview Practice worksheets accompany these lessons.

UNIT RESOURCES

Worksheets:
Unit B Writing Practice
Unit B Reading Practice
Interview Practice Worksheets 7–10

Audio Program:
CD 1: Tracks 13–19

RELATED PRACTICE

Foundations: Unit 1
Word by Word Basic: pages 2–7, 34, 40–41, 240–241
Word by Word: pages 1–3, 15, 18, 160
Side by Side / Side by Side Plus: Book 1, Units 3, 4
Side by Side Interactive CD-ROM / Side by Side TV: Level 1A, Segments 4, 5
ExpressWays: Book 1, Unit 1
Access: Units 3, 4

KEY VOCABULARY

PERSONAL INFORMATION

address	home address
apartment number	home telephone number
area code	information
birth	middle name
birth date	name
born	nationality
city	native country
country	place of birth
country of birth	social security number
country of nationality	state
current address	street
date	telephone number
date of birth	town
e-mail address	work phone number
family name	zip code
first name	

FAMILY MEMBERS

aunt
brother
daughter
father
grandfather
grandmother
husband
mother
sister
son
uncle
wife

TIME EXPRESSIONS

date
day
month
year

MONTHS

January
February
March
April
May
June
July
August
September
October
November
December

IMMIGRATION STATUS

citizen
citizenship
naturalization
permanent resident

GRAMMAR

TO BE

My name **is** Maria Lopez.
I'm from Mexico.
My mother and father **are** in Monterrey.

WH-QUESTIONS

What's your place of birth?
Where were you born?
When were you born?

YES/NO QUESTIONS

Are you still living at 86 Central Avenue?
Is your zip code 10715?

SHORT ANSWERS

Yes, I am.
No, I'm not.
Yes, it is.
No, it isn't.

FUNCTIONAL EXPRESSIONS

ASKING FOR REPETITION

Excuse me?
Could you please say that again?

CLARIFYING

On *May 4, 1979?*

EXPRESSING LACK OF UNDERSTANDING

I'm sorry. I didn't understand.

VERIFYING INFORMATION

Is that right?
Is that correct?
   Yes. That's right.
   No. That's not correct.

TEXT PAGE 13 VOCABULARY PREVIEW

You may want to introduce these words before beginning the unit, or you may choose to wait until they first occur in a specific lesson. If you choose to introduce them at this point, here are some suggestions:

1. Have students look at the calendar and the date on text page 13. Have them identify the months they already know, and have them identify the parts of the date (month, day, year) they already know.

2. Present the vocabulary. Say each word and have the class repeat it chorally and individually. Check students' understanding and pronunciation of the words.

3. Practice the vocabulary as a class, in pairs, or in small groups. Have students cover the word list and look at the calendar and the date. Practice the words in the following ways:

   • Say a word and have students tell the number of that word in the illustration.
   • Give the number of a month on the calendar or the number of a part of the date and have students say the word.

FOCUS

TOPICS

Personal information	Dates
Months of the year	Family members

GRAMMAR

To Be

My name **is** Maria Lopez.
I'm from Mexico.
My mother and father **are** in Monterrey.

NEW VOCABULARY

are	grandmother	now
aunt	husband	on
born	in	sister
brother	May	son
daughter	Mexican	uncle
father	mother	was
grandfather	naturalization	wife

GETTING READY

Introduce dates.

Show a calendar. Point to today's date and say, "Today is (month) (date), (year)." For example, "Today is December 12, 2010."

PREVIEWING THE READING

Have students talk about the title and the photograph to establish the context of the passage.

Ask some or all of the following questions:

Where is she? (She's at the USCIS office. / She's at the office of U.S. Citizenship and Immigration Services.)
Why? (She's applying for citizenship.)
Where is she from? (Have students guess.)
Is she happy? nervous? Why?
What's the name of our city?
What's the name of our state?
What's the name of our country?
What country are you from?

READING THE PASSAGE

1. Have students read the passage silently. (If you wish, you may read the passage aloud or play the audio program as students read along silently.)

2. **Check reading comprehension:** Ask students a question about each line of the passage. For beginning-level students, ask these questions in the order below so that the questions follow the sequence of the passage. For higher-level students, ask the questions in random order.

What's her name?
Where is she from?
Is she a permanent resident?
What's the name of her city?
Where is Houston?

What nationality is she?
Where was she born?
Where is Monterrey?
Where is Nuevo León?

When was she born?
What's her mother's name?
What's her father's name?
Where are her mother and father?

What's she applying for?
What does she want to be?

3. Ask students if they have any questions about the passage; check understanding of vocabulary.

4. **Choral Repetition:** Read aloud each line of the passage and have students repeat.

5. **Class Circle Reading:** Have students read the passage aloud as a class, with different students reading each line. (You can assign each line to a particular student or by seating patterns, or by letting students take turns spontaneously. In large classes, have a different group or row of students read each line.)

6. **Pair Practice:** Have students work in pairs, reading the passage to each other, section by section. Circulate around the room and check students' reading and pronunciation, focusing more attention on students who need more assistance.

CHECK-UP

MATCHING		VOCABULARY CHECK	
1. d	4. e	1. name	4. born
2. c	5. b	2. city	5. mother
3. a		3. state	

FILL OUT THE FORM

New Vocabulary: country of birth, date of birth, day, month, year

This exercise offers students practice with a simulated section of a USCIS form. Have students fill in the boxes with their own information. Make sure that each student knows how to fill in his or her date of birth. Low-beginning-level students may need to copy this information from a model.

SHARING

Have students bring in photographs of family members and describe them by saying, "This is my _____. His/her name is _____. He/she is in _____." Teach words for other family members as necessary.

FOCUS

TOPIC

Giving personal information about place of birth and native country

GRAMMAR

WH-Questions

What's your place of birth?
Where were you born?

FUNCTIONAL INTERVIEW SKILLS

Reporting personal information
Asking for repetition

NEW VOCABULARY

city	were
native country	where
or	
place of birth	Excuse me?
town	

PRACTICING THE MODEL DIALOG

1. **Setting the Scene:** Have students look at the photograph and determine who is talking: a USCIS officer and an applicant for citizenship. Establish the context: "The USCIS officer is asking about where the applicant was born."

2. **Listening:** With books closed, have students listen to the dialog—presented by you, by a pair of students, or on the audio program.

3. **Choral Repetition:** With books still closed, model each line and have the whole class repeat in unison.

4. **Reading:** With books open, have students follow along as two students present the model dialog. Ask students if they have any questions and check understanding of vocabulary.

5. **Choral Conversation Practice:** Divide the class in half. Have Group 1 ask the questions and Group 2 give the answers; then reverse. (Or: You ask the questions and have the whole class answer in unison; then reverse.)

6. Call on one or two pairs of students to present the model dialog.

PRACTICING NEW DIALOGS

1. Call on one or two pairs of students to present new dialogs, using the skeletal dialog as a guide and filling in the blanks with the appropriate information.

2. **Pair Practice:** Have students practice making new dialogs in pairs, taking turns being the USCIS officer and the applicant.

3. Call on one or two more pairs of students to present their new dialogs to the class.

CHECK-UP

QUESTIONS AND ANSWERS

This exercise offers students important practice with the multiple ways a question might be posed by the USCIS officer. First, have students repeat each question after you. Then, have students practice asking and answering the questions with other students. Finally, have students write their answers to questions 1, 2, and 3.

GRAMMAR CHECK

1. What
2. Where
3. What
4. What
5. Where

LISTENING

In order to do the listening activity, students will first need to write their place of birth on line A and date of birth on line B. Low-beginning-level students may have to copy this information from a model.

Have students complete the exercises as you play the audio program or read the following:

Listen carefully and circle A or B.

1. Where were you born?
2. What's your date of birth?
3. What's your place of birth?
4. When were you born?
5. Where are you from?
6. What's your birth date?

ANSWERS

1. A
2. B
3. A
4. B
5. A
6. B

FOCUS

TOPICS

Giving personal information about date of birth
Months of the year
Dates

GRAMMAR

WH-Questions

What's your date of birth?
When were you born?

FUNCTIONAL INTERVIEW SKILLS

Reporting personal information
Asking for repetition
Checking understanding

NEW VOCABULARY

again	Could you please say that again?
didn't	I didn't understand.
say	I'm sorry.
understand	That's right.
when	

January
February
March
April
May
June
July
August
September
October
November
December

GETTING READY

1. **Use a calendar to introduce the months of the year.**

   a. Point to January on the calendar. Say "January" and have students repeat.

   b. Continue with all twelve months.

2. **Practice dates.**

   a. Tell students when your birthday is. Say, "I was born on (month) (day)."

   b. Ask a student, "When were you born?"

   c. Write that student's birthday on the board—for example, June 9. Have that student ask another student.

d. Continue by having students ask each other. Write the dates on the board.

e. Have students practice saying their birth dates. Teach each student how to say the ordinal number in the student's birth date.

PRACTICING THE MODEL DIALOG

1. **Setting the Scene:** Have students look at the photograph and determine who is talking: a USCIS officer and an applicant. Establish the context: "The USCIS officer is asking about the applicant's birth date."

2. **Listening:** With books closed, have students listen to the dialog—presented by you, by a pair of students, or on the audio program.

3. **Choral Repetition:** With books still closed, model each line and have the whole class repeat in unison.

4. **Reading:** With books open, have students follow along as two students present the model dialog. Ask students if they have any questions and check understanding of vocabulary.

5. **Choral Conversation Practice:** Divide the class in half. Have Group 1 ask the questions and Group 2 give the answers; then reverse. (Or: You ask the questions and have the whole class answer in unison; then reverse.)

6. Call on one or two pairs of students to present the model dialog.

PRACTICING NEW DIALOGS

1. Call on one or two pairs of students to present new dialogs, using the skeletal dialog as a guide and filling in the blanks with the appropriate information.

2. **Pair Practice:** Have students practice making new dialogs in pairs, taking turns being the USCIS officer and the applicant.

3. Call on one or two more pairs of students to present their new dialogs to the class.

EXPANSION

Birthday Line-up

Tell students to line up in the order of their birthdays (month and day). The students will have to talk among themselves to determine who should be first, second, third, etc.

CHECK-UP

MONTHS AND YEARS

Say the months of the year and have students repeat. Then, model for students how to read the years listed in the second box.

QUESTIONS AND ANSWERS

This exercise offers students important practice with the multiple ways a question might be posed by the USCIS officer. First, have students repeat each question after you. Then, have students practice asking and answering the questions with other students. Finally, have students write their answers to questions 1, 2, and 3.

CALENDAR ACTIVITY

Have students fill in calendars with information about students' birthdays and holidays. (You can often get free calendar books at gift and card shops, or students can make their own.)

    a. Ask students:

> Do any students have birthdays in January?
> What's the date?
> Are there any United States holidays in
>   January?
> What's the date?
> Are there any holidays in your native country in
>   January?
> What's the date?

    Have students record this information on their calendars.

    b. Follow the same procedure for the other months.

FOCUS

TOPIC
Verifying personal information about address

GRAMMAR

Yes/No Questions

Are you still living at 86 Central Avenue?
Is your zip code 10715?

Short Answers

Yes, I am.
No, I'm not.

Yes, it is.
No, it isn't.

WH-Questions

What's the zip code?

FUNCTIONAL INTERVIEW SKILLS
Verifying information
Reporting personal information
Correcting

NEW VOCABULARY

at	new
current	no
it	still
live	

GETTING READY

Introduce Yes/No questions and short answers.

a. Write on the board:

    Are you from Mexico?   Yes, I am.
                                 No, I'm not.

b. Ask the question and model the answer for each student. Then ask each student the question, and have him/her respond appropriately.

c. Write on the board:

    Is your name Maria?   Yes, it is.
                              No, it isn't.

d. Ask the question and model the answer for each student. Then ask each student the question and have him/her respond appropriately.

PRACTICING THE MODEL DIALOGS

For each dialog:

1. **Setting the Scene:** Have students look at the photograph and determine who is talking: a USCIS officer and an applicant. Establish the context: "The USCIS officer is asking about the applicant's address."

2. **Listening:** With books closed, have students listen to the dialog—presented by you, by a pair of students, or on the audio program.

3. **Choral Repetition:** With books still closed, model each line and have the whole class repeat in unison.

4. **Reading:** With books open, have students follow along as two students present the model dialog. Ask students if they have any questions and check understanding of vocabulary.

5. **Choral Conversation Practice:** Divide the class in half. Have Group 1 ask the questions and Group 2 give the answers; then reverse. (Or: You ask the questions and have the whole class answer in unison; then reverse.)

6. Call on one or two pairs of students to present the model dialog.

PRACTICING NEW DIALOGS

1. Call on one or two pairs of students to present new dialogs, using one of the skeletal dialogs as a guide and filling in the blanks with the appropriate information.

2. **Pair Practice:** Have students practice making new dialogs in pairs, taking turns being the USCIS officer and the applicant.

3. Call on one or two more pairs of students to present their new dialogs to the class.

FOCUS

TOPICS

Verifying information about name, nationality, and date of birth

Dates

GRAMMAR

Yes/No Questions

Is your date of birth November 20, 1975?

Is that correct?

Short Answers

Yes, it is.

No, it isn't.

WH-Questions

What's your social security number?

FUNCTIONAL INTERVIEW SKILLS

Verifying Information

Correcting

NEW VOCABULARY

correct	All right.
some	I see.
verify	Let me. . .

PRACTICING THE MODEL DIALOG

1. **Setting the Scene:** Have students look at the photograph and determine who the person is: an applicant for citizenship. Establish the context: "The USCIS officer is asking the applicant for some personal information."

2. **Listening:** With books closed, have students listen to the dialog—presented by you, by a pair of students, or on the audio program.

3. **Choral Repetition:** With books still closed, model each line and have the whole class repeat in unison.

4. **Reading:** With books open, have students follow along as two students present the model dialog. Ask students if they have any questions and check understanding of vocabulary.

5. **Choral Conversation Practice:** Divide the class in half. Have Group 1 ask the questions and Group 2 give the answers; then reverse. (Or: You ask the questions and have the whole class answer in unison; then reverse.)

6. Call on one or two pairs of students to present the model dialog.

PRACTICING NEW DIALOGS

1. Call on one or two pairs of students to present new dialogs, using the skeletal dialog as a guide and filling in the blanks with the appropriate information.

2. **Pair Practice:** Have students practice making new dialogs in pairs, taking turns being the USCIS officer and the applicant.

3. Call on one or two more pairs of students to present their new dialogs to the class.

CHECK-UP

QUESTIONS AND ANSWERS

This exercise offers students important practice with the multiple ways a question might be posed by the USCIS officer. First, have students repeat each question after you. Then, have students practice asking and answering the questions with other students. Finally, have students write their answers to questions 1–4 on a separate sheet of paper.

WRITING: *Fill Out the Form*

Have students fill out the form with their personal information. Low-beginning-level students may need to copy the information from a model. Make sure students write in capital letters.

INFORMATION EXCHANGE

Have the entire class practice asking the questions in the box at the top of the page. Then have students circulate around the room and interview six other students, writing the information they gather in the appropriate place on the grid. (For additional speaking practice, students can later report back to the class and tell about the students they interviewed.)

ADDITIONAL PRACTICE

Have students work in pairs, taking turns asking and answering the nine questions. (For additional practice, students can write the answers to the questions on a separate sheet of paper.)

TEXT PAGE 24

CIVICS ENRICHMENT

PERFORMANCE-BASED ASSESSMENT

These civics enrichment activities are designed to promote students' active participation in class and in the civic life of the community—through projects, issues discussions, community tasks, field trips, and Internet activities. Reproducible performance-based assessment forms for use in evaluating and documenting student participation in these activities are included in the Teacher's Resources section.

CIVIC PARTICIPATION

First have students practice introducing themselves in class. Then have them go around the school and introduce themselves to various school personnel in the office, in the library, and other places. They should tell their name, their nationality, where they were born, when they came to the United States, and other information they would like to share.

PROJECT

Bulletin Board Project: In this project students first work individually. They bring in a map of their native country (a real map or one they have drawn), and they write a paragraph about themselves. In the paragraph, they tell their name, nationality, country of birth, and the city or town where they were born. Then students work as a class to make a bulletin board display of their work. Have students take responsibility for all aspects of this project. Have them identify the particular tasks involved in the project, who will accomplish each task, what resources are needed, and what form the final bulletin board display will take. Use the project as a basis for building students' skills in leadership, teamwork, and communicating information—key SCANS* skills useful for success in the workplace.

*Secretary's Commission on Achieving Necessary Skills.

PROJECT

Calendar Project: Students work as a class to make a calendar with separate pages for each month that they will study together in your class. On the calendar they should indicate their birthdays, U.S. holidays, native country holidays, and other special dates. Have students take responsibility for all aspects of this project. Have them identify the particular tasks involved in the project, who will accomplish each task, what resources are needed, and what form the final calendar will take. Use the project as a basis for building students' leadership and teamwork skills.

UNIT SUMMARY

KEY VOCABULARY

Have students review the lists of words they have learned in this unit. Encourage students to get a small notebook where they can write down vocabulary that is new for them.

GRAMMAR

Have students review the sentence-examples of grammar in this unit. For enrichment, have higher-level students look for more examples of this grammar in the unit and write additional sentences.

FUNCTIONAL EXPRESSIONS

Have students review the sentences and find where they occur in this unit. For enrichment, have students make up new conversations that use these functional expressions and present them to the class.

UNIT REVIEW WORKSHEETS

Unit B Writing Practice
Unit B Reading Practice

FOCUS

TOPICS

Requirements of the English Speaking Test
Giving information about name, other names used, or
    the desire to change name
Giving information about eligibility for citizenship

FUNCTIONAL INTERVIEW SKILLS

Reporting information
Asking for repetition
Showing confidence and pride during the interview

KEY VOCABULARY

ABOUT THE ENGLISH SPEAKING TEST

answer questions	information
Application for	interview
Naturalization	look down
chair	nervous
change	officer
confident	proud
Excuse me.	shoulders
eye contact	sit up straight
Form N-400	smile
friendly	tell the truth
head	words
I'm sorry.	

GIVING YOUR NAME

change your name	legally change your name
family name	middle name
first name	surname
full name	use another name
given name	use other name
last name	

GIVING INFORMATION ABOUT YOUR ELIGIBILITY

for ___ years	married
how long	permanent resident
husband	U.S. citizen
lawful permanent	wife
resident	

ABOUT THE ENGLISH SPEAKING TEST

As a class, have students read the information in the blue box. Emphasize that officers might ask about any of the information on the student's N-400 form. Students should especially prepare to talk about any unusual information on their form, such as trips outside the United States, a change in marital status, and a change in the student's name. Practice the functional expressions for asking for repetition. Make sure students understand the guidance about demonstrating confidence and pride during the interview. Have them practice the specific suggestions in class.

ROLE PLAY

Have students work in pairs and role-play the dialogs in Section 5 (Giving Your Name) and Section 6 (Giving Information about Your Eligibility). Have students take turns being the USCIS officer and the applicant. Then have pairs of students present their role plays to the class.

WORKSHEETS

Interview Practice Worksheets 7–10

LESSONS & UNIT ACTIVITIES	OBJECTIVES	STUDENT TEXT	TEACHER'S GUIDE
Vocabulary Preview	Interpreting a map of North America; Compass directions	25	27
A Map of the United States of America	Interpreting a map of the United States; Identifying states that border Canada and Mexico; Identifying the Atlantic and Pacific Oceans, the Missouri and Mississippi Rivers	26–29	28–29
Famous U.S. Landmarks	Identifying location of the Statue of Liberty; Identifying famous U.S. landmarks	30–31	30–31
U.S. Territories	Identifying and locating U.S. territories	32–33	32–33
Civics Test: Are You Ready for Some Civics Questions?	Answering civics questions about U.S. geography; Asking for repetition; Asking for clarification	34	34
Song of Freedom: *America the Beautiful*	Reciting the lyrics and singing *America the Beautiful*	35	35
Unit Test	Preparing for USCIS civics, reading, and writing test questions	36–37	35
Civics Enrichment	Finding locations and information on a local street map and other community maps; Project: Making a tourist map of places to visit in the community; Internet Activity: Visiting U.S. states and territories online	38	36
The English Test (Speaking)*	Giving information about yourself; Giving information about address and telephone numbers; Asking for clarification; Saying you don't understand	218–219	37

* This interview preparation lesson is in the Appendix for students' convenience. It can be introduced in this unit and then reviewed along with the other interview preparation lessons as students get ready for their appointment at USCIS. If you prefer, you can do these lessons later in the course if that is more appropriate for the timing of your students' interviews. Interview Practice worksheets accompany these lessons.

UNIT RESOURCES

Worksheets:
Unit 1 Writing Practice
Unit 1 Reading Practice
Interview Practice Worksheets 11–16

Audio Program:
CD 1: Tracks 20–33

RELATED PRACTICE

Foundations: Unit 3
Word by Word Basic: pages 22–25, 248–251
Word by Word: pages 9–10, 167–171
Side by Side / Side by Side Plus: Book 1, Units 5, 6
Side by Side Interactive CD-ROM / Side by Side TV: Level 1A, Segments 6–8
ExpressWays: Book 1, Unit 2

KEY VOCABULARY

READING	WRITING	GEOGRAPHY	STATES	CITIES
capital	Alaska	Atlantic Ocean	Alaska	Hollywood
city	Canada	Canada	Arizona	New York City
country	capital	capital	California	Philadelphia
has	has	city	Idaho	St. Louis
is	is	country	Maine	San Antonio
largest	largest	East Coast	Michigan	San Francisco
most	Mexico	Hudson River	Minnesota	Washington, D.C.
north	most	island	Missouri	
of	New York City	Liberty Island	Montana	**U.S. TERRITORIES**
people	north	map	New Hampshire	American Samoa
south	of	Mexico	New Jersey	Guam
the	people	Mississippi River	New Mexico	Northern Mariana
United States	south	Missouri River	New York	Islands
what	the	New York Harbor	North Dakota	Puerto Rico
	United States	ocean	Ohio	U.S. Virgin Islands
	Washington, D.C.	Pacific Ocean	Pennsylvania	
		river	South Dakota	**COMPASS DIRECTIONS**
		state	Texas	east
		United States of America	Vermont	north
		West Coast	Washington	south
				west

GRAMMAR

TO BE

The United States **is** a large country.

WH-QUESTIONS

What is the capital of the U.S.?
Where is the Statue of Liberty?
Which states do you want to visit?
Why?

YES/NO QUESTIONS

Is the United States a large country?
Are you ready for some civics questions?

SHORT ANSWERS

Yes, it is.
No, it isn't.

FUNCTIONAL EXPRESSIONS

ASKING FOR REPETITION

I'm sorry. Please repeat the question.

CLARIFYING

I'm sorry. Did you say ____?

TEXT PAGE 25 VOCABULARY PREVIEW

You may want to introduce these words before beginning the unit, or you may choose to wait until they first occur in a specific lesson. If you choose to introduce them at this point, here are some suggestions:

1. Have students look at the map on text page 25 and identify the words they already know.

2. Present the vocabulary. Say each word and have the class repeat it chorally and individually. Check students' understanding and pronunciation of the words.

3. Practice the vocabulary as a class, in pairs, or in small groups. Have students cover the word list and look at the map. Practice the words in the following ways:

   • Say a word and have students tell the number of the word on the map.
   • Give the number of something on the map and have students say the word.

FOCUS

TOPICS

Maps & Geography
Cities, States, & Capitals

GRAMMAR

To Be

The United States **is** a large country.
Canada **is** north of the United States.

WH-Questions

What's the name of your state?

KEY VOCABULARY

COUNTRIES

Canada	the United States
Mexico	

STATES

Alaska	New Mexico
Arizona	New York
California	North Dakota
Idaho	Ohio
Maine	Pennsylvania
Michigan	Texas
Minnesota	Vermont
Montana	Washington
New Hampshire	

BODIES OF WATER / **COMPASS DIRECTIONS**

Atlantic Ocean	east
Mississippi River	north
Missouri River	south
Pacific Ocean	west

OTHER VOCABULARY

between	map
border (v.)	other
capital	state
country	state capital
East Coast	Washington, D.C.
large	West Coast
long	

GETTING READY

Introduce directions.

a. Use the map on page 26. Point to the top of the map and say, "This is north." Repeat for south, east, and west.

b. Have students identify the direction as you point north, south, east, and west in random order several times.

PREVIEWING THE READING

Have students talk about the map to establish the context of the passage. Ask some or all of the following questions:

What country is this?
How many states are there in the United States?
Where is Texas? / Point to Texas.
Where is California? / Point to California.
Where is Florida? / Point to Florida.
Where is New York? / Point to New York.
Where is our state? / Point to our state.
What state is north of (your state)?
What state is south of (your state)?
What state is east of (your state)?
What state is west of (your state)?

READING THE PASSAGE

1. Have students read the passage silently. (If you wish, you may read the passage aloud or play the audio program as students read along silently.)

2. **Check Reading Comprehension**: Ask students a question about each line of the passage. For beginning-level students, ask these questions in the order below so that the questions follow the sequence of the passage. For higher-level students, ask the questions in random order.

Is the United States a large country or a small country?
How many other countries is the United States between?
What country is north of the United States?
What country is south of the United States?
Name some states that border Canada.
Name some states that border Mexico.
How many oceans is the United States between?
What ocean is on the East Coast of the United States?
What ocean is on the West Coast of the United States?
What is the longest river in the United States?
What is the second longest river in the United States?
What is the capital of the United States?

3. Ask students if they have any questions about the passage; check understanding of vocabulary.

4. **Choral Repetition:** Read aloud each line of the passage and have students repeat.

5. **Class Circle Reading:** Have students read the passage aloud as a class, with different students reading each line. (You can assign each line to a particular student or by seating patterns, or by letting students take turns spontaneously. In large classes,

have a different group or row of students read each line.)

6. Have students work in pairs, reading the passage to each other section by section. Circulate around the room and check students' reading and pronunciation, focusing more attention on students who need more assistance.

MAP ACTIVITY

Have students answer the questions as a class as they point to the correct locations on the map on page 26.

EXPANSION

Map Reading

Use a large classroom map (a pull-down map or a map on a bulletin board) if available, or use the map on text page 26. Point to a state and have students identify what is north, south, east, and west of the state you pointed to. Ask individual students to point to states and have the rest of the class identify what is north, south, east, and west of that state.

CHECK-UP (Pages 28–29)

VOCABULARY CHECK

1. country   3. capital   5. west
2. north   4. east   6. south

GRAMMAR CHECK

1. Yes, it is.   3. Yes, it is.   5. Yes, it is.
2. No, it isn't.   4. No, it isn't.   6. Yes, it is.

MAP GAME

Students can look at the map on page 26 or a large classroom map as they play this game. For a more challenging game, don't allow students to refer to a map as they play.

CIVICS CHECK

The Civics Check activities throughout the text are presented in an easy-to-use chart format that enables students to easily practice the 100 official USCIS civics test questions. The interactive classroom practice prepares students to extend learning outside of class by working with a study partner. Students can also practice alone, with or without the audio. Using the audio, students hear the question, a pause (for them to give an answer), and then the correct answer(s).

Note: Since many questions have multiple acceptable answers, encourage low beginners to consistently practice a single answer to a question, while higher-level students can practice the multiple answers.

First, practice each question separately:

1. **Listening:** Have students read along silently as they listen to the question and answer(s)—presented by you, by a pair of students, or on the audio program.

2. **Choral Repetition:** Model the question and answer(s) and have the whole class repeat in unison.

3. **Choral Conversation Practice:** Divide the class in half. Have Group 1 ask the question and Group 2 give the answer(s); then reverse. (Or: You ask the question and have the whole class answer in unison; then reverse.)

4. **Pair Practice:** Have students practice the question and answer(s) in pairs.

5. **Presentation:** Call on one or two pairs of students to present the question and answer(s) to the class.

Then practice all the questions together:

6. **Choral Answers:** Ask any question and have students give the answer in unison. (If there are multiple answers, have them give the first answer in the text.)

7. **Pair Practice:** Have students work in pairs, taking turns asking and answering all the questions in random order.

For more practice or for review during the next class session, do one of these activities:

LINE PRACTICE: Have students stand in two lines facing each other. Each pair of facing students should take turns asking and answering a question. After sufficient time for this practice, say "Move," and have one line of students move down one position while the other line remains in place. (The student at the end of the line moves to the beginning of the line.) In this way, new pairs are created and students practice with another partner. Continue until students have practiced all the questions.

"ROUND ROBIN": Have students circulate around the room and ask each other the questions. Students should move on to another person after they have taken turns asking and answering a question.

MAP DISCUSSION

Have students answer the questions in a class discussion. As they share their answers, have them point to the different states. (If available, a large classroom map would be useful for this activity.)

YOUR NATIVE COUNTRY

Have students write the answers to these questions about their native countries. (Low-beginning-level students may need help providing this information.) Then have students draw a map of their country. Students should indicate the location of their country's capital, their city or town, and the countries or bodies of water that are next to their countries.

TEXT PAGES 30–31 FAMOUS U.S. LANDMARKS

FOCUS

TOPICS

The Statue of Liberty
Famous U.S. Landmarks

GRAMMAR

To Be

The Statue of Liberty **is** in New York.

KEY VOCABULARY

CITIES AND TOWNS	BODIES OF WATER
Hollywood	Hudson River
Keystone	Mississippi River
New York	New York Harbor
Philadelphia	
St. Louis	**FAMOUS U.S. LANDMARKS**
San Antonio	Alamo
San Francisco	Gateway Arch
Washington, D.C.	Golden Gate Bridge
	Grand Canyon National Park
STATES	Hollywood sign
Arizona	Liberty Bell
California	Mount Rushmore
Missouri	Statue of Liberty
New Jersey	Washington Monument
New York	
Pennsylvania	**OTHER VOCABULARY**
South Dakota	border (v.)
Texas	freedom
	island
	symbol

PREVIEWING THE READING

Have students look at all the photographs on pages 30–31. Introduce the word *landmark*. Have students identify which landmarks they are familiar with. Then ask these questions about the top two photographs on page 30:

Look at the picture on the left. What is this? (The Statue of Liberty)
Look at the picture on the right. The Statue of Liberty is on a small piece of land with water all around it. What do we call this? (An island.)
Where is the Statue of Liberty? (In New York.)

READING THE PASSAGE

Note: The complete passage includes the captions under the photographs on pages 30–31.

1. Have students read the passage silently. (If you wish, you may read the passage aloud or play the audio program as students read along silently.)
2. **Check Reading Comprehension:** Ask students a question about each line of the passage. For beginning-level students, ask these questions in the order below so that the questions follow the sequence of the passage. For higher-level students, ask the questions in random order.

   Where is the Statue of Liberty?
   What is it on?
   Which states does New York Harbor border?
   The Statue of Liberty is at the southern end of what river?
   What is the Statue of Liberty a symbol of?
   What famous landmark is in Washington, D.C.?
   What famous landmark is in Philadelphia, Pennsylvania?
   What famous landmark is in San Francisco, California?
   Where is Mount Rushmore?
   Where is the Alamo?
   Where is Grand Canyon National Park?
   What famous landmark is in St. Louis, Missouri?
   Where is the Hollywood sign?

3. Ask students if they have any questions about the passage; check understanding of vocabulary.
4. **Choral Repetition:** Read aloud each line of the passage and have students repeat.
5. **Class Circle Reading:** Have students read the passage aloud as a class, with different students reading each line. (You can assign each line to a particular student or by seating patterns, or by letting students take turns spontaneously. In large classes, have a different group or row of students read each line.)
6. **Pair Practice:** Have students work in pairs, reading the passage to each other. Circulate around the room and check students' reading and pronunciation, focusing more attention on students who need more assistance.

MAP ACTIVITY

Have students answer the questions as a class as they point to the correct locations on the map on page 26 or on a large classroom map, if available.

EXPANSION

1. U.S. Landmark Facts

Ask if students know the answers to these questions:

a. Who is the Washington Monument named for? (President George Washington.)

b. Who are the U.S. presidents on Mount Rushmore? (From left to right: George Washington, Thomas Jefferson, Theodore Roosevelt, Abraham Lincoln)

c. Which do you think is taller—the Washington Monument or the Gateway Arch? (The Gateway Arch is 630 feet tall. The Washington Monument is 555 feet, 5 1/8 inches tall.)

2. Research Project about a U.S. Landmark

You may want to assign higher-level students to do a research project about one of the U.S. landmarks in this lesson or another landmark that interests them. Students can work on their own, in pairs, or as a small group. They can use the Internet to find information about the landmark's history, its features, how to visit, and other interesting facts. Have students prepare a presentation for the class.

TEXT PAGES 32–33 U.S. TERRITORIES

FOCUS

TOPIC
U.S. Territories

GRAMMAR

To Be

Puerto Rico **is** an island in the Caribbean.
The Northern Mariana Islands **are** in the western Pacific Ocean.

KEY VOCABULARY

U.S. TERRITORIES
American Samoa	Puerto Rico
Guam	U.S. Virgin Islands
Northern Mariana Islands	

BODIES OF WATER
Atlantic Ocean	Pacific Ocean
Caribbean Sea	South Pacific

OTHER VOCABULARY
Caribbean	island
group	territory

PREVIEWING THE READING

Have students look at the maps on page 32. Ask the following questions:

> What do you see on this page? (Two maps.)
> What do you see on the maps? (Bodies of water and islands.)
> Look at the words in blue on the maps. What are the names of these bodies of water?
> (If a large world map is available in the classroom, have students locate these places on the map.)

READING THE PASSAGE

1. Have students read the passage silently. (If you wish, you may read the passage aloud or play the audio program as students read along silently.)
2. **Check Reading Comprehension:** Ask students a question about each line of the passage. For beginning-level students, ask these questions in the order below so that the questions follow the sequence of the passage. For higher-level students, ask the questions in random order.

> Some places that are part of the United States are not states. What are they?
> What is Puerto Rico?
> Where is Puerto Rico?

> What is the U.S. Virgin Islands?
> Where are the Northern Mariana Islands?
> What is Guam?
> Where is American Samoa?

3. Ask students if they have any questions about the passage; check understanding of vocabulary.
4. **Choral Repetition:** Read aloud each line of the passage and have students repeat.
5. **Class Circle Reading:** Have students read the passage aloud as a class, with different students reading each line. (You can assign each line to a particular student or by seating patterns, or by letting students take turns spontaneously. In large classes, have a different group or row of students read each line.)
6. **Pair Practice:** Have students work in pairs, reading the passage to each other, section by section. Circulate around the room and check students' reading and pronunciation, focusing more attention on students who need more assistance.

CHECK-UP

VOCABULARY CHECK

1. River
2. Harbor
3. Canyon
4. Ocean
5. Islands
6. Coast

CIVICS CHECK

Note: Since many questions have multiple acceptable answers, encourage low beginners to consistently practice a single answer to a question, while higher-level students can practice the multiple answers.

First, practice each question separately:

1. **Listening:** Have students read along silently as they listen to the question and answer(s)—presented by you, by a pair of students, or on the audio program.
2. **Choral Repetition:** Model the question and answer(s) and have the whole class repeat in unison.
3. **Choral Conversation Practice:** Divide the class in half. Have Group 1 ask the question and Group 2 give the answer(s); then reverse. (Or: You ask the question and have the whole class answer in unison; then reverse.)
4. **Pair Practice:** Have students practice the question and answer(s) in pairs.
5. **Presentation:** Call on one or two pairs of students to present the question and answer(s) to the class.

Then practice all the questions together:

6. **Choral Answers:** Ask any question and have students give the answer in unison. (If there are multiple answers, have them give the first answer in the text.)

7. **Pair Practice:** Have students work in pairs, taking turns asking and answering all the questions in random order.

For more practice or for review during the next class session, do one of these activities:

LINE PRACTICE: Have students stand in two lines facing each other. Each pair of facing students should take turns asking and answering a question. After sufficient time for this practice, say "Move," and have one line of students move down one position while the other line remains in place. (The student at the end of the line moves to the beginning of the line.) In this way, new pairs are created and students practice with another partner. Continue until students have practiced all the questions.

"ROUND ROBIN": Have students circulate around the room and ask each other the questions. Students should move on to another person after they have taken turns asking and answering a question.

A LANDMARK IN YOUR NATIVE COUNTRY

Have students describe famous landmarks in their native countries. Encourage them to bring in photos, books, brochures, or other material to share with the class.

FOCUS

TOPIC
U.S. Geography

GRAMMAR

To Be

What ocean **is** on the West Coast?

WH-Questions

What ocean is on the East Coast?

FUNCTIONAL INTERVIEW SKILLS

Asking for repetition
Asking for clarification

NEW VOCABULARY

Are you ready . . . ?
Did you say . . . ?
I'm sorry.
Okay.
Please repeat the question.
That's correct.
That's right.
Very good.

PRACTICING THE DIALOG

Notes:
- This dialog is in three parts. Practice each part separately.
- Most Civics Test dialogs in the text have blank lines and answer-choice boxes since many questions have multiple acceptable answers. Encourage low beginners to consistently practice one answer to a question so that they master it—the first answer in the text or another answer they prefer. Higher-level students can practice the multiple answers. (The audio always contains the first answer.)

1. **Setting the Scene:** Have students look at the photograph and determine who is talking: a USCIS officer and an applicant for citizenship. Establish the context: "The USCIS officer is asking some civics questions."
2. **Listening:** With books closed, have students listen to the dialog—presented by you, by a pair of students, or on the audio program.
3. **Choral Repetition:** With books still closed, model each line and have the whole class repeat in unison.
4. **Reading:** With books open, have students follow along as two students present the dialog. Ask students if they have any questions and check understanding of vocabulary.
5. **Choral Conversation Practice:** Divide the class in half. Have Group 1 ask the questions and Group 2 give the answers; then reverse. (Or: You ask the questions and have the whole class answer in unison; then reverse.)
6. **Pair Practice:** Have students practice the dialog in pairs, taking turns being the USCIS officer and the applicant.
7. **Presentations:** Call on pairs of students to present the dialog to the class.

PRACTICING THE SONG

1. **Listening to the Lyrics:** Have students listen to the lyrics of the song by playing the audio or saying the lyrics yourself.
2. **Choral Repetition:** Read aloud each line of the song and have students repeat in unison.
3. **Listening to the Song:** Have students listen to the song by playing the audio or singing it yourself.
4. **Singing Aloud:** Have students sing along as you play the audio or sing the song.

EXPANSION

Discuss with students the photo of Pike's Peak and the information in the caption.

TEXT PAGES 36–37　Unit Test

The end-of-unit assessment evaluates student achievement of the unit's learning objectives while developing the specific test-taking skills required for success during the USCIS English and civics exam. Students can practice and complete the tests in class or at home.

A. CIVICS

This section contains the official USCIS questions that appear in the unit. Students can practice the questions and answers outside of class on their own or with a study partner. (Since many questions have multiple acceptable answers, encourage low beginners to consistently practice a single answer to a question, while higher-level students can practice the multiple answers.) For in-class assessment, call on students to answer different questions, or observe students as they test each other through pair practice.

B. CIVICS MATCHING

1. b
2. c
3. a

C. KEY VOCABULARY

1. Washington, D.C.
2. Canada
3. Mexico
4. Alaska
5. New York
6. United States
7. California

D. READING AND WRITING

This section contains the types of reading and writing questions on the USCIS test. You can assess students' reading skills by their ability to read aloud the questions. You can assess their writing skills by their ability to write the sentences from dictation. (The dictation sentences appear below, in the text on page 239, and on the audio program. Each dictation sentence is on a separate audio track so that the audio can be paused while students write.)

1. Canada is north of the United States.
2. The capital of the United States is Washington, D.C.
3. Mexico is south of the United States.
4. Alaska is the largest state.
5. New York City has the most people.

CIVICS ENRICHMENT

> ### PERFORMANCE-BASED ASSESSMENT
>
> These civics enrichment activities are designed to promote students' active participation in class and in the civic life of the community—through projects, issues discussions, community tasks, field trips, and Internet activities. Reproducible performance-based assessment forms for use in evaluating and documenting student participation in these activities are included in the Teacher's Resources section.

CIVIC PARTICIPATION

Bring to class one or more local street maps of your community. (If possible, bring in a sufficient number of maps so that students can work in pairs or in small groups.) Have students identify the kind of information they see on the map. Have them find the location of their school on the map. Then have them find the locations where they live. Have students bring in other kinds of maps of the community, such as bus route maps, subway maps, and maps of parks, bicycle routes, or other local features. (Brainstorm with students where they can find these maps, and then have students obtain them. While it may seem easier for you to supply them, a key goal of the activity is for students to access community resources such as the library, city hall, or parks and recreation department in order to locate the materials.) When students have brought in the maps, have a class discussion about the kinds of information the maps provide.

PROJECT

In this project, students work as a class to make a big tourist map for visitors to your community. Students should draw all the important places to visit and show where they are located. They should try to show all the important streets and also show any bus or train routes tourists can use to visit the places on the map. (You can use a tourist map of another city as an example. Don't use a tourist map of your own city as students might replicate it.) Have students take responsibility for all aspects of this project. Have them identify the particular tasks involved in the project, who will accomplish each task, what resources are needed, and what form the final tourist map will take. Use the project as a basis for building students' skills in leadership, teamwork, and communicating information—key SCANS* skills useful for success in the workplace.

*Secretary's Commission on Achieving Necessary Skills.

INTERNET ACTIVITY

Have students visit the indicated website to find links to tourism information for all the U.S. states and territories. Students should select a place, gather information about it, and share with the class.

TECHNOLOGY ENRICHMENT

See Teacher's Guide page 311 for additional Internet enrichment activities related to this unit.

UNIT SUMMARY

KEY VOCABULARY

Have students review the lists of words they have learned in this unit. Encourage students to get a small notebook where they can write down vocabulary that is new for them.

GRAMMAR

Have students review the sentence-examples of grammar in this unit. For enrichment, have higher-level students look for more examples of this grammar in the unit and write additional sentences.

FUNCTIONAL EXPRESSIONS

Have students review the sentences and find where they occur in this unit. For enrichment, have students make up new conversations that use these functional expressions and present them to the class.

UNIT REVIEW WORKSHEETS

Unit 1 Writing Practice
Unit 1 Reading Practice
Unit 1 Civics Practice

FOCUS

TOPICS

Giving information about yourself
Giving information about address and telephone
   numbers

FUNCTIONAL INTERVIEW SKILLS

Asking for clarification
Saying you don't understand

KEY VOCABULARY

GIVING INFORMATION ABOUT YOURSELF

become	marital status
birth date	married
born	mother
citizen	nationality
country	parents
country of birth	permanent resident
country of nationality	single
date of birth	social security number
divorced	U.S. citizen
either	widowed
father	

GIVING INFORMATION ABOUT ADDRESS AND TELEPHONE NUMBERS

address	live
change address	move
current address	new address
daytime phone number	now
email address	same address
evening phone number	still
home address	

FUNCTIONAL EXPRESSIONS

Could you please say that another way?
Do you mean . . . ?
I don't understand.
I'm sorry.

ROLE PLAY

Have students work in pairs and role-play USCIS
interviews using many of the questions that appear on
pages 218–219 (Sections 7 and 8). Have students
take turns being the USCIS officer and the applicant.
Then have pairs of students present their role plays to
the class.

WORKSHEETS

Interview Practice Worksheets 11–16

UNIT 2   THE FLAG

LESSONS & UNIT ACTIVITIES	OBJECTIVES	STUDENT TEXT	TEACHER'S GUIDE
Vocabulary Preview	The flag of the United States	39	39
The Flag of the United States	Identifying what the stars and stripes on the flag represent; Identifying the colors of the flag	40–41	40–41
Voice of Freedom: The Pledge of Allegiance	Reciting the Pledge of Allegiance	42	42
Civics Test: Why Does the Flag Have Fifty Stars?	Answering questions about the flag; Apologizing; Asking for repetition	43	43
Unit Test	Preparing for USCIS civics, reading, and writing test questions	44–45	44
Civics Enrichment	Discussing where the flag can be found in the community, the state flag, and other flags; Project: Drawing a native country flag and writing about it; Internet Activity: Searching online for information about the American flag	46	44–45
The English Test (Speaking)*	Giving information for criminal records search: height, weight, race, hair color, eye color	219	45

* This interview preparation lesson is in the Appendix for students' convenience. It can be introduced in this unit and then reviewed along with the other interview preparation lessons as students get ready for their appointment at USCIS. If you prefer, you can do these lessons later in the course if that is more appropriate for the timing of your students' interviews. Interview Practice worksheets accompany these lessons.

UNIT RESOURCES

Worksheets:

Unit 2 Writing Practice
Unit 2 Reading Practice
Unit 2 Civics Practice
Interview Practice Worksheets 17–18

Audio Program:
CD 1: Tracks 34–43

RELATED PRACTICE

Foundations: Units 2, 9
Word by Word Basic: pages 10–17, 128–141
Word by Word: pages 4–7, 65–71
Side by Side / Side by Side Plus: Book 1, Units 7, 8
Side by Side Interactive CD-ROM / Side by Side TV: Level 1A, Segments 9–12
ExpressWays: Book 1, Unit 4

KEY VOCABULARY

READING	WRITING	THE FLAG	PLACES	OTHER WORDS
American flag	Alaska	American flag	island	because
are	and	flag	Iwo Jima	colonies
colors	blue	Pledge of Allegiance	moon	loyalty
country	California	star	Mount Suribachi	native country
does	capital	stripe	mountain	original
have/has	fifty (50)	U.S. flag	New York City	plant (v.)
how many	flag		United States	raise (v.)
in	has	**COLORS**	World Trade Center	represent
is	is	blue		show (v.)
largest	largest	red	**EVENTS**	site
most	most	white	battle	state
on	of		terrorist attack	top
people	people	**PEOPLE**	World War II	
state	red	astronaut		
the	state	firefighter	**NUMBERS**	
United States	the	U.S. Marines	one (1)	
Washington, D.C.	United States		thirteen (13)	
what	Washington, D.C.		fifty (50)	
	white			

GRAMMAR

THERE IS/THERE ARE

There is one star for each state.
There are fifty stars on the flag.

SINGULAR/PLURAL

There is one stripe.
There are thirteen stripe**s**.

HAVE/HAS

How many stars does the flag **have**?
The flag **has** fifty stars.

WH-QUESTIONS

What are the colors of the flag?
How many stars are there?
Why does the flag have fifty stars?

FUNCTIONAL EXPRESSIONS

APOLOGIZING

I'm sorry.

ASKING FOR REPETITION

Could you please repeat the
    question?
Could you please say that again?
Could you please repeat that?

TEXT PAGE 39 VOCABULARY PREVIEW

You may want to introduce these words before beginning the unit, or you may choose to wait until they first occur in a specific lesson. If you choose to introduce them at this point, here are some suggestions:

1. Have students look at the photographs on text page 39 and identify the words they already know.

2. Present the vocabulary. Say each word and have the class repeat it chorally and individually. Check students' understanding and pronunciation of the words.

3. Practice the vocabulary as a class, in pairs, or in small groups. Have students cover the word list and look at the photographs. Practice the words in the following ways:

   • Say a word and have students tell the correct number on the photograph.
   • Give a number on a photograph and have students say the word.

FOCUS

TOPIC
The Flag

GRAMMAR

There Is / There Are

There is one star for each state.
There are fifty stars on the American flag.

Singular / Plural

Each star represents a state.
The star**s** are white.

Have / Has

The flag **has** fifty stars.

NEW VOCABULARY

American	one
blue	red
call	represent
colonies	star
color	stripe
each	there
fifty	thirteen
first	three
flag	white

GETTING READY

1. Introduce singular and plural.

Give examples of singular and plural nouns by pointing out objects in the room. For example:

a book—books
a window—windows

2. Introduce *there is/there are*.

Using the singular and plural nouns from the first Getting Ready activity, make sentences using *there is* or *there are*. For example:

There is one book on the desk.
There are ten books on the shelf.

3. Introduce colors.

Use colored paper or objects in the room to introduce the colors red, white, and blue.

a. Show students the red paper or object and say "Red." Have students repeat. Continue for white and blue.

b. Ask about the color of objects or articles of clothing in the room that are red, white, or blue. For example, point to a student and ask, "What color is his shirt?" ("White.")

PREVIEWING THE READING

Have students talk about the title and the photograph to establish the context of the passage. Ask some or all of the following questions:

What is this? (The flag of the United States)
Where do you see it? (At school / In the community / At sporting events / On TV)
What are the colors of the American flag?
What is on the American flag?

READING THE PASSAGE

1. Have students read the passage silently. (If you wish, you may read the passage aloud or play the audio program as students read along silently.)

2. **Check Reading Comprehension:** Ask students a question about each line of the passage. For beginning-level students, ask these questions in the order below so that the questions follow the sequence of the passage. For higher-level students, ask the questions in random order.

How many colors are there on the flag of the United States?
What color is the American flag?

How many states are there in the United States?
How many stars are there on the American flag?
Why does the flag have fifty stars?
What does each star represent?
What color are the stars?

How many stripes does the American flag have?
What do the stripes represent?
What were the first thirteen states called?
Why are there thirteen stripes on the American flag?
What color are the stripes?

3. Ask students if they have any questions about the passage; check understanding of vocabulary.

4. **Choral Repetition:** Read aloud each line of the passage and have students repeat.

5. **Class Circle Reading:** Have students read the passage aloud as a class, with different students reading each line. (You can assign each line to a particular student or by seating patterns, or by letting students take turns spontaneously. In large classes, have a different group or row of students read each line.)

6. **Pair Practice:** Have students work in pairs, reading the passage to each other section by section. Circulate around the room and check students' reading and pronunciation, focusing more attention on students who need more assistance.

EXPANSION

There Is / There Are

Have students practice *there is / there are* as they describe objects in the classroom and locations around the school. For example:

> There is a pencil on my desk.
> There are books on the shelf.
> There is a post office next to our school.

CHECK-UP

VOCABULARY CHECK

1. blue
2. stripes
3. stars
4. red
5. colonies

GRAMMAR CHECK

1. There are
2. There is
3. There are
4. There are
5. There is

CIVICS CHECK

Note: Since many questions have multiple acceptable answers, encourage low beginners to consistently practice a single answer to a question, while higher-level students can practice the multiple answers.

Practice each question separately:

1. **Listening:** Have students read along silently as they listen to the question and answer(s)—presented by you, by a pair of students, or on the audio program.

2. **Choral Repetition:** Model the question and answer(s) and have the whole class repeat in unison.

3. **Choral Conversation Practice:** Divide the class in half. Have Group 1 ask the question and Group 2 give the answer(s); then reverse. (Or: You ask the question and have the whole class answer in unison; then reverse.)

4. **Pair Practice:** Have students practice the question and answer(s) in pairs.

5. **Presentation:** Call on one or two pairs of students to present the question and answer(s) to the class.

YOUR NATIVE COUNTRY'S FLAG

Have each student draw his or her native country's flag. (If possible, have crayons or colored pencils available so that students can depict the flags' colors. If not, ask students to color the flags at home.) Have students write answers to the questions about their flags and then share this information with other students. To expand students' vocabulary, make a list on the board of the names of additional colors, shapes, animals, and other symbols on these flags.

INTRODUCING THE PLEDGE OF ALLEGIANCE

Point out the important fact at the beginning of this lesson. (It is one of the 100 USCIS civics test questions.) Have students read the sentence silently as you read it aloud.

PRACTICING THE PLEDGE OF ALLEGIANCE

(Note: You may want to have students stand and place their right hands on their chests while practicing the Pledge in parts or in its entirety.)

1. **Listening:** Have students listen to the Pledge of Allegiance recited by you or by playing the audio.

2. **Choral Repetition (line by line):** Read aloud each separate line of the Pledge as it appears in the text and have students repeat in unison.

3. **Choral Repetition (phrase by phrase):** Read aloud each phrase and have students repeat in unison, as follows:

   I pledge allegiance to the flag of the United States of America /
   and to the republic for which it stands, /
   one nation, under God, indivisible, /
   with liberty and justice for all.

4. **Reading:** Have students practice reading the Pledge as a class, in small groups, or on their own.

5. **Reciting:** Have students memorize the Pledge and practice reciting it as a class, in small groups, and on their own.

EXPANSION

1. Discuss with students the photos and information in the captions:

   PHOTO 1: Astronauts Neil Armstrong and Buzz Aldrin planting the U.S. flag on the moon on July 20, 1969.

   PHOTO 2: U.S. Marines raising the U.S. flag on Iwo Jima during World War II. Tell students about the Marine memorial in the nation's capital that depicts this scene, and bring in a photo of the memorial if available.

   PHOTO 3: Firefighters raising the flag at the site of the World Trade Center in New York City after the terrorist attack on September 11, 2001. Ask students what they remember about that day, and have them discuss their thoughts and feelings about the events.

2. Tell students about when *you* say/said the Pledge of Allegiance: as a child (school? scout troop?) and as an adult (meetings? assemblies?).

3. Ask students to recite pledges of their native countries in their native languages and then explain in English what they mean.

FOCUS

TOPIC
The Flag

GRAMMAR

Have/Has

Why does the flag **have** fifty stars?

WH-Questions

Why does the flag have thirteen stripes?
What do we show loyalty to when we say the Pledge of Allegiance?

FUNCTIONAL INTERVIEW SKILLS
Apologizing
Asking for repetition

KEY VOCABULARY

loyalty	Certainly.
Pledge of	Could you please repeat that?
Allegiance	Could you please repeat the
say	question?
stars	Could you please say that again?
stripes	I'm sorry.
	Sure.
	That's correct.
	That's right.
	Very good.

GETTING READY

1. **Introduce *have*.**

   a. Write on the board:

      How many stars does the American flag have?

   b. Model the question for students, and have them repeat chorally and individually. Then have them answer the question: "Fifty."

   c. Ask other questions about the flag:

      How many stripes does the American flag have?
      How many colors does the American flag have?

   d. Ask other questions, such as:

      How many pages does our book have?
      How many windows does our classroom have?
      How many rooms does your apartment have?

2. **Introduce different ways to ask for repetition.**

   Point out that the dialogs contain three different ways to ask for repetition:

      Could you please repeat the question?
      Could you please say that again?
      Could you please repeat that?

   Model these sentences for students, and have them repeat chorally and individually.

PRACTICING THE DIALOG

Notes:

- There are three dialogs. Practice each dialog separately.

- 3rd dialog: Before practicing this dialog, point out that when the USCIS officer repeats the question, the word order changes.

   1st Line A: What do we show loyalty to when we say the Pledge of Allegiance?
   2nd Line A: When we say the Pledge of Allegiance, what do we show loyalty to?

   Explain to students that the officer is rephrasing the question (saying the question a different way) to make it more understandable. When students ask the officer to repeat a question, they should know that the officer might or might not repeat the question exactly word-for-word. If the sentence sounds different, it is because the officer is trying to be helpful.

- These dialogs have blank lines and answer-choice boxes since the questions have multiple acceptable answers. Encourage low beginners to consistently practice one answer to a question so that they master it—the first answer in the text or another answer they prefer. Higher-level students can practice the multiple answers. (The audio contains the first answer.)

1. **Setting the Scene:** Have students look at the photograph and determine the topic of the conversation:

   1st dialog: The stars on the flag
   2nd dialog: The stripes on the flag
   3rd dialog: The Pledge of Allegiance

2. **Listening:** With books closed, have students listen to the dialog—presented by you, by a pair of students, or on the audio program.

3. **Choral Repetition:** With books still closed, model each line and have the whole class repeat in unison.

4. **Reading:** With books open, have students follow along as two students present the dialog. Ask students if they have any questions and check understanding of vocabulary.

5. **Choral Conversation Practice:** Divide the class in half. Have Group 1 ask the questions and Group 2 give the answers; then reverse. (Or: You ask the questions and have the whole class answer in unison; then reverse.)

6. **Pair Practice:** Have students practice the dialog in pairs, taking turns being the USCIS officer and the applicant.

7. **Presentations:** Call on pairs of students to present the dialog to the class.

The end-of-unit assessment evaluates student achievement of the unit's learning objectives while developing the specific test-taking skills required for success during the USCIS English and civics exam. Students can practice and complete the tests in class or at home.

A. CIVICS

This section contains the official USCIS questions that appear in the unit. Students can practice the questions and answers outside of class on their own or with a study partner. (Since many questions have multiple acceptable answers, encourage low beginners to consistently practice a single answer to a question, while higher-level students can practice the multiple answers.) For in-class assessment, call on students to answer different questions, or observe students as they test each other through pair practice.

B. CIVICS MATCHING

1. c   2. b   3. a

C. GRAMMAR

1. are   4. are   6. are
2. has   5. has   7. are
3. is

D. KEY VOCABULARY

1. flag   4. blue   6. state
2. states   5. white   7. fifty
3. red

E. READING AND WRITING

This section contains the types of reading and writing questions on the USCIS test. You can assess students' reading skills by their ability to read aloud the questions. You can assess their writing skills by their ability to write the sentences from dictation. (The dictation sentences appear below, in the text on page 239, and on the audio program. Each dictation sentence is on a separate audio track so that the audio can be paused while students write.)

1. The flag is red, white, and blue.
2. The United States has fifty (50) states.
3. The state of California has the most people.
4. Washington, D.C. is the capital of the United States.
5. Alaska is the largest state.

TEXT PAGE 46

CIVICS ENRICHMENT

PERFORMANCE-BASED ASSESSMENT

These civics enrichment activities are designed to promote students' active participation in class and in the civic life of the community—through projects, issues discussions, community tasks, field trips, and Internet activities. Reproducible performance-based assessment forms for use in evaluating and documenting student participation in these activities are included in the Appendix.

CIVIC PARTICIPATION

Have students discuss where they see the flag of the United States in your community and what other kinds of flags they see. Then have them discuss the symbols and colors on your state flag.

PROJECT

Bulletin Board "Flags of the World" Project: In this project, students draw color pictures of the flags of their native countries, they write some sentences that describe the flags, and then they work as a class to make a bulletin board display containing their drawings,

their sentences, and perhaps their photographs labeled with their names and native countries. Have students take responsibility for all aspects of this project. Have them identify the particular tasks involved in the project, who will accomplish each task, what resources are needed, and what form the final bulletin board display will take. Use the project as a basis for building students' skills in leadership, teamwork, and communicating information—key SCANS* skills useful for success in the workplace. (If possible, use a bulletin board in the school cafeteria, near the main office, or in another highly visible location so that the display is seen by the greatest number of people.)

*Secretary's Commission on Achieving Necessary Skills.

INTERNET ACTIVITY

In this activity, students use an Internet search engine to find information to answer questions about the flag. This activity enables students to develop basic computer research skills, such as using an Internet browser, typing search words to find information, and typing URLs to access websites. Make sure students have the skills to access the Internet and to use the computer to search for the information about the flag. Students can use www.google.com, www.bing.com, www.yahoo.com, or another search engine for this activity.

Answers to the questions are as follows:

- The flag flies at half-mast when public officials request it after someone in the government dies.
- If you want to fly the flag at night, you must have a light shine on it.
- The flag flies in front of the White House only when the President is staying there.

TECHNOLOGY ENRICHMENT

See Teacher's Guide page 311 for additional Internet enrichment activities related to this unit.

UNIT SUMMARY

KEY VOCABULARY

Have students review the lists of words they have learned in this unit. Encourage students to get a small notebook where they can write down vocabulary that is new for them.

GRAMMAR

Have students review the sentence-examples of grammar in this unit. For enrichment, have higher-level students look for more examples of this grammar in the unit and write additional sentences.

FUNCTIONAL EXPRESSIONS

Have students review the sentences and find where they occur in this unit. For enrichment, have students make up new conversations that use these functional expressions and present them to the class.

UNIT REVIEW WORKSHEETS

Unit 2 Writing Practice
Unit 2 Reading Practice
Unit 2 Civics Practice

TEXT PAGE 219 (SECTION 9) THE ENGLISH TEST (SPEAKING)

FOCUS

> ### TOPIC
> Giving information for criminal records search
>
> ### FUNCTIONAL INTERVIEW SKILLS
> Reporting information

KEY VOCABULARY

> ### DESCRIBING PHYSICAL FEATURES
> height
> how tall
> I'm ___ feet ___ inches tall.
> tall
>
> weight
> weigh
> how much
> I weigh ___ pounds.
>
> eyes
> eye color
> hair
> hair color

> ### RACE
> African-American
> Alaskan Native
> American Indian
> Asian
> Black
> Native Hawaiian
> Other Pacific Islander
> White

ROLE PLAY

Have students work in pairs and role-play dialogs using the questions in Section 9 (Giving Information for Criminal Records Search). Have students take turns being the USCIS officer and the applicant. Then have pairs of students present their role plays to the class.

WORKSHEETS

Interview Practice Worksheets 17–18

UNIT 3

BRANCHES OF GOVERNMENT

LESSONS & UNIT ACTIVITIES	OBJECTIVES	STUDENT TEXT	TEACHER'S GUIDE
Vocabulary Preview	Identifying the three branches of government	47	47
Branches of Government	Identifying the three branches of government; Understanding the concepts of separation of powers / checks and balances	48–49	48–49
Making, Enforcing, and Explaining the Laws of the United States	Identifying the functions of and public officials in the three branches of government	50–52	50–51
Civics Test: Name One Branch of the Government	Answering questions about the branches of government; Asking for repetition; Apologizing; Interpreting paraphrased questions	53	52
Unit Test	Preparing for USCIS civics, reading, and writing test questions	54–55	53
Civics Enrichment	Preparing for a field trip to the local office of a U.S. representative; Discussing problems, issues, and opinions to share with a U.S. representative; Internet Activity: Visiting a U.S. representative's website	56	53
The English Test (Speaking)*	Asking the officer to paraphrase a question; Giving information about residence and employment; Talking about time outside the United States	220–221	54–55

* This interview preparation lesson is in the Appendix for students' convenience. It can be introduced in this unit and then reviewed along with the other interview preparation lessons as students get ready for their appointment at USCIS. If you prefer, you can do these lessons later in the course if that is more appropriate for the timing of your students' interviews. Interview Practice worksheets accompany these lessons.

UNIT RESOURCES

Worksheets:
Unit 3 Writing Practice
Unit 3 Reading Practice
Unit 3 Civics Practice
Interview Practice Worksheets 19–21

Audio Program:
CD 1: Tracks 44–54

RELATED PRACTICE

Foundations: Unit 5
Word by Word Basic: pages 44–53, 58–67, 242–243
Word by Word: pages 20–24, 27–31, 161
Side by Side / Side by Side Plus: Book 1, Units 9–11
Side by Side Interactive CD-ROM / Side by Side TV: Levels 1A & 1B, Segments 13–17
ExpressWays: Book 1, Unit 3

UNIT OVERVIEW

KEY VOCABULARY

READING	WRITING	GOVERNMENT	PEOPLE	QUESTION WORDS
Congress	Congress	branches	Congress	what
do	in	courts	President	where
does	is	enforce the laws	representative	which
in	lives	executive	senator	who
is	meet/meets	explain the laws	Supreme Court justice	
lives	of	judicial	Vice President	**OTHER WORDS**
meet	President	laws		called
of	Senators	legislative	**BUILDINGS & PLACES**	can
President	the	make the laws	Capitol	have/has
Senators	United States	parts	Supreme Court	in charge of
the	Washington, D.C.	separation of powers	Washington, D.C.	live
United States	White House	system of checks and	White House	name (v.)
where		balances		powerful
White House				work
who				

GRAMMAR

SIMPLE PRESENT TENSE

They **work** in the Capitol.
The President **works** in the White House.

HAVE/HAS

The government **has** three branches.

CAN

Can you name one part of the government?

TO BE

The White House **is** in Washington, D.C.
Senators **are** in the Congress.

FUNCTIONAL EXPRESSIONS

APOLOGIZING

I'm sorry.

ASKING FOR REPETITION

Could you please repeat the question?
Could you say that one more time?

TEXT PAGE 47 VOCABULARY PREVIEW

You may want to introduce these words before beginning the unit, or you may choose to wait until they first occur in a specific lesson. If you choose to introduce them at this point, here are some suggestions:

1. Have students look at the photographs on text page 47 and identify the words they already know.
2. Present the vocabulary. Say each word and have the class repeat it chorally and individually. Check students' understanding and pronunciation of the words.

3. Practice the vocabulary as a class, in pairs, or in small groups. Have students cover the word list and look at the photographs. Practice the words in the following ways:

   • Say a word and have students tell the correct number on the photograph.
   • Give a number on a photograph and have students say the word.

FOCUS

TOPICS

Branches of Government
Separation of Powers/Checks and Balances

GRAMMAR

Have/Has

The government of the United States **has** three
  parts.

To Be

The Congress **is** the legislative branch.
The courts **are** in the judicial branch.

NEW VOCABULARY

branch	legislative branch
checks and balances	part
Congress	powerful
courts	President
executive branch	separation of powers
government	stop
in charge of	system
judicial branch	

PREVIEWING THE READING

Have students talk about the title and the photographs
to establish the context of the passage. Ask some or all
of the following questions. (Students may have previous
knowledge of some of the vocabulary, and some words
appear in the Vocabulary Preview on text page 47.)

(Point to the first picture.)
What is this? (The U.S. Capitol Building.)
Where is this? (In Washington, D.C.)
Who works there? (The Congress.)

(Point to the second picture.)
What is this? (The White House.)
Where is this? (In Washington, D.C.)
Who works there? (The President.)
Who lives there? (The President.)

(Point to the third picture.)
What is this? (The Supreme Court Building.)
Where is this? (In Washington, D.C.)
Who works there? (The Supreme Court.)

READING THE PASSAGE

1. Have students read the passage silently. (If you
   wish, you may read the passage aloud or play the
   audio program as students read along silently.)

2. **Check Reading Comprehension:** Ask students
   a question about each line of the passage. For
   beginning-level students, ask these questions in
   the order below so that the questions follow the
   sequence of the passage. For higher-level students,
   ask the questions in random order.

   How many parts does the government of the
     United States have?
   What are these parts called?

   What are the names of the three branches of
     government?

   Which branch is the Congress?
   Who is in charge of the executive branch?
   In which branch are the courts?

   What kind of separation is there between the
     branches of government?
   What kind of system is this?
   What does the system of checks and balances
     do?

3. Ask students if they have any questions about the
   passage; check understanding of vocabulary.

4. **Choral Repetition:** Read aloud each line of the
   passage and have students repeat.

5. **Class Circle Reading:** Have students read the
   passage aloud as a class, with different students
   reading each line. (You can assign each line to a
   particular student or by seating patterns, or by letting
   students take turns spontaneously. In large classes,
   have a different group or row of students read each
   line.)

6. **Pair Practice:** Have students work in pairs, reading
   the passage to each other section by section.
   Circulate around the room and check students'
   reading and pronunciation, focusing more attention
   on students who need more assistance.

CHECK-UP

VOCABULARY CHECK

1. government
2. branches
3. executive
4. legislative
5. judicial
6. powers
7. balances

CIVICS CHECK

Note: Since many questions have multiple acceptable answers, encourage low beginners to consistently practice a single answer to a question, while higher-level students can practice the multiple answers.

First, practice each question separately:

1. **Listening:** Have students read along silently as they listen to the question and answer(s)—presented by you, by a pair of students, or on the audio program.
2. **Choral Repetition:** Model the question and answer(s) and have the whole class repeat in unison.
3. **Choral Conversation Practice:** Divide the class in half. Have Group 1 ask the question and Group 2 give the answer(s); then reverse. (Or: You ask the question and have the whole class answer in unison; then reverse.)
4. **Pair Practice:** Have students practice the question and answer(s) in pairs.
5. **Presentation:** Call on one or two pairs of students to present the question and answer(s) to the class.

Then practice all the questions together:

6. **Choral Answers:** Ask any question and have students give the answer in unison. (If there are multiple answers, have them give the first answer in the text.)
7. **Pair Practice:** Have students work in pairs, taking turns asking and answering all the questions in random order.

For more practice or for review during the next class session:

"ROUND ROBIN": Have students circulate around the room and ask each other the questions. Students should move on to another person after they have taken turns asking and answering a question.

DISCUSSION

Have students describe the structure of the government in their native countries, including the branches of government, what they are called, who works in them, and where the government is located.

FOCUS

TOPIC
Branches of Government

GRAMMAR

Simple Present Tense
They **work** in the Capitol.
The President **works** in the White House.

NEW VOCABULARY

building	senators
Capitol	Supreme Court
enforce the laws	Supreme Court justices
explain the laws	they
make the laws	Vice President
representatives	White House

GETTING READY

Introduce the third person singular form of the simple present tense.

a. Write on the board:

    I work at (name of school).
    The President works in the White House.

b. Model the sentences for students.

c. Have students repeat chorally and individually.

PREVIEWING THE READING

Have students talk about the title and the photographs to establish the context of the passage. Ask some or all of the following questions to review the previous lesson's content:

(Point to the top picture.)
What building is this? (The U.S. Capitol Building.)
Where is it? (In Washington, D.C.)
What branch of government works there?
  (The legislative branch.)
Who works there? (The Congress.)

(Point to the middle picture.)
What building is this? (The White House.)
Where is it? (In Washington, D.C.)
What branch of government works there?
  (The executive branch.)
Who works there? (The President.)

(Point to the bottom picture.)
What building is this? (The Supreme Court Building.)
Where is it? (In Washington, D.C.)
What branch of government works there? (The
  judicial branch.)
Who works there? (The Supreme Court.)

READING THE PASSAGE

1. Have students read the passage silently. (If you wish, you may read the passage aloud or play the audio program as students read along silently.)

2. **Check Reading Comprehension:** Ask students a question about each line of the passage. For beginning-level students, ask these questions in the order below so that the questions follow the sequence of the passage. For higher-level students, ask the questions in random order.

    What is the legislative branch of the government
      called?
    Who is in the Congress?
    What do they do?
    Where do they work?
    What is the Capitol?

    Who is in charge of the executive branch?
    Who also works in the executive branch?
    What do the President and the Vice President do?
    Where does the President live and work?
    Where is the White House?

    Who works in the judicial branch?
    What do they do?
    Where do they work?
    Where is the Supreme Court?

3. Ask students if they have any questions about the passage; check understanding of vocabulary.

4. **Choral Repetition:** Read aloud each line of the passage and have students repeat.

5. **Class Circle Reading:** Have students read the passage aloud as a class, with different students reading each line. (You can assign each line to a particular student or by seating patterns, or by letting students take turns spontaneously. In large classes, have a different group or row of students read each line.)

6. **Pair Practice:** Have students work in pairs, reading the passage to each other section by section. Circulate around the room and check students' reading and pronunciation, focusing more attention on students who need more assistance.

CHECK-UP (Pages 51–52)

MATCHING I

1. b
2. c
3. a

MATCHING II

1. b
2. c
3. a

MATCHING III

1. c
2. a
3. b

ANSWER THESE QUESTIONS

1. The legislative branch / The Congress / Senators and representatives
2. The judicial branch / The Supreme Court / The Supreme Court justices
3. The executive branch / The President and Vice President

DISCUSSION

Have students discuss how the government works in their native countries. Have them also discuss U.S. laws they know about.

GRAMMAR CHECK

1. lives
2. work
3. works
4. explain
5. enforces
6. has

QUESTIONS AND ANSWERS

1. The legislative branch
2. The judicial branch
3. The executive branch

LISTENING

Have students complete the exercises as you play the audio program or read the following:

Listen and circle the correct answer.

1. Where does the President work?
2. Where does the Congress work?
3. Who makes the laws of the United States?
4. Who explains the laws of the United States?
5. Who enforces the laws of the United States?
6. Who works in the Congress of the United States?

ANSWERS

1. White House
2. Capitol
3. Congress
4. Supreme Court
5. the President
6. senators

FOCUS

> ### TOPIC
> Branches of Government
>
> ### GRAMMAR
>
> **Can**
>
> **Can** you name one part of the government?
>
> ### FUNCTIONAL INTERVIEW SKILLS
> Asking for repetition
> Apologizing
> Interpreting paraphrased questions

NEW VOCABULARY

All right.	Could you say that one
Can you name . . . ?	more time?
civics questions	Do you know . . . ?
Could you please repeat	going to
the question?	I'm sorry.
	Name . . . .

GETTING READY

1. Introduce *can*.

Write on the board:

Can you _____? Yes, I can.

a. Model the question and answer and have students repeat both chorally and individually.

b. Have several students answer as you ask about their ability to speak their native language:

Can you speak *Spanish*? (Yes, I can.)

2. Introduce different ways to ask for repetition.

Point out that the dialog contains two different ways to ask for repetition:

Could you please repeat the question?
I'm sorry. Could you say that one more time?

Model these sentences for students, and have them repeat chorally and individually.

3. Prepare students for paraphrased questions.

Point out that when the applicant asks the officer to repeat the question, the officer *paraphrases*—the officer says the question using different words or different word order.

2nd Line A: Name one branch of the government.
3rd Line A: Can you name one part of the government?

5th Line A: And do you know what stops one branch of government from becoming too powerful?
6th Line A: Something stops one branch of government from having more power than the other branches. Do you know what it is?

Explain to students that the officer is rephrasing the question (saying the question a different way) to make it more understandable. In the first example, the officer changes the word *branch* to the word *part* and also adds the words "Can you . . . " at the beginning of the question. In the second example, the officer changes the long question into a statement followed by a shorter question.

When students ask the officer to repeat a question, they should know that the officer might or might not repeat the question exactly word-for-word. If the sentence sounds different, it is because the officer is trying to be helpful.

PRACTICING THE DIALOG

Note: The dialog has blank lines and answer-choice boxes since the questions have multiple acceptable answers. Encourage low beginners to consistently practice one answer to a question so that they master it—the first answer in the text or another answer they prefer. Higher-level students can practice the multiple answers. (The audio contains the first answer.)

1. **Setting the Scene:** Have students look at the photograph and determine who is talking: a USCIS officer and an applicant for citizenship. Establish the context: "The USCIS officer is asking about the branches of government."

2. **Listening:** With books closed, have students listen to the dialog—presented by you, by a pair of students, or on the audio program.

3. **Choral Repetition:** With books still closed, model each line and have the whole class repeat in unison.

4. **Reading:** With books open, have students follow along as two students present the dialog. Ask students if they have any questions and check understanding of vocabulary.

5. **Choral Conversation Practice:** Divide the class in half. Have Group 1 ask the questions and Group 2 give the answers; then reverse. (Or: You ask the questions and have the whole class answer in unison; then reverse.)

6. **Pair Practice:** Have students practice the dialog in pairs, taking turns being the USCIS officer and the applicant.

7. **Presentations:** Call on pairs of students to present the dialog to the class.

The end-of-unit assessment evaluates student achievement of the unit's learning objectives while developing the specific test-taking skills required for success during the USCIS English and civics exam. Students can practice and complete the tests in class or at home.

A. CIVICS

This section contains the official USCIS questions that appear in the unit. Students can practice the questions and answers outside of class on their own or with a study partner. (Since many questions have multiple acceptable answers, encourage low beginners to consistently practice a single answer to a question, while higher-level students can practice the multiple answers.) For in-class assessment, call on students to answer different questions, or observe students as they test each other through pair practice.

B. CIVICS MATCHING

1. d   2. a   3. b   4. c

C. GRAMMAR

1. is   2. work   3. lives   4. has

D. KEY VOCABULARY

1. President   4. White House
2. Congress   5. Senators
3. Washington, D.C.   6. United States

E. READING AND WRITING

This section contains the types of reading and writing questions on the USCIS test. You can assess students' reading skills by their ability to read aloud the questions. You can assess their writing skills by their ability to write the sentences from dictation. (The dictation sentences appear below, in the text on page 239, and on the audio program. Each dictation sentence is on a separate audio track so that the audio can be paused while students write.)

1. The Congress meets in Washington, D.C.
2. The President of the United States lives in the White House.
3. The White House is in Washington, D.C.
4. United States Senators meet in Washington, D.C.
5. The President lives in the White House in Washington, D.C.

TEXT PAGE 56

CIVICS ENRICHMENT

> ### PERFORMANCE-BASED ASSESSMENT
> Reproducible performance-based assessment forms for use in evaluating and documenting student participation in these activities are included in the Appendix.

CIVIC PARTICIPATION

Field Trip Preparation: Prepare students for a visit the class will make to the local office of your representative in the U.S. Congress. (The best timing for the visit is while students are working in the next unit of the text.) Have students practice conversations in which they introduce themselves, tell where they are from, tell about when and why they came to the United States, describe what they are learning in school, and tell about their plans for the future.

COMMUNITY ISSUES

Have students brainstorm as a class problems or issues that are important to them. Have them discuss what they want to talk about and what opinions they want to share when they visit their representative.

INTERNET ACTIVITY

Have students go to the website listed in the text, find the link for their U.S. representative, go to the representative's website, and write down the kinds of information they find. Students can do this Internet activity individually, in pairs, or in small groups based on the computer resources available. Make sure students have the basic skills needed to access the Internet.

TECHNOLOGY ENRICHMENT

See Teacher's Guide page 311 for additional Internet enrichment activities related to this unit.

UNIT SUMMARY

KEY VOCABULARY

Have students review the lists of words they have learned in this unit. Encourage students to get a small notebook where they can write down vocabulary that is new for them.

GRAMMAR

Have students review the sentence-examples of grammar in this unit. For enrichment, have higher-level students look for more examples of this grammar in the unit and write additional sentences.

FUNCTIONAL EXPRESSIONS

Have students review the sentences and find where they occur in this unit. For enrichment, have students make up new conversations that use these functional expressions and present them to the class.

UNIT REVIEW WORKSHEETS

Unit 3 Writing Practice
Unit 3 Reading Practice
Unit 3 Civics Practice

FOCUS

> ### TOPICS
>
> Giving information about residence and employment
> Talking about time outside the United States
>
> ### FUNCTIONAL INTERVIEW SKILLS
>
> Asking the officer to paraphrase a question
> Reporting information

KEY VOCABULARY

> **ASKING THE OFFICER TO PARAPHRASE A QUESTION**
>
> | | |
> |---|---|
> | a different way | paraphrase |
> | another way | politely |
> | apologize | question |
> | different words | repeat |
> | explain | sentence |
> | meaning | understand |
> | means | word |
>
> **GIVING INFORMATION ABOUT RESIDENCE AND EMPLOYMENT**
>
> | | |
> |---|---|
> | address | name (v.) |
> | attend | occupation |
> | current address | position |
> | employed | previous address |
> | employer | previous job |
> | how long | school |
> | job | week |
> | live | work |
> | month | year |
>
> **TALKING ABOUT TIME OUTSIDE THE UNITED STATES**
>
> | | |
> |---|---|
> | 24 hours or more | lawful permanent |
> | absent | resident |
> | away | leave |
> | before | most recent trip |
> | during the past ___ years | outside the United |
> | for ___ days | States |
> | go | reason |
> | gone | take trip |
> | last | travel |
> | (the) last time | trip |

ASKING THE OFFICER TO PARAPHRASE A QUESTION

As a class, have students read the information in the blue box. Make sure they understand that asking the officer to paraphrase is different from asking for repetition. If students want the officer to rephrase the question using different words, they need to say that they don't understand and ask the officer to explain the question or use different words. Model each way to ask for paraphrasing and have the whole class repeat in unison.

ROLE PLAY: Section 10

Notes: Before practicing this dialog, point out the following examples of what happens when the student asks the officer to paraphrase:

- In the first dialog, the officer rephrases a short question by asking the question two different ways using different words:

  1st Line A: What was your previous address?
  2nd Line A: What was your address before your current address—the address before where you live now?

- In the second dialog, the applicant asks for the meaning of a word, and the officer answers by giving the meaning and also by rephrasing the original question two different ways:

  1st Line A: Are you employed?
  2nd Line A: It means "working." Do you work now? Do you have a job?

- Also in the second dialog (5th, 6th, and 7th lines), the applicant shows that she doesn't understand the word "position" by simply repeating the word with question intonation: "My position?" The officer answers by giving a synonym for the word and also by rephrasing the original question:

  A. What's your position there?
  B. My "position"?
  A. Yes—your occupation. What's your job?

Have students work in pairs and role-play the dialog. Have students take turns being the USCIS officer and the applicant. Then have pairs of students present their role plays to the class.

ROLE PLAY: Section 11

Note: Before practicing this dialog, have students write on a separate sheet of paper complete information about any trips they have made outside the United States during the past five years and since becoming a permanent resident. Have them list the trips in order beginning with the most recent one. They should write the date they left, the date they returned, the amount of time they were away, the place where they went, and the reason for the trip. Then have students put this information into sentences that they can say to explain these trips to the USCIS officer. Students can write these sentences in the space available on text page 221 or on a separate sheet of paper. Students should use this information as they practice the dialog, and the list they create can also be a reference for them to bring to their USCIS interview.

Have students work in pairs and role-play the dialog. Have students take turns being the USCIS officer and the applicant. Then have pairs of students present their role plays to the class.

For additional practice, have students work in other pairs and role-play the dialog again, this time using some of the expressions on text page 220 to ask the officer to paraphrase. (Five of the questions in the dialog have bracketed alternative ways that the officer might ask the question when paraphrasing.)

WORKSHEETS

Interview Practice Worksheets 19–21

UNIT 4

THE SENATE
THE HOUSE OF
REPRESENTATIVES

THE PRESIDENT
THE PRESIDENT'S CABINET
THE SUPREME COURT

LESSONS & UNIT ACTIVITIES	OBJECTIVES	STUDENT TEXT	TEACHER'S GUIDE
Vocabulary Preview	Identifying the three branches of government and public officials	57	57
The Senate	Identifying the legislative branch of government: U.S. senators	58–59	58–59
The House of Representatives	Identifying the legislative branch of government: U.S. representatives	60–61	60–61
The President of the United States	Identifying the executive branch of government: the President and Vice President	62–65	62–63
The President's Cabinet	Identifying the functions of the President's Cabinet and the Cabinet-level positions	66–67	64–65
The Supreme Court	Identifying the judicial branch of government: the Supreme Court and the Chief Justice	68–69	66–67
Review	Identifying different ways to ask questions; Reviewing facts about the branches of government	70	68
Civics Test: What Are the Two Parts of the U.S. Congress?	Answering questions about the branches of government; Asking for repetition; Asking for clarification; Interpreting paraphrased questions	71	69–70
Civic Participation	Writing a letter to a public official; Role-playing the U.S. Supreme Court; Meeting with a U.S. representative	72	71
Unit Test	Preparing for USCIS civics, reading, and writing test questions	73–75	71
Civics Enrichment	Making a field trip to the local office of a U.S. representative; Internet Activity: Visiting the website of the U.S. Capitol Visitor Center; Internet Activity: Visiting the website of the White House	76	72
The English Test (Speaking)*	Recognizing how the USCIS officer might check the applicant's understanding; Asking for an explanation or paraphrasing; Giving information about marital history and children	222	73

* This interview preparation lesson is in the Appendix for students' convenience. It can be introduced in this unit and then reviewed along with the other interview preparation lessons as students get ready for their appointment at USCIS. If you prefer, you can do these lessons later in the course if that is more appropriate for the timing of your students' interviews. Interview Practice worksheets accompany these lessons.

UNIT RESOURCES

Worksheets:
Unit 4 Writing Practice
Unit 4 Reading Practice
Unit 4 Civics Practice
Interview Practice Worksheet 22

Audio Program:
CD 1: Tracks 55–71

RELATED PRACTICE

Foundations: Unit 4
Word by Word Basic: pages 36–37, 212–215, 242–243
Word by Word: pages 16, 116–117, 161
Side by Side / Side by Side Plus: Book 1, Unit 12
Side by Side Interactive CD-ROM / Side by Side TV: Level 1B, Segments 18, 19
ExpressWays: Book 1, Unit 5

KEY VOCABULARY

READING	WRITING	PEOPLE	GOVERNMENT	ACTIONS
can	can	chief executive	bill	advise
citizens	citizens	Chief Justice of the	Congressional district	appoint
Congress	Congress	United States	document	approve
do/does	elect	Commander-in-Chief	executive branch	become
elects	fifty (50)	Congress	federal courts	elect
for	for	congressman	government	enforce the laws
government	has	congressperson	House of	explain the laws
have	in	congresswoman	Representatives	go
how many	November	people	judicial branch	go against
in	of	President	law	live
of	one hundred (100)	President's Cabinet	legislative branch	make the federal
people	people	representative	legislature	laws
President	President	senator	military	pass
Senators	Senators	Speaker of the House	national legislature	represent
the	states	of Representatives	Senate	resolve
United States	the	Supreme Court	Supreme Court	review
United States Senators	United States	justices	U.S. legislature	serve
vote	vote	Vice President	White House	sign
when		voting member		veto
who				vote
				work

GRAMMAR

SIMPLE PRESENT TENSE VS. TO BE

The President **lives** in the White House.
The President **is** the chief executive.

THERE ARE

There are one hundred senators.

TIME EXPRESSIONS

The President's term is **four years**.
We elect a senator **for six years**.
We elect a President for **how many years**?
In what month do we vote for President?

FUNCTIONAL EXPRESSIONS

ASKING FOR REPETITION

Excuse me. Could you please say that again?

CLARIFYING

Do you mean . . . ?

TEXT PAGE 57 VOCABULARY PREVIEW

You may want to introduce these words before beginning the unit, or you may choose to wait until they first occur in a specific lesson. If you choose to introduce them at this point, here are some suggestions:

1. Have students look at the photographs on text page 57 and identify the words they already know.
2. Present the vocabulary. Say each word and have the class repeat it chorally and individually. Check students' understanding and pronunciation of the words.

3. Practice the vocabulary as a class, in pairs, or in small groups. Have students cover the word list and look at the photographs. Practice the words in the following ways:

   • Say a word and have students tell the correct number on the photograph.
   • Give a number on a photograph and have students say the word.

FOCUS

TOPIC
The Senate

GRAMMAR

There Are

There are one hundred U.S. senators.

Simple Present Tense vs. To Be

U.S. senators **work** in the Senate.
The Congress **is** the legislative branch.

Time Expressions

We elect a U.S. senator **for six years**.

NEW VOCABULARY

elect	represent
federal laws	Senate
House of Representatives	U.S. senators
national legislature	year

PREVIEWING THE READING

Have students talk about the title and the photograph to establish the context of the passage. Ask some or all of the following questions:

Which branch of government do you think these people work in—the legislative branch, the executive branch, or the judicial branch? (The legislative branch.)

Where do they work? In what city? (In Washington, D.C.)

They are United States senators. Do you know the names of our state's United States senators? (Ignore this question in the District of Columbia and in U.S. territories.)

READING THE PASSAGE

1. Have students read the passage silently. (If you wish, you may read the passage aloud or play the audio program as students read along silently.)

2. **Check Reading Comprehension:** Ask students a question about each line of the passage. For beginning-level students, ask these questions in the order below so that the questions follow the sequence of the passage. For higher-level students, ask the questions in random order.

   What is the Congress of the United States?
   Is it the legislature of a *state*?
   Who makes the federal laws of the United States?
   What are the two parts of the Congress?

   Who works in the Senate?
   How many U.S. senators are there?
   How many U.S. senators are there from each state?
   Who does a senator represent?
   For how long do we elect a U.S. senator?

3. Ask students if they have any questions about the passage; check understanding of vocabulary.

4. **Choral Repetition:** Read aloud each line of the passage and have students repeat.

5. **Class Circle Reading:** Have students read the passage aloud as a class, with different students reading each line. (You can assign each line to a particular student or by seating patterns, or by letting students take turns spontaneously. In large classes, have a different group or row of students read each line.)

6. **Pair Practice:** Have students work in pairs, reading the passage to each other section by section. Circulate around the room and check students' reading and pronunciation, focusing more attention on students who need more assistance.

CHECK-UP

VOCABULARY CHECK

1. legislative
2. senators
3. six
4. two
5. laws

CIVICS CHECK

Note: Since many questions have multiple acceptable answers, encourage low beginners to consistently practice a single answer to a question, while higher-level students can practice the multiple answers.

First, practice each question separately:

1. **Listening:** Have students read along silently as they listen to the question and answer(s)—presented by you, by a pair of students, or on the audio program.

2. **Choral Repetition:** Model the question and answer(s) and have the whole class repeat in unison.

3. **Choral Conversation Practice:** Divide the class in half. Have Group 1 ask the question and Group 2 give the answer(s); then reverse. (Or: You ask the question and have the whole class answer in unison; then reverse.)

4. **Pair Practice:** Have students practice the question and answer(s) in pairs.

5. **Presentation:** Call on one or two pairs of students to present the question and answer(s) to the class.

Then practice all the questions together:

6. **Choral Answers:** Ask any question and have students give the answer in unison. (If there are multiple answers, have them give the first answer in the text.)

7. **Pair Practice:** Have students work in pairs, taking turns asking and answering all the questions in random order.

For more practice or for review during the next class session, do one of these activities:

LINE PRACTICE: Have students stand in two lines facing each other. Each pair of facing students should take turns asking and answering a question. After sufficient time for this practice, say "Move," and have one line of students move down one position while the other line remains in place. (The student at the end of the line moves to the beginning of the line.) In this way, new pairs are created and students practice with another partner. Continue until students have practiced all the questions.

"ROUND ROBIN": Have students circulate around the room and ask each other the questions. Students should move on to another person after they have taken turns asking and answering a question.

EXPANSION

Bring in, or have students bring in, newspaper and magazine pictures of a U.S. senator from your state.

TEXT PAGES 60–61 THE HOUSE OF REPRESENTATIVES

FOCUS

TOPIC

The House of Representatives

GRAMMAR

Simple Present Tense vs. To Be

The legislative branch **makes** the federal laws.
The Congress **is** the legislative branch.

Have/Has

Some states **have** more people.
The Congress **has** two parts.

Time Expressions

We elect a U.S. representative **for two years**.

NEW VOCABULARY

Congressional district	more
congressman	population
congressperson	Speaker of the House
congresswoman	of Representatives
female	U.S. representative
House of Representatives	voting member
leader	

PREVIEWING THE READING

Have students talk about the title and the photograph to establish the context of the passage.

Ask some or all of the following questions:

Which branch of government do you think these
people work in—the legislative branch, the
executive branch, or the judicial branch?
(The legislative branch.)
Where do they work? In what city?
(In Washington, D.C.)
They are United States representatives. Do
you know the name of your United States
representative?

READING THE PASSAGE

1. Have students read the passage silently. (If you wish, you may read the passage aloud or play the audio program as students read along silently.)

2. **Check Reading Comprehension:** Ask students a question about each line of the passage. For beginning-level students, ask these questions in the order below so that the questions follow the sequence of the passage. For higher-level students, ask the questions in random order.

   What is the Congress of the United States?
   Who makes the federal laws of the United States?
   What are the two parts of the Congress?

   Who works in the House of Representatives?
   What is a representative also called?
   How many voting members does the House of
   Representatives have?

   Do all states have the same number of
   representatives?
   Why?
   Do some states have more people?
   Which states have more representatives?
   Who does a representative represent?
   For how long do we elect a U.S. representative?

3. Ask students if they have any questions about the passage; check understanding of vocabulary.

4. **Choral Repetition:** Read aloud each line of the passage and have students repeat.

5. **Class Circle Reading:** Have students read the passage aloud as a class, with different students reading each line. (You can assign each line to a particular student or by seating patterns, or by letting students take turns spontaneously. In large classes, have a different group or row of students read each line.)

6. **Pair Practice:** Have students work in pairs, reading the passage to each other section by section. Circulate around the room and check students' reading and pronunciation, focusing more attention on students who need more assistance.

PHOTO CAPTION

Have students read the photo caption about the Speaker of the House of Representatives. The name of the Speaker is one of the 100 USCIS civics test questions.

CHECK-UP

VOCABULARY CHECK

1. Congress
2. representatives
3. two
4. district
5. House

CIVICS CHECK

Note: Since many questions have multiple acceptable answers, encourage low beginners to consistently practice a single answer to a question, while higher-level students can practice the multiple answers.

First, practice each question separately:

1. **Listening:** Have students read along silently as they listen to the question and answer(s)—presented by you, by a pair of students, or on the audio program.

2. **Choral Repetition:** Model the question and answer(s) and have the whole class repeat in unison.

3. **Choral Conversation Practice:** Divide the class in half. Have Group 1 ask the question and Group 2 give the answer(s); then reverse. (Or: You ask the question and have the whole class answer in unison; then reverse.)

4. **Pair Practice:** Have students practice the question and answer(s) in pairs.

5. **Presentation:** Call on one or two pairs of students to present the question and answer(s) to the class.

Then practice all the questions together:

6. **Choral Answers:** Ask any question and have students give the answer in unison. (If there are multiple answers, have them give the first answer in the text.)

7. **Pair Practice:** Have students work in pairs, taking turns asking and answering all the questions in random order.

For more practice or for review during the next class session, do one of these activities:

LINE PRACTICE: Have students stand in two lines facing each other. Each pair of facing students should take turns asking and answering a question. After sufficient time for this practice, say "Move," and have one line of students move down one position while the other line remains in place. (The student at the end of the line moves to the beginning of the line.) In this way, new pairs are created and students practice with another partner. Continue until students have practiced all the questions.

"ROUND ROBIN": Have students circulate around the room and ask each other the questions. Students should move on to another person after they have taken turns asking and answering a question.

EXPANSION

1. Bring in, or have students bring in, newspaper and magazine pictures of U.S. representatives from your state.

2. Bring in a map of Congressional districts in the United States and discuss the number of representatives there are from various states. Have students find out the name of the representative for their Congressional district and the names of your state's senators in the U.S. Senate.

FOCUS

TOPIC

The President

GRAMMAR

Simple Present Tense vs. To Be

The President **is** the chief executive.
The President **lives** and **works** in the White House.

Time Expressions

The President's term is **four years**.
The President can serve **two terms**.
We vote for President **in November**.
We elect the President and the Vice President
   at the same time.

NEW VOCABULARY

approve	head	serve
bill	military	sign
chief executive	no longer	term
Commander-in-Chief	pass the bill	veto
document		

GETTING READY

Write on the board:

2001	2005	2009	2013
2002	2006	2010	2014
2003	2007	2011	2015
2004	2008	2012	2016

Say, "We elected a President in 2004 and in 2008. We are going to elect a President in 2012 and 2016. We elect a President every four years. The President's term is four years."

PREVIEWING THE READING

Have students talk about the title and the photographs to establish the context of the passage. Ask some or all of the following questions:

(The first photograph)
Who is this? (The President.)
What's his name? (Barack Obama.)
Why is he raising his right hand? (He's taking the oath of office.)

(The second photograph)
The President is saluting. Who is he saluting? (Members of the military / the armed forces.)

(The third photograph)
What is the President doing? (He's signing a document / a bill / a law.)

(The fourth photograph)
Who do you see? (The President and his family)

(The fifth photograph)
Who do you see? (The President and the Vice President)

READING THE PASSAGE

1. Have students read the passage silently. (If you wish, you may read the passage aloud or play the audio program as students read along silently.)

2. **Check Reading Comprehension:** Ask students a question about each line of the passage. For beginning-level students, ask these questions in the order below so that the questions follow the sequence of the passage. For higher-level students, ask the questions in random order.

   Who is the head of the executive branch of the government?
   What does the executive branch do?
   Who is the chief executive?
   Who is the Commander-in-Chief of the military?

   When the Congress wants to make a new law, what does it do?
   Who must pass the bill to approve it?
   After the Senate and the House of Representatives approve the bill, who does it go to?
   If the President approves it, what happens?
   If the President doesn't approve it, what happens?

   Where does the President live and work?
   For how long do the American people elect a President?
   How long is the President's term?
   How many terms can the President serve?
   When do we vote for President?

   What does the Vice President do?
   When do the American people elect the Vice President?
   If the President can no longer serve, who becomes the new President?
   If both the President and the Vice President can no longer serve, who becomes the new President?

   What is the name of the President of the United States now?
   What is the name of the Vice President of the United States now?

3. Ask students if they have any questions about the passage; check understanding of vocabulary.

4. **Choral Repetition:** Read aloud each line of the passage and have students repeat.

5. **Class Circle Reading:** Have students read the passage aloud as a class, with different students reading each line. (You can assign each line to a particular student or by seating patterns, or by letting students take turns spontaneously. In large classes,

have a different group or row of students read each line.)

6. **Pair Practice:** Have students work in pairs, reading the passage to each other section by section. Circulate around the room and check students' reading and pronunciation, focusing more attention on students who need more assistance.

CHECK-UP (Pages 64–65)

VOCABULARY CHECK
1. White House   3. military   5. executive
2. elect   4. serve

GRAMMAR CHECK
1. is   3. vote   5. signs
2. lives   4. work

THE ANSWER IS "THE PRESIDENT!"
1. The President.   3. The President.
2. The President.   4. The President.

WHAT'S THE NUMBER?
1. 6   3. 2   5. 100
2. 2   4. 4   6. 435

CIVICS CHECK

First, practice each question separately:

1. **Listening:** Have students read along silently as they listen to the question and answer—presented by you, by a pair of students, or on the audio program.

2. **Choral Repetition:** Model the question and answer and have the whole class repeat in unison.

3. **Choral Conversation Practice:** Divide the class in half. Have Group 1 ask the question and Group 2 give the answer; then reverse. (Or: You ask the question and have the whole class answer in unison; then reverse.)

4. **Pair Practice:** Have students practice the question and answer in pairs.

5. **Presentation:** Call on one or two pairs of students to present the question and answer to the class.

Then practice all the questions together:

6. **Choral Answers:** Ask any question and have students give the answer in unison.

7. **Pair Practice:** Have students work in pairs, taking turns asking and answering all the questions in random order.

For more practice or for review during the next class session, do one of these activities:

LINE PRACTICE: Have students stand in two lines facing each other. Each pair of facing students should take turns asking and answering a question. After sufficient time for this practice, say "Move," and have one line of students move down one position while the other line remains in place. (The student at the end of the line moves

to the beginning of the line.) In this way, new pairs are created and students practice with another partner. Continue until students have practiced all the questions.

"ROUND ROBIN": Have students circulate around the room and ask each other the questions. Students should move on to another person after they have taken turns asking and answering a question.

EXPANSION

1. Vocabulary Expansion

a. Have students look again at the top photograph on page 62. Ask:

> What day is this? (Inauguration Day. / The day the President takes the oath of office.)
> What's happening in the photograph? (The President is raising his right hand. / The President is taking the oath of office.)

Have students point to the Chief Justice, the First Lady, and the President's children.

b. Have students look at the photograph at the bottom of page 65. Ask:

> What is this? (The seal of the President of the United States.)
> When do you see it? (When the President speaks on TV / at a meeting / etc.)

2. Language Experience Letter

As a class, have students dictate to you a letter to the President expressing their opinion on a national or world issue. As you ask students for the following information, write what they say on the board or on a large sheet of paper. You can write one letter for the entire class, various letters for small groups, or letters for individual students.

a. Have students discuss what national or world issue they wish to write about to the President.

b. Ask students the following questions, writing down the answers in correct letter format:

> What's today's date?
> Who are you writing to? (Write "Dear President _____")
> What is your opinion?
> Why do you think that?

Finish the letter by adding "Thank you for your attention" and "Sincerely, (Name)."

c. Read the letter to the class (or small group). Point to each word or sentence as you read. Then have students repeat each sentence after you.

d. Write down the letters on regular-sized paper. Make copies for each student in the class.

e. You may want to consider sending students' letters to the President. The address is:

> The White House
> 1600 Pennsylvania Avenue NW
> Washington, DC 20500

FOCUS

TOPIC
The President's Cabinet

NEW VOCABULARY

advise
Attorney General
Cabinet
Secretary of Agriculture
Secretary of Commerce
Secretary of Defense
Secretary of Education
Secretary of Energy
Secretary of Health and Human Services
Secretary of Homeland Security
Secretary of Housing and Urban Development
Secretary of the Interior
Secretary of Labor
Secretary of State
Secretary of Transportation
Secretary of the Treasury
Secretary of Veterans Affairs
Vice President

PREVIEWING THE LESSON

Have students talk about what they see in the photographs to understand the work of the different government departments. Students' ability to describe the photographs will depend on their language skill level.

Page 66 (from left to right and top to bottom):

A farm / A field / A field of wheat
A highway / An interstate highway / A road / A truck
The army / The military / The armed forces /
  A soldier
A classroom / A teacher and students / A school
Solar panels on a roof / Solar energy
A doctor's office / A clinic / A doctor and a patient
The U.S. Border Patrol / The border
A new building / A construction project
A national park
A car factory / An automobile factory

Page 67 (from left to right and top to bottom):

A meeting between an American official and people
  in another country
An airport / An airplane and a train
Printing money / A printing press for money
Veterans / People who were in the military /
  A parade of older soldiers
A prison
The Vice President

READING THE LESSON

1. Have students read the lesson silently. (If you wish, you may read the lesson aloud or play the audio program as students read along silently.)

2. **Choral Repetition:** Read aloud the first line of the lesson and the name of each Cabinet-level position and have students repeat.

3. **Check Understanding of the Cabinet-Level Positions:** Ask students a question about each Cabinet-level position as they look at the lesson for reference. For beginning-level students, ask these questions in the order below so that the questions follow the sequence of the photographs. For higher-level students, ask the questions in random order.

    Who is in charge of farms? (The Secretary of
      Agriculture)
    Who is in charge of highways and trucks?
      (The Secretary of Commerce)
    Who is in charge of the army? (The Secretary of
      Defense)
    Who is in charge of teachers and schools?
      (The Secretary of Education)
    Who is in charge of solar power? (The Secretary
      of Energy)
    Who is in charge of clinics, hospitals, and
      medicine? (The Secretary of Health and
      Human Services)
    Who is in charge of the U.S. Border Patrol and
      Citizenship and Immigration Services?
      (The Secretary of Homeland Security)
    Who is in charge of construction and new
      buildings? (The Secretary of Housing and
      Urban Development)
    Who is in charge of national parks?
      (The Secretary of the Interior)
    Who is in charge of factories and other places
      where people work? (The Secretary of Labor)
    Who is in charge of meeting with officials in other
      countries? (The Secretary of State)
    Who is in charge of airports and trains?
      (The Secretary of Transportation)
    Who is in charge of printing money?
      (The Secretary of the Treasury)
    Who is in charge of people who were in the
      military? (The Secretary of Veterans Affairs)
    Who is in charge of federal prisons? (The Attorney
      General)
    Who works with the President? (The Vice
      President)

4. **Pair Practice:** Have students work in pairs, reading the names of the Cabinet-level positions to each other. Circulate around the room and check students' reading and pronunciation, focusing more attention on students who need more assistance.

CIVICS CHECK

Practice each question separately:

1. **Listening:** Have students read along silently as they listen to the question and answer—presented by you, by a pair of students, or on the audio program.

2. **Choral Repetition:** Model the question and answer and have the whole class repeat in unison.

3. **Choral Conversation Practice:** Divide the class in half. Have Group 1 ask the question and Group 2 give the answer; then reverse. (Or: You ask the question and have the whole class answer in unison; then reverse.)

4. **Pair Practice:** Have students practice the question and answer in pairs.

5. **Presentation:** Call on one or two pairs of students to present the question and answer to the class.

EXPANSION

1. **Who Is It?**

   Repeat the activity in step 3 of the "Reading the Lesson" instructions above. This time, have students close their books so they don't rely on the photographs as they answer the questions about the Cabinet-level positions.

2. **Who Are They?**

   As a class, have students use their knowledge of current events, the Internet, the library, and other sources to make a list of the people who currently serve in all the Cabinet-level positions.

3. **Research Project about a Department of the Federal Government**

   Assign higher-level students to do a research project about one of the Cabinet-level departments. Students can work on their own, in pairs, or as a small group. They can use the Internet, the library, and other sources to find information about the responsibilities of the department, the agencies that exist in the department, the kinds of jobs related to the department's work, and how this work is important. Have students prepare a presentation for the class about their research.

FOCUS

TOPIC

The Supreme Court

GRAMMAR

Simple Present Tense vs. To Be

The judicial branch **explains** the laws of the United States.

They **serve** for life.

The American people **don't elect** the Supreme Court justices.

The Supreme Court **is** the highest court in the United States.

There Are

There are nine justices on the Supreme Court.

Time Expressions

They serve **for life.**

NEW VOCABULARY

appoint	federal court
approve	highest
Chief Justice	life
don't	

PREVIEWING THE READING

Have students talk about the title and the photograph to establish the context of the passage. Ask some or all of the following questions:

How many people are there in this photograph?
Who are they?
What do they do?
Where is the Supreme Court?
Is there a supreme court in your native country?

READING THE PASSAGE

1. Have students read the passage silently. (If you wish, you may read the passage aloud or play the audio program as students read along silently.)

2. **Check Reading Comprehension:** Ask students a question about each line of the passage. For beginning-level students, ask these questions in the order below so that the questions follow the sequence of the passage. For higher-level students, ask the questions in random order.

   What is the judicial branch of the government?
   What does the judicial branch do?

   What is the highest court in the United States?
   What does it do?
   What does it decide?

How many justices are there on the Supreme Court?
How long do they serve?
Do the American people elect the Supreme Court justices?
Who appoints them? Who approves them?
What is the head of the Supreme Court called?
What is the name of the Chief Justice of the United States now?

3. Ask students if they have any questions about the passage; check understanding of vocabulary.

4. **Choral Repetition:** Read aloud each line of the passage and have students repeat.

5. **Class Circle Reading:** Have students read the passage aloud as a class, with different students reading each line. (You can assign each line to a particular student or by seating patterns, or by letting students take turns spontaneously. In large classes, have a different group or row of students read each line.)

6. **Pair Practice:** Have students work in pairs, reading the passage to each other section by section. Circulate around the room and check students' reading and pronunciation, focusing more attention on students who need more assistance.

CHECK-UP

FACT CHECK

1. explains
2. nine
3. appoints
4. life
5. Chief Justice

GRAMMAR CHECK

First, have students write the words to complete the questions.

1. What
2. How many
3. Who
4. How long
5. Which

Then have students practice asking and answering the questions.

1. The Supreme Court.
2. Nine.
3. John Roberts.
4. They serve for life.
5. The judicial branch.

CIVICS CHECK

Note: Since many questions have multiple acceptable answers, encourage low beginners to consistently practice a single answer to a question, while higher-level students can practice the multiple answers.

First, practice each question separately:

1. **Listening:** Have students read along silently as they listen to the question and answer(s)—presented by you, by a pair of students, or on the audio program.

2. **Choral Repetition:** Model the question and answer(s) and have the whole class repeat in unison.

3. **Choral Conversation Practice:** Divide the class in half. Have Group 1 ask the question and Group 2 give the answer(s); then reverse. (Or: You ask the question and have the whole class answer in unison; then reverse.)

4. **Pair Practice:** Have students practice the question and answer(s) in pairs.

5. **Presentation:** Call on one or two pairs of students to present the question and answer(s) to the class.

Then practice all the questions together:

6. **Choral Answers:** Ask any question and have students give the answer in unison. (If there are multiple answers, have them give the first answer in the text.)

7. **Pair Practice:** Have students work in pairs, taking turns asking and answering all the questions in random order.

For more practice or for review during the next class session, do one of these activities:

LINE PRACTICE: Have students stand in two lines facing each other. Each pair of facing students should take turns asking and answering a question. After sufficient time for this practice, say "Move," and have one line of students move down one position while the other line remains in place. (The student at the end of the line moves to the beginning of the line.) In this way, new pairs are created and students practice with another partner. Continue until students have practiced all the questions.

"ROUND ROBIN": Have students circulate around the room and ask each other the questions. Students should move on to another person after they have taken turns asking and answering a question.

EXPANSION

1. **Who Are They?**

   As a class, have students use their knowledge of current events, the Internet, the library, and other sources to make a list of the people who currently serve in all the Cabinet-level positions.

2. **Research Project: Mini-Biography**

   Assign higher-level students to do a research project about one of the current Supreme Court justices. Students can work on their own, in pairs, or as a small group. They can use the Internet, the library, and other sources to find biographical information about the person. Have students prepare a presentation for the class about their research.

3. **Research Project: An Important Supreme Court Decision**

   Assign higher-level students to do a research project about an important Supreme Court ruling. Students can work on their own, in pairs, or as a small group. They can use the Internet, the library, and other sources to find information about the ruling and why it was important. Have students prepare a presentation for the class about their research.

QUESTIONS AND ANSWERS

This exercise offers students important practice with the multiple ways a question might be posed by the USCIS officer. First, have students repeat each question after you. Then have students practice asking and answering the questions with other students. Finally, have students write their answers to questions 1–5.

INFORMATION EXCHANGE: Branches of Government

1. Help students read the chart by pointing out the vertical and horizontal headings and reviewing what they mean.

2. Point to a particular cell in the chart and have students give a full sentence containing that information. For example:

Point to:	Full Sentence:
100	There are 100 United States senators.
6 years	A United States senator's term is six years.
Senate	United States senators work in the Senate.
Make the laws	The legislative branch makes the laws of the United States.

3. Have students practice asking and answering the questions with other students.

FOCUS

TOPIC

Branches of Government

GRAMMAR

WH-Questions

What are the two parts of the U.S. Congress?
How many U.S. senators are there?
Who is one of your state's U.S. senators now?

FUNCTIONAL INTERVIEW SKILLS

Asking for repetition
Asking for clarification
Interpreting paraphrased questions

KEY VOCABULARY

Excuse me.
Could you please say that again?
Do you mean . . . ?

GETTING READY

1. **Preview asking for repetition.**

   Point out that in the sixth line of the dialog, the applicant asks for repetition:

   > Could you please say that again?

   Model the sentence for students, and have them repeat it chorally and individually.

2. **Preview asking for clarification.**

   Explain to students the difference between asking for repetition and asking for clarification.

   > Asking for repetition: You want the USCIS officer to say the question again using the same words.

   > Asking for clarification: You want to make sure you understand the question, so you ask about the meaning of the question.

   One way to ask for clarification is to ask directly. (See text page 220 for a list of questions.)
   For example:

   > Could you please explain what that means?
   > Could you please explain that?

Another way to ask for clarification is to tell the officer what you think the question means and ask if your understanding is correct. For example, in the twelfth line of this dialog, the applicant asks:

> Do you mean who is my U.S. representative?

Model the sentence for students, and have them repeat it chorally and individually.

3. **Preview dealing with a question that does not use the official wording.**

   Point out to students that the officer's question in the eleventh line of the dialog is not worded using the language in the official question:

   > And who represents your Congressional district in Washington?

   The official question is:

   > Name your U.S. representative.

   Explain to students that if this happens during their test, they should ask for clarification to find out what the question means.

4. **Prepare students for paraphrased questions.**

   When the applicant asks the officer to repeat a question, the officer might *paraphrase*—saying the question using different words or different word order. Sometimes this might actually make the original question more difficult to understand. For example:

   > 3rd Line A: We elect a U.S. senator for how many years?
   > 4th Line A: For how many years do we elect a U.S. senator? What is a U.S. senator's term?

   Explain to students that the officer is rephrasing the question (saying the question a different way) to make it more understandable. In this example, the officer changes the word order of the question, and then the officer asks the question a different way using vocabulary that the student might not know ("a U.S. senator's *term*").

   When students ask the officer to repeat a question, they should know that the officer might or might not repeat the question exactly word-for-word. The officer might change the word order, use new words, or even ask the question two different ways. The officer does this to help the applicant understand the question.

PRACTICING THE DIALOG

Note: Students should fill in the name of one of their U.S. senators and the name of their U.S. representative when practicing the dialog. Students living in the District of Columbia or a U.S. territory can answer: "We don't have a U.S. senator."

1. **Setting the Scene:** Have students look at the photograph and determine who is talking: a USCIS officer and an applicant for citizenship. Establish the context: "The USCIS officer is asking about the legislative branch of the government."

2. **Listening:** With books closed, have students listen to the dialog—presented by you, by a pair of students, or on the audio program.

3. **Choral Repetition:** With books still closed, model each line and have the whole class repeat in unison.

4. **Reading:** With books open, have students follow along as two students present the dialog. Ask students if they have any questions and check understanding of vocabulary.

5. **Choral Conversation Practice:** Divide the class in half. Have Group 1 ask the questions and Group 2 give the answers; then reverse. (Or: You ask the questions and have the whole class answer in unison; then reverse.)

6. **Pair Practice:** Have students practice the dialog in pairs, taking turns being the USCIS officer and the applicant.

7. **Presentations:** Call on pairs of students to present the dialog to the class.

TEXT PAGE 72 CIVIC PARTICIPATION

WRITE A LETTER

Have each student write and send a letter to the President, a representative, or a senator. Check students' first drafts of their letters for comprehensibility and form, and have students use your corrections and suggestions to create a final version.

YOU'RE THE JUDGE!

Simulation: Have the class appoint nine Supreme Court justices to decide on an issue relating to immigrant rights or another matter of interest to your students. Give the "justices" time to deliberate and then have them report their decisions to the class.

MEET WITH YOUR REPRESENTATIVE IN CONGRESS

Invite your district's representative or a staff person to visit your school, or arrange a class visit to your representative's local office. Have students introduce themselves, give some personal background information, and talk about what they are learning in your class. Have them also prepare questions to ask the representative about his or her job.

TEXT PAGES 73–75 UNIT TEST

The end-of-unit assessment evaluates student achievement of the unit's learning objectives while developing the specific test-taking skills required for success during the USCIS English and civics exam. Students can practice and complete the tests in class or at home.

A. CIVICS

This section contains the official USCIS questions that appear in the unit. Students can practice the questions and answers outside of class on their own or with a study partner. (Since many questions have multiple acceptable answers, encourage low beginners to consistently practice a single answer to a question, while higher-level students can practice the multiple answers.) For in-class assessment, call on students to answer different questions, or observe students as they test each other through pair practice.

B. KEY VOCABULARY

1. President
2. Senators
3. Congress
4. States

C. READING AND WRITING

This section contains the types of reading and writing questions on the USCIS test. You can assess students' reading skills by their ability to read aloud the questions. You can assess their writing skills by their ability to write the sentences from dictation. (The dictation sentences appear below, in the text on page 239, and on the audio program. Each dictation sentence is on a separate audio track so that the audio can be paused while students write.)

1. Citizens of the United States can vote for the President.
2. People vote for President in November.
3. The Congress of the United States has one hundred (100) Senators.
4. Citizens in the fifty (50) states elect the Senators.
5. Citizens of the United States vote in November.

CIVICS ENRICHMENT

PERFORMANCE-BASED ASSESSMENT
These civics enrichment activities are designed to promote students' active participation in class and in the civic life of the community—through projects, issues discussions, community tasks, field trips, and Internet activities. Reproducible performance-based assessment forms for use in evaluating and documenting student participation in these activities are included in the Appendix.

CIVIC PARTICIPATION
Field Trip or Classroom Visitor: As suggested for the activity on text page 72, visit the local office of your students' representative in the U.S. Congress, or invite the representative (or someone in the representative's office) to visit your class. During the visit, have students introduce themselves, tell where they are from, tell about when and why they came to the United States, describe what they are learning in school, and tell about their plans for the future. Have students also share some of the problems, issues, and opinions that they brainstormed in class (a civics enrichment activity in the previous unit).

INTERNET ACTIVITY
Online Field Trip to the U.S. Capitol: Have students go to the website listed in the text for the U.S. Capitol Visitor Center. Have students click on "About Congress" to learn about what Congress does. Then have them click on "About the Capitol" to learn about the Capitol Building. Students should make a list or write short sentences about what they see on the website. Students can do this Internet activity individually, in pairs, or in small groups based on the computer resources available. Make sure students have the basic skills needed to access the Internet.

INTERNET ACTIVITY
Visiting the White House Online: Have students go to the website listed in the text for the President of the United States. Have them click on "The Administration" and then click on the links to learn about the President, the Vice President, and the Cabinet. Students should make a list or write short sentences about the information on the website. Students can do this Internet activity individually, in pairs, or in small groups.

TECHNOLOGY ENRICHMENT
See Teacher's Guide page 311 for additional Internet enrichment activities related to this unit.

UNIT SUMMARY

KEY VOCABULARY
Have students review the lists of words they have learned in this unit. Encourage students to get a small notebook where they can write down vocabulary that is new for them.

GRAMMAR
Have students review the sentence-examples of grammar in this unit. For enrichment, have higher-level students look for more examples of this grammar in the unit and write additional sentences.

FUNCTIONAL EXPRESSIONS
Have students review the functional expressions and find where they occur in this unit. For enrichment, have students make up new conversations that use these functional expressions and present them to the class.

UNIT REVIEW WORKSHEETS
Unit 4 Writing Practice
Unit 4 Reading Practice
Unit 4 Civics Practice

FOCUS

TOPICS

Giving information about marital history
Giving information about children

FUNCTIONAL INTERVIEW SKILLS

Recognizing how the USCIS officer might check the
applicant's understanding
Asking for an explanation or paraphrasing

KEY VOCABULARY

HOW THE OFFICER MIGHT ASK IF YOU UNDERSTAND

another way	know
ask	mean
different	question
different way	say
example	understand/understood
explain	words
give	

GIVING INFORMATION ABOUT MARITAL HISTORY

apply for citizenship	marriage
become	married
citizenship	now
currently	spouse
date	U.S. citizen
how many times	wife
husband	

GIVING INFORMATION ABOUT CHILDREN

born	live
children	name
current address	now
date of birth	oldest child
daughter	son
how old	

HOW THE OFFICER MIGHT ASK IF YOU UNDERSTAND

As a class, have students read and practice the
information in the blue box.

First, explain that the USCIS officer might ask if the
applicant understands a question. Model each way the
officer might ask this and have the whole class repeat in
unison.

Then explain that asking for an explanation or
paraphrasing is different from asking for repetition. If
students don't understand a question, they should ask
the officer to say the question a different way. Point out
that this is different from asking for repetition. Model
each way to ask for an explanation or paraphrasing and
have the whole class repeat in unison.

Finally, have students practice with a partner the
dialog in the blue box ("What's your spouse's name?").
Have them take turns being the USCIS officer and the
applicant.

ROLE PLAY: Sections 12 and 13

Have students work in pairs and role-play dialogs using
the questions in Sections 12 and 13 and some of the
lines in the blue box above. Have students take turns
being the USCIS officer and the applicant. Then have
pairs of students present their role plays to the class.

WORKSHEET

Interview Practice Worksheet 22

UNIT 5

TYPE OF GOVERNMENT & ECONOMY
THE RULE OF LAW
FEDERAL & STATE GOVERNMENT

PUBLIC OFFICIALS
THE CONSTITUTION
THE BILL OF RIGHTS

LESSONS & UNIT ACTIVITIES	OBJECTIVES	STUDENT TEXT	TEACHER'S GUIDE
Vocabulary Preview	Identifying federal and state government and voting	77	75
Government, Economy, & the Rule of Law	Identifying the type of government in the United States (republic, democratic); Identifying the rule of law; Identifying the economic system (market economy)	78–79	76–77
Federal and State Government	Differentiating federal and state government powers; Identifying the governor and capital of one's state	80–81	78–79
The Constitution	Identifying the Constitution as the supreme law of the land; Identifying what the Constitution does	82	80
The Bill of Rights	Identifying the Bill of Rights as the first ten amendments; Naming rights or freedoms from the First Amendment	83–85	81–82
Document of Freedom: The Preamble to the Constitution	Identifying the first three words of the Constitution: We the People; Reciting the Preamble; Describing the idea of self-government	86	83
Civics Test: Can You Tell Me . . . ?	Answering questions about the Constitution and the rule of law; Asking for clarification	87	84
Unit Test	Preparing for USCIS civics, reading, and writing test questions	88–89	85
Civics Enrichment	Making a field trip to city hall or a town government office; Project: Having an election day in class; Internet Activity: Searching a state's official website for information	90	86
The English Test (Speaking)*	Answering Form N-400 "Part 10" questions during the USCIS interview	223	87

* This interview preparation lesson is in the Appendix for students' convenience. It can be introduced in this unit and then reviewed along with the other interview preparation lessons as students get ready for their appointment at USCIS. If you prefer, you can do these lessons later in the course if that is more appropriate for the timing of your students' interviews. Interview Practice worksheets accompany these lessons.

UNIT RESOURCES

Worksheets:
Unit 5 Writing Practice
Unit 5 Reading Practice
Unit 5 Civics Practice
Interview Practice Worksheets 23–25

Audio Program:
CD 1: Tracks 72–78
CD 2: Tracks 1–9

RELATED PRACTICE

Foundations: Unit 6
Word by Word Basic: pages 72–83, 160–161, 244–245
Word by Word: pages 36–41, 84, 162
Side by Side / Side by Side Plus: Book 1, Units 13, 14
Side by Side Interactive CD-ROM / Side by Side TV: Level 1B, Segments 20–23
ExpressWays: Book 1, Unit 5

KEY VOCABULARY

READING	WRITING	GOVERNMENT	PUBLIC OFFICIALS	THE CONSTITUTION & BILL OF RIGHTS
Bill of Rights	citizens	branch	Governor	amendment
Congress	Congress	democratic	leader	Bill of Rights
do/does	elect	federal	official	Constitution
elects	for	form of government	President	First Amendment
for	freedom of	House of	public official	freedom of assembly
in	speech	Representatives	representative	freedom of religion
is	have	powers	senator	freedom of speech
live	in	representative	Vice President	freedom of the press
of	lives	republic		freedoms
one	November	self-government	**GOVERNMENT POWERS**	law
people	of	Senate	army	meet together
President	people	state	driver's license	petition
right	President	Supreme Court	education	Preamble
the	the		land use	rights
United States	United States	**ECONOMIC SYSTEM**	money	rules
vote/votes	vote	capitalist economy	police	say
what	we	goods	protection	supreme law of the
when	White House	market economy	safety	land
where		prices	schooling	worship
who		services	treaties	write
			zoning	

GRAMMAR

TO BE

The United States **is** a republic.
The first three words of the
 Constitution **are** *We the People.*

SIMPLE PRESENT TENSE

The people **vote** for officials.

HAVE/HAS

The Constitution **has** 27 amendments.

CAN

Americans **can** say what they want to.

MUST

Everyone **must** follow the law.

FUNCTIONAL EXPRESSIONS

CLARIFYING

Do you mean . . . ?
I'm sorry. Did you say ___?

INDICATING UNDERSTANDING

I understand.

TEXT PAGE 77 VOCABULARY PREVIEW

You may want to introduce these words before beginning the unit, or you may choose to wait until they first occur in a specific lesson. If you choose to introduce them at this point, here are some suggestions:

1. Have students look at the photographs on text page 77 and identify the words they already know.

2. Present the vocabulary. Say each word and have the class repeat it chorally and individually. Check students' understanding and pronunciation of the words.

3. Practice the vocabulary as a class, in pairs, or in small groups. Have students cover the word list and look at the photographs. Practice the words in the following ways:

   • Say a word and have students tell the correct number on the photograph.
   • Give a number on a photograph and have students say the word.

FOCUS

TOPICS

Type of Government
The Rule of Law
The Economic System

GRAMMAR

To Be

The United States **is** a republic.
The producers of most goods and services **are** privately owned.

Have/Has

It **has** a democratic form of government.

Simple Present Tense

The American people **vote** for public officials.

Must

Everyone **must** follow the law.

NEW VOCABULARY

above the law	market economy
American democracy	obey the law
capitalist economy	principle
control	privately owned
decide	producers
democratic	public official
economic system	representative form
follow the law	of government
form of government	republic
goods and services	rule of law
leader	serve
market	

PREVIEWING THE READING

Have students talk about the title and the photographs to establish the context of the passage. Ask some or all of the following questions:

(The top photograph)

What are they doing? (They're voting.)
What are they using to vote? (Voting machines.)

(The bottom photograph)

What is this? (A stock exchange.)
Where is it? (In New York City. / On Wall Street.)

READING THE PASSAGE

1. Have students read the passage silently. (If you wish, you may read the passage aloud or play the audio program as students read along silently.)

2. **Check Reading Comprehension:** Ask students a question about each line of the passage. For beginning-level students, ask these questions in the order below so that the questions follow the sequence of the passage. For higher-level students, ask the questions in random order.

   What is the United States?
   What form of government does the United States have?
   Does the United States have a representative form of government?
   Who votes for public officials?
   Who do the American people elect?
   Who do these officials serve?

   What is a basic principle of American democracy?
   What must everyone do?
   What must leaders do?
   What must government do?
   Is anyone above the law?

   What is the economic system in the United States?
   Who owns the producers of most goods and services?
   Does the government control the producers of most goods and services?
   What are other words for *capitalist economy*?
   In a market economy, what does the market itself decide?

3. Ask students if they have any questions about the passage; check understanding of vocabulary.

4. **Choral Repetition:** Read aloud each line of the passage and have students repeat.

5. **Class Circle Reading:** Have students read the passage aloud as a class, with different students reading each line. (You can assign each line to a particular student or by seating patterns, or by letting students take turns spontaneously. In large classes, have a different group or row of students read each line.)

6. **Pair Practice:** Have students work in pairs, reading the passage to each other section by section. Circulate around the room and check students' reading and pronunciation, focusing more attention on students who need more assistance.

CHECK-UP

VOCABULARY CHECK

1. democratic
2. vote
3. law
4. capitalist
5. rule

GRAMMAR CHECK

1. has
2. elect
3. is
4. is
5. serve

CIVICS CHECK

Note: Since many questions have multiple acceptable answers, encourage low beginners to consistently practice a single answer to a question, while higher-level students can practice the multiple answers.

Practice each question separately:

1. **Listening:** Have students read along silently as they listen to the question and answer(s)—presented by you, by a pair of students, or on the audio program.

2. **Choral Repetition:** Model the question and answer(s) and have the whole class repeat in unison.

3. **Choral Conversation Practice:** Divide the class in half. Have Group 1 ask the question and Group 2 give the answer(s); then reverse. (Or: You ask the question and have the whole class answer in unison; then reverse.)

4. **Pair Practice:** Have students practice the question and answer(s) in pairs.

5. **Presentation:** Call on one or two pairs of students to present the question and answer(s) to the class.

DISCUSSION

Have students discuss the forms of government, elections, and types of economic systems in their countries.

FOCUS

TOPICS

Federal and State Government Powers
The Governor
The State Capital

GRAMMAR

Simple Present Tense

Some powers **belong** to the federal government.

To Be

The governor **is** the head of a state's government.

NEW VOCABULARY

approve land use	Governor
approve zoning	make treaties
create an army	police
declare war	print money
driver's license	provide protection
education	provide safety
federal government	provide schooling
fire department	state government

PREVIEWING THE READING

Have students talk about what they see in the photographs so that they understand the information about the powers of federal and state government. Students' ability to describe the photographs will depend on their language skill level.

Top (from left to right):

Printing money / A printing press for money
The President speaking to the Congress (The photo shows President George H.W. Bush speaking to the Congress when the United States declared war against Iraq during the first Gulf War on January 12, 1991.)
Soldiers / The army / The armed forces / The military
The President signing a treaty with another country / The President and an official from another country signing an agreement

Bottom (from left to right and top to bottom):

A classroom / A teacher and students / A school
A police officer / A (California) highway patrol
A fire engine / A fire department
A registry (department) of motor vehicles / A place to get a driver's license
A zoning sign / A land use sign

READING THE PASSAGE

1. Have students read the passage silently. (If you wish, you may read the passage aloud or play the audio program as students read along silently.)

2. **Check Reading Comprehension:** Ask students a question about each line of the passage. For beginning-level students, ask these questions in the order below so that the questions follow the sequence of the passage. For higher-level students, ask the questions in random order.

> What is one power of the federal government?*
> What's another power of the federal government? etc.
> * As alternative questions for low-beginners, have students complete these phrases:
>> The power to print _____ (money)
>> The power to declare _____ (war)
>> The power to create _____ (an army)
>> The power to make _____ (treaties)

> What is one power of the states?*
> What's another power of the states? etc.
> * As alternative questions for low-beginners, have students complete these phrases:
>> The power to provide schooling and _____ (education)
>> The power to provide protection—for example, _____ (police)
>> The power to provide safety—for example, _____ (fire departments)
>> The power to give _____ (a driver's license)
>> The power to approve _____ (zoning and land use)

> Who is the head of a state's government?
> What's the name of our state?
> Who is the Governor of our state now?
> What is the capital of our state?

3. Ask students if they have any questions about the passage; check understanding of vocabulary.

4. **Choral Repetition:** Read aloud each line of the passage and have students repeat.

5. **Class Circle Reading:** Have students read the passage aloud as a class, with different students reading each line. (You can assign each line to a particular student or by seating patterns, or by letting students take turns spontaneously. In large classes, have a different group or row of students read each line.)

6. **Pair Practice:** Have students work in pairs, reading the passage to each other section by section. Circulate around the room and check students' reading and pronunciation, focusing more attention on students who need more assistance.

CHECK-UP

VOCABULARY CHECK

1. government
2. war
3. zoning
4. governor
5. money

FEDERAL OR STATE POWERS?

1. state
2. federal
3. federal
4. state
5. state
6. federal

CIVICS CHECK

Note: Since many questions have multiple acceptable answers, encourage low beginners to consistently practice a single answer to a question, while higher-level students can practice the multiple answers.

First, practice each question separately:

1. **Listening:** Have students read along silently as they listen to the question and answer(s)—presented by you, by a pair of students, or on the audio program.

2. **Choral Repetition:** Model the question and answer(s) and have the whole class repeat in unison.

3. **Choral Conversation Practice:** Divide the class in half. Have Group 1 ask the question and Group 2 give the answer(s); then reverse. (Or: You ask the question and have the whole class answer in unison; then reverse.)

4. **Pair Practice:** Have students practice the question and answer(s) in pairs.

5. **Presentation:** Call on one or two pairs of students to present the question and answer(s) to the class.

Then practice all the questions together:

6. **Choral Answers:** Ask any question and have students give the answer in unison. (If there are multiple answers, have them give the first answer in the text.)

7. **Pair Practice:** Have students work in pairs, taking turns asking and answering all the questions in random order.

For more practice or for review during the next class session, do one of these activities:

LINE PRACTICE: Have students stand in two lines facing each other. Each pair of facing students should take turns asking and answering a question. After sufficient time for this practice, say "Move," and have one line of students move down one position while the other line remains in place. (The student at the end of the line moves to the beginning of the line.) In this way, new pairs are created and students practice with another partner. Continue until students have practiced all the questions.

"ROUND ROBIN": Have students circulate around the room and ask each other the questions. Students should move on to another person after they have taken turns asking and answering a question.

EXPANSION

A Letter to a Local Government Official

As a class, have students write a letter to a local government official. Have them explain that they are studying English and Civics, and have them request a meeting with the official and a tour of the local government offices. (This letter sets up the Civic Participation Field Trip on text page 90.)

FOCUS

TOPIC
The Constitution

GRAMMAR

Simple Present Tense vs. To Be

It **defines** the rules.
The Constitution **is** the supreme law of the land.

NEW VOCABULARY

basic rights	protect
Constitution	set up
define the rules	supreme law
highest	tell

PREVIEWING THE READING

Have students talk about the title and the photograph to establish the context of the passage. Ask some or all of the following questions:

This is a very important document in the United States. What is the name of this document?
Why is it important?
Does your native country have a constitution?

READING THE PASSAGE

1. Have students read the passage silently. (If you wish, you may read the passage aloud or play the audio program as students read along silently.)

2. **Check Reading Comprehension:** Ask students a question about each line of the passage. For beginning-level students, ask these questions in the order below so that the questions follow the sequence of the passage. For higher-level students, ask the questions in random order.

   What is the supreme law of the land?
   Why is it the supreme law of the land?

   What does the Constitution do?
   What does it define the rules for?
   What does it say about the branches of government?
   What does the Constitution tell the Senate and the House of Representatives?
   What does the Constitution tell the President and the Vice President?
   What does it help the Supreme Court do?
   What does it say about the states?

   What does the Constitution protect?

3. Ask students if they have any questions about the passage; check understanding of vocabulary.

4. **Choral Repetition:** Read aloud each line of the passage and have students repeat.

5. **Class Circle Reading:** Have students read the passage aloud as a class, with different students reading each line. (You can assign each line to a particular student or by seating patterns, or by letting students take turns spontaneously. In large classes, have a different group or row of students read each line.)

6. **Pair Practice:** Have students work in pairs, reading the passage to each other section by section. Circulate around the room and check students' reading and pronunciation, focusing more attention on students who need more assistance.

EXPANSION

1. Bring in a copy of the Constitution. Show students the various articles of the Constitution and describe what the articles are about. Pocket-sized copies of the Constitution can be obtained at many federal offices.

2. Have a "Constitutional Convention" in class. Have students write a constitution for their class or their school. Have them decide who should have which powers and responsibilities.

3. Have students describe their native country's constitution.

FOCUS

TOPIC

The Bill of Rights

GRAMMAR

Simple Present Tense

We **call** the first ten amendments the Bill of Rights.
It **guarantees** freedom of speech.

To Be

A change to the Constitution **is** an amendment.

Have/Has

How many amendments does the Constitution
   have?
The Constitution **has** 27 amendments.

Can

Americans **can** say what they want to.

NEW VOCABULARY

addition	guarantee
amendment	important
ask to do something	meet together
Bill of Rights	petition
call	petition the government
change	practice a religion
First Amendment	rights
freedom of assembly	signed document
freedom of religion	want to
freedom of speech	worship
freedom of the press	write
freedoms	

PREVIEWING THE READING

Have students talk about the title and the photograph to
establish the context of the passage. Ask some or all of
the following questions:

> The document on page 82 is the U.S. Constitution.
>   It has many pages. But the document on page 83
>   is short. It is just this one page. What is it called?
>   (The Bill of Rights)
> What are rights?
> What rights and freedoms do you have because you
>   live in the United States?
> Does the United States government control the
>   newspapers?
> Can you go to any church or other place of worship
>   you want to?
> What can you do if you do not agree with the
>   President?

READING THE PASSAGE

1. Have students read the passage silently. (If you
   wish, you may read the passage aloud or play the
   audio program as students read along silently.)

2. **Check Reading Comprehension:** Ask students
   a question about each line of the passage. For
   beginning-level students, ask these questions in
   the order below so that the questions follow the
   sequence of the passage. For higher-level students,
   ask the questions in random order.

   > Can the people of the United States change the
   >   Constitution?
   > What is a change to the Constitution called?
   > What is an amendment?
   > How many amendments does the Constitution
   >   have?
   > What do we call the first ten amendments to the
   >   Constitution?
   > What does the Bill of Rights give to all people in
   >   the United States?
   > Which amendment gives Americans many
   >   important rights and freedoms?
   > What is one right or freedom from the First
   >   Amendment?
   > What is freedom of speech?
   > What is another right or freedom from the First
   >   Amendment?
   > What is freedom of the press?
   > What is another right or freedom from the First
   >   Amendment?
   > What is freedom of religion?
   > What is another right or freedom from the First
   >   Amendment?
   > What is freedom of assembly?
   > What is another right or freedom from the First
   >   Amendment?
   > What is the right to petition the government?

3. Ask students if they have any questions about the
   passage; check understanding of vocabulary.

4. **Choral Repetition:** Read aloud each line of the
   passage and have students repeat.

5. **Class Circle Reading:** Have students read the
   passage aloud as a class, with different students
   reading each line. (You can assign each line to a
   particular student or by seating patterns, or by letting
   students take turns spontaneously. In large classes,
   have a different group or row of students read each
   line.)

6. **Pair Practice:** Have students work in pairs, reading
   the passage to each other section by section.
   Circulate around the room and check students'
   reading and pronunciation, focusing more attention
   on students who need more assistance.

EXPANSION

Have students discuss as a class: Do people have the same freedoms and rights in your native country?

CHECK-UP (Pages 84–85)

"MIRROR" QUESTIONS

Point out to students that the questions in the box are two different ways of asking about the same information. Have students practice both questions and answers, chorally and individually.

After students have written the answers to the questions on a separate sheet of paper, have them work in pairs, asking and answering the questions. Students can provide short answers to these questions.

1. The Constitution.
2. The supreme law of the land.
3. A change to the Constitution.
4. An amendment.
5. The Bill of Rights.
6. The first ten amendments to the Constitution.

FIRST AMENDMENT RIGHTS

1. freedom of speech
2. freedom of the press
3. freedom of religion
4. the right to petition the government
5. freedom of assembly

FIRST AMENDMENT MATCHING

1. b
2. e
3. a
4. c
5. d

CIVICS CHECK

Note: Since many questions have multiple acceptable answers, encourage low beginners to consistently practice a single answer to a question, while higher-level students can practice the multiple answers.

First, practice each question separately:

1. **Listening:** Have students read along silently as they listen to the question and answer(s)—presented by you, by a pair of students, or on the audio program.
2. **Choral Repetition:** Model the question and answer(s) and have the whole class repeat in unison.

3. **Choral Conversation Practice:** Divide the class in half. Have Group 1 ask the question and Group 2 give the answer(s); then reverse. (Or: You ask the question and have the whole class answer in unison; then reverse.)
4. **Pair Practice:** Have students practice the question and answer(s) in pairs.
5. **Presentation:** Call on one or two pairs of students to present the question and answer(s) to the class.

Then practice all the questions together:

6. **Choral Answers:** Ask any question and have students give the answer in unison. (If there are multiple answers, have them give the first answer in the text.)
7. **Pair Practice:** Have students work in pairs, taking turns asking and answering all the questions in random order.

For more practice or for review during the next class session, do one of these activities:

LINE PRACTICE: Have students stand in two lines facing each other. Each pair of facing students should take turns asking and answering a question. After sufficient time for this practice, say "Move," and have one line of students move down one position while the other line remains in place. (The student at the end of the line moves to the beginning of the line.) In this way, new pairs are created and students practice with another partner. Continue until students have practiced all the questions.

"ROUND ROBIN": Have students circulate around the room and ask each other the questions. Students should move on to another person after they have taken turns asking and answering a question.

DISCUSSION AND DEBATE

Lead a student discussion about equal rights and freedoms in the United States. Then lead a second discussion about limits on freedom of speech or other rights. You may want to conduct class debates on one or both issues.

FOCUS

TOPICS

We the People
The Preamble to the Constitution

GRAMMAR

To Be

The idea of self-government **is** in the first three
words of the Constitution.
These words **are** *We the People.*

Simple Present Tense

The people **give** power to the government.
The government **serves** the people.

NEW VOCABULARY

famous	Preamble
introduction	self-government
power	We the People

PREVIEWING THE READING

Have students talk about the title and the photograph to
establish the context of the passage. Ask some or all of
the following questions:

> Look at the photo on page 86. What do these words
> say? (We the People)
> Look at the photo on page 82. Where can you find
> these words? (In the Constitution)
> What is the Constitution? (The supreme law of the
> land)
> What is the Preamble to the Constitution?
> (The introduction / The first part)

READING THE PASSAGE

Note: Practice the first three sections of the passage
first. (Don't practice the Preamble yet.)

1. Have students read the passage silently. (If you
   wish, you may read the passage aloud or play the
   audio program as students read along silently. Stop
   the audio after the third paragraph of the passage.)
2. **Check Reading Comprehension:** Ask students
   a question about each line of the passage. For
   beginning-level students, ask these questions in
   the order below so that the questions follow the
   sequence of the passage. For higher-level students,
   ask the questions in random order.

> What idea is in the first three words of the
> Constitution?
> What are these words?

What do these three words describe?
Who gives power to the government?
Who does the government serve?

> What is the introduction to the Constitution called?
> What three famous words does the Preamble
> begin with?

3. Ask students if they have any questions about the
   passage; check understanding of vocabulary.
4. **Choral Repetition:** Read aloud each line of the
   passage and have students repeat.
5. **Class Circle Reading:** Have students read the
   passage aloud as a class, with different students
   reading each line. (You can assign each line to a
   particular student or by seating patterns, or by letting
   students take turns spontaneously. In large classes,
   have a different group or row of students read each
   line.)
6. **Pair Practice:** Have students work in pairs, reading
   the passage to each other section by section.
   Circulate around the room and check students'
   reading and pronunciation, focusing more attention
   on students who need more assistance.

PRACTICING THE PREAMBLE*

* Note: The Preamble is not required for the USCIS
civics test. It is provided for enrichment and speaking
practice.

1. **Listening:** Have students read along silently as you
   recite the Preamble or play the audio.
2. **Choral Repetition (line by line):** Read aloud each
   separate line of the Preamble as it appears in the
   text and have students repeat in unison.
3. **Reading:** Have students practice reading aloud the
   Preamble as a class, in small groups, or on their
   own.
4. Ask students if they understand the general meaning
   of the Preamble. (They do not have to know the
   exact meaning of unfamiliar words.)
5. **Public Speaking Practice:** Have individual students
   present the Preamble to the class. If you feel it is
   appropriate to do so, help students with their diction
   and projection to improve their public speaking skills
   in English.
6. **Reciting:** Have students memorize the Preamble
   and practice reciting it (without the text) as a class,
   in small groups, and on their own.

EXPANSION

Oratorical Contest: Have interested students memorize
the Preamble and recite it for the class. Have class
members vote on the best rendition, and award a prize
to the winner.

FOCUS

TOPICS

The Constitution
The Rule of Law

GRAMMAR

Can

Can you tell me the first three words of the
  Preamble?

Simple Present Tense

What **does** the Constitution do?

Have/Has

Do you know how many amendments the
  Constitution **has**?

To Be

What **is** the rule of law?

FUNCTIONAL INTERVIEW SKILLS

Asking for clarification

KEY VOCABULARY

Can you tell me . . . ?
Did you say . . . ?
Do you know . . . ?
Do you mean . . . ?
I understand.
I'm sorry.

GETTING READY

**Introduce different reasons and ways to ask for
clarification.**

Point out that the dialogs contain two different reasons
and two different ways to ask for clarification:

In the first dialog, the applicant isn't sure of the meaning
of a word in the question. The applicant thinks she
knows the meaning, but she isn't sure. So she asks:

> The Preamble? Do you mean the first three words of
>   the Constitution?

In the third dialog, the applicant isn't sure what the
officer said. The applicant heard the word "law", but
there are two short civics test questions that use this
word:

> What is the "rule of law"?
> What is the supreme law of the land?

So the applicant asks:

> I'm sorry. Did you say "the supreme law"?

The applicant didn't hear correctly, so the officer repeats
the correct question:

> No. The rule of law. What is the rule of law?

Encourage students to ask for clarification when they
don't understand the meaning of a word and when they
aren't sure they heard correctly.

PRACTICING THE DIALOG

Notes:

- There are three dialogs. Practice each dialog
  separately.

- These dialogs have blank lines and answer-
  choice boxes since the questions have multiple
  acceptable answers. Encourage low beginners to
  consistently practice one answer to a question so
  that they master it—the first answer in the text or
  another answer they prefer. Higher-level students
  can practice the multiple answers. (The audio
  contains the first answer.)

1. **Setting the Scene:** Have students look at the
   photograph and determine who is talking: a USCIS
   officer and an applicant for citizenship. Establish
   the context: "The USCIS officer is asking about the
   Constitution."

2. **Listening:** With books closed, have students
   listen to the dialog—presented by you, by a pair of
   students, or on the audio program.

3. **Choral Repetition:** With books still closed, model
   each line and have the whole class repeat in unison.

4. **Reading:** With books open, have students follow
   along as two students present the dialog. Ask
   students if they have any questions and check
   understanding of vocabulary.

5. **Choral Conversation Practice:** Divide the class in
   half. Have Group 1 ask the questions and Group
   2 give the answers; then reverse. (Or: You ask
   the questions and have the whole class answer in
   unison; then reverse.)

6. **Pair Practice:** Have students practice the dialog in
   pairs, taking turns being the USCIS officer and the
   applicant.

7. **Presentations:** Call on pairs of students to present
   the dialog to the class.

The end-of-unit assessment evaluates student achievement of the unit's learning objectives while developing the specific test-taking skills required for success during the USCIS English and civics exam. Students can practice and complete the tests in class or at home.

A. CIVICS

This section contains the official USCIS questions that appear in the unit. Students can practice the questions and answers outside of class on their own or with a study partner. (Since many questions have multiple acceptable answers, encourage low beginners to consistently practice a single answer to a question, while higher-level students can practice the multiple answers.) For in-class assessment, call on students to answer different questions, or observe students as they test each other through pair practice.

B. READING AND WRITING

This section contains the types of reading and writing questions on the USCIS test. You can assess students' reading skills by their ability to read aloud the questions. You can assess their writing skills by their ability to write the sentences from dictation. (The dictation sentences appear below, in the text on page 239, and on the audio program. Each dictation sentence is on a separate audio track so that the audio can be paused while students write.)

1. The people of the United States elect the President.
2. Citizens of the United States vote for the Congress.
3. We vote for the Congress in November.
4. People in the United States have freedom of speech.
5. The President lives in the White House.

CIVICS ENRICHMENT

> ### PERFORMANCE-BASED ASSESSMENT
>
> These civics enrichment activities are designed to promote students' active participation in class and in the civic life of the community—through projects, issues discussions, community tasks, field trips, and Internet activities. Reproducible performance-based assessment forms for use in evaluating and documenting student participation in these activities are included in the Appendix.

CIVIC PARTICIPATION

Field Trip: Arrange for your class to visit your city hall or town government office and to meet with a local official. The visit should include a tour of the building and an explanation of the services available in different departments of the local government. As preparation for the field trip, or as an alternative, students can visit the local government's website and learn about the different services available.

PROJECT

"Class Election Day" Simulation: In this simulation, students conduct an election in class for the offices of class president and class vice president. Students nominate other students (or themselves) to be candidates. All students should participate in some aspect of the election process: candidates should give campaign speeches, students who serve on the Board of Elections should supervise the voting and count the ballots, some students should be TV news reporters who interview the candidates and report the election results, and other students should be voters. Have students take responsibility for all aspects of the Election Day simulation. Have them identify and assign the roles to be played and determine how to proceed with each stage of the election process. Be available to answer students' questions or to give advice when needed. Use the simulation as a basis for building students' skills in leadership, teamwork, and communicating information—key SCANS* skills useful for success in the workplace.

*Secretary's Commission on Achieving Necessary Skills

INTERNET ACTIVITY

Visiting Your State Government Online: Have students visit your state's official website (or, if appropriate, the website of the District of Columbia or your U.S. territory). Have them explore the website and make a list or write short sentences about the information they find. Students can do this Internet activity individually, in pairs, or in small groups, and then they should share what they have learned as a class.

TECHNOLOGY ENRICHMENT

See Teacher's Guide page 311 for additional Internet enrichment activities related to this unit.

UNIT SUMMARY

KEY VOCABULARY

Have students review the lists of words they have learned in this unit. Encourage students to get a small notebook where they can write down vocabulary that is new for them.

GRAMMAR

Have students review the sentence-examples of grammar in this unit. For enrichment, have higher-level students look for more examples of this grammar in the unit and write additional sentences.

FUNCTIONAL EXPRESSIONS

Have students review the functional expressions and find where they occur in this unit. For enrichment, have students make up new conversations that use these functional expressions and present them to the class.

UNIT REVIEW WORKSHEETS

Unit 5 Writing Practice
Unit 5 Reading Practice
Unit 5 Civics Practice

FOCUS

TOPIC
Answering Form N-400 "Part 10" questions during the USCIS interview

FUNCTIONAL INTERVIEW SKILL
Reporting information

KEY VOCABULARY

become
citizen
claim
country
election
fail to
federal, state, or local election
federal, state, or local taxes
file a required federal, state, or local tax return
Have you ever . . . ?
in the future
lawful permanent resident
on time
overdue
owe
pay my taxes
register to vote
required
send in
since
tax form
tell / told
U.S. citizen
vote
want to

ANSWERING THE FORM N-400 "PART 10" QUESTIONS

As a class, have students read and discuss the information in the blue box about how to answer questions that relate to Part 10 of their Application for Citizenship. Explain that they should try to give complete answers that show that they understand the officer's questions. Make sure students understand that they must always tell the truth during the interview. The answers in the book are samples. If a student's answer is different, the student should write it out and practice it.

ROLE PLAY: Questions 1–6

Have students work in pairs and role-play interviews using questions 1–6. Have them use in their conversations some of the expressions that appear in the blue boxes on pages 216, 220, and 222 to practice asking for repetition and clarification. Have students take turns being the USCIS officer and the applicant. Then have pairs of students present their role plays to the class.

WORKSHEETS

Interview Practice Worksheets 23–25

**NATIVE AMERICANS
CHRISTOPHER COLUMBUS**

**DISCOVERY
COLONIZATION**

LESSONS & UNIT ACTIVITIES	OBJECTIVES	STUDENT TEXT	TEACHER'S GUIDE
Vocabulary Preview	Identifying vocabulary of discovery and colonization	91	89
Native Americans (American Indians) & Columbus	Identifying American Indian tribes; Identifying Columbus; Using a map to trace a journey	92–95	90–91
The Colonies	Identifying reasons colonists came to America; Identifying colonists in Jamestown, Plymouth, Massachusetts Bay Colony, and Rhode Island	96–101	92–94
Holidays and History: Thanksgiving	Identifying reasons for the first Thanksgiving, conflicting histories about its location, and how the holiday is celebrated today	102–103	95–96
Civics Test: Tell Me One Reason . . .	Recognizing different ways a question may be asked	104	96
Song of Freedom: America (My Country 'Tis of Thee)	Reciting the lyrics and singing *America*	105	97
Unit Test	Preparing for USCIS civics, reading, and writing test questions	106–107	97
Civics Enrichment	Field Trip: Visiting a local supermarket; Project: Celebrating Thanksgiving in the classroom; Internet Activity: Visiting Plimoth Plantation online	108	98
The English Test (Speaking)*	Answering Form N-400 "Part 10" questions during the USCIS interview	223–224	99

* This interview preparation lesson is in the Appendix for students' convenience. It can be introduced in this unit and then reviewed along with the other interview preparation lessons as students get ready for their appointment at USCIS. If you prefer, you can do these lessons later in the course if that is more appropriate for the timing of your students' interviews. Interview Practice worksheets accompany these lessons.

UNIT RESOURCES

Worksheets:
Unit 6 Writing Practice
Unit 6 Reading Practice
Unit 6 Civics Practice
Interview Practice Worksheets 26–28

Audio Program:
CD 2: Tracks 10–25

RELATED PRACTICE

Foundations: Unit 8
Word by Word Basic: 96–103, 110–111
Word by Word: 48–51, 55, 163
Side by Side / Side by Side Plus: Book 1, Unit 15
Side by Side Interactive CD-ROM / Side by Side TV: Level 1B, Segment 24
ExpressWays: Book 1, Unit 6

KEY VOCABULARY

READING	WRITING	PEOPLE	PLACES	OTHER WORDS
America	American Indians	Alaska Natives	America	celebration
Columbus	be	American Indians	Atlantic Coast	church
Day	Columbus Day	children	Atlantic Ocean	colonial
come	first	colonists	colony	Columbus Day
do	free	Europeans	England	economic opportunity
first	here	family	Europe	freedom
in	in	Indians	homesite	gold
is	is	Native Americans	(the) Indies	holiday
lived	lived	native people	island	holiday tradition
people	November	Pilgrims	Jamestown Colony	*Mayflower*
Thanksgiving	October	Puritans	Jamestown, Virginia	national holiday
the	people	settler	Massachusetts Bay Colony	parade
to	Thanksgiving	slave	North America	political liberty
was	the	tribe	Plimoth Plantation	religious beliefs
when	to		Plymouth Colony	religious freedom
who	want	**FOOD**	Plymouth, Massachusetts	religious persecution
why	was	corn	Providence Plantation	rights
		cranberries	Rhode Island	ship
		potatoes	Spain	Thanksgiving (Day)
		squash	state	tobacco
		turkey	village	tribal government

GRAMMAR

PAST TENSE: REGULAR VERBS

[t]	[d]	[ɪd]
hope**d**	sail**ed**	want**ed**
like**d**	live**d**	land**ed**
punish**ed**	die**d**	invite**d**

PAST TENSE: IRREGULAR VERBS

bring – brought	is/are – was/were
come – came	leave – left
eat – ate	grow – grew
go – went	speak – spoke
have – had	teach – taught

FUNCTIONAL EXPRESSIONS

WAYS TO ASK QUESTIONS

Who . . . ?
Tell me who . . . .
Can you tell me who . . . ?
What is one reason . . . ?
(Can you) tell me one reason . . . ?
(Can you) give me one reason . . . ?
Why . . . ? Give me one reason.

TEXT PAGE 91 VOCABULARY PREVIEW

You may want to introduce these words before beginning the unit, or you may choose to wait until they first occur in a specific lesson. If you choose to introduce them at this point, here are some suggestions:

1. Have students look at the photographs on text page 91 and identify the words they already know.

2. Present the vocabulary. Say each word and have the class repeat it chorally and individually. Check students' understanding and pronunciation of the words.

3. Practice the vocabulary as a class, in pairs, or in small groups. Have students cover the word list and look at the photographs. Practice the words in the following ways:

   • Say a word and have students tell the correct number on the photograph.
   • Give a number on a photograph and have students say the word.

FOCUS

TOPICS

Christopher Columbus
Discovery
American Indian Tribes

GRAMMAR

Past Tense: Regular Verbs

Christopher Columbus sail**ed** from Spain.
He want**ed** to go to the Indies.
People in Europe like**d** things from the Indies.

Did/Didn't

He **didn't** land in the Indies.

NEW VOCABULARY

across	Indies
after	kill
already	land (v.)
America	learn
American Indians	like
arrive	most
Atlantic Coast	Native Americans
back	native people
better way	near
by land	North America
call	on the way
children	order (v.)
die	people
discover	punish
enough	sail
Europe	school
Europeans	sell
far	ship (v.)
federally recognized	slave
find	soon
get	Spain
gold	story
hope	things
however	travel
hundreds	tribal government
hundreds of thousands	tribe
Indians	way

AMERICAN INDIAN TRIBES

Apache	Crow	Navajo
Arawak	Hopi	Oneida
Blackfeet	Huron	Pueblo
Cherokee	Inuit	Seminole
Cheyenne	Iroquois	Shawnee
Chippewa	Lakota	Sioux
Choctaw	Mohegan	Teton
Creek		

GETTING READY

Introduce the past tense of regular verbs.

Write on the board:

hope	hoped
live	lived
want	wanted

a. Read each form of the verb and have students repeat chorally and individually.

b. Point out that "-ed" has three final sounds: [t], [d], and [ɪd].

PREVIEWING THE READING

Have students talk about the title and the pictures to establish the context of the passage. Ask some or all of the following questions:

(Page 92 top photograph)

How did these people come to this place?
(By boat / ship.)
Who do you think the person is in the middle of the group? (Their leader. / Christopher Columbus.)
Who do you see on the left side of the picture?
(People who lived there. / Natives. / Native Americans.

(Page 93 map)

Is this a map of the United States today? How do you know? (No. There aren't states. / The map shows names of Indian tribes.)

READING THE PASSAGE

1. Have students read the passage silently. (If you wish, you may read the passage aloud or play the audio program as students read along silently.)

2. **Check Reading Comprehension:** Ask students a question about each line of the passage. For beginning-level students, ask these questions in the order below so that the questions follow the sequence of the passage. For higher-level students, ask the questions in random order.

When did Christopher Columbus sail from Spain?
Where did he want to go?
Why did Columbus want to go there?
Before Columbus, how did Europeans travel to the Indies?
What did Columbus hope to find?
How did he want to get to the Indies?
What ocean did he sail across?
Did he land in the Indies?
Where did he land?

What do children often learn about Columbus in stories and in school?

Did people already live in America before Columbus?

What did Columbus call the native people?

What do we call them today?

Why did Columbus ship hundreds of native people to Spain?

What happened to most of them?

What did Columbus order them to find?

What did he do if they didn't find enough gold each year?

How many Indians died in the years after 1492?

How many federally recognized tribal governments of American Indian tribes and Alaska natives are there in the United States today?

3. Ask students if they have any questions about the passage; check understanding of vocabulary.

4. **Choral Repetition:** Read aloud each line of the passage and have students repeat.

5. **Class Circle Reading:** Have students read the passage aloud as a class, with different students reading each line. (You can assign each line to a particular student or by seating patterns, or by letting students take turns spontaneously. In large classes, have a different group or row of students read each line.)

6. **Pair Practice:** Have students work in pairs, reading the passage to each other section by section. Circulate around the room and check students' reading and pronunciation, focusing more attention on students who need more assistance.

CIVICS CHECK

Note: Encourage low beginners to consistently practice a single answer to each of these questions. Higher-level students can practice the multiple answers, including the names of all the American Indian tribes in the second question.

Practice each question separately:

1. **Listening:** Have students read along silently as they listen to the question and answer(s)—presented by you, by a pair of students, or on the audio program.

2. **Choral Repetition:** Model the question and answer(s) and have the whole class repeat in unison.

3. **Choral Conversation Practice:** Divide the class in half. Have Group 1 ask the question and Group 2 give the answer(s); then reverse. (Or: You ask the question and have the whole class answer in unison; then reverse.)

4. **Pair Practice:** Have students practice the question and answer(s) in pairs.

5. **Presentation:** Call on one or two pairs of students to present the question and answer(s) to the class.

CHECK-UP (Pages 94–95)

VOCABULARY CHECK

1. Spain	4. islands	6. Europeans
2. the Indies	5. Indians	7. gold
3. Atlantic		

GRAMMAR CHECK

1. sailed	3. lived	5. called
2. wanted	4. landed	6. ordered

PRONUNCIATION PRACTICE

First, have students listen to the pairs of words presented by you or on the audio program. Ask them to listen carefully to the sounds of the endings of these words. Then have students listen again and practice saying the pairs of words chorally and individually.

PRONUNCIATION CHECK

Have students say each word and then write it in the correct column.

[t]	[d]	[ɪd]
shipped	arrived	wanted
liked	discovered	landed
hoped	traveled	
punished	sailed	
	lived	
	called	

After students write the words in the correct columns, have them practice saying the three columns of words chorally and individually.

MAPS, JOURNEYS, AND DISCOVERIES

1. Using a world map, have students trace Columbus's route. Then have students trace their own route to the United States.

2. Have students write about their routes and experiences during their journey to the United States. Publish a collection of student stories. Make copies for the school and for students to take home. (Or, if possible, put these stories on your school's website!)

3. Have students write a passage about Columbus from the perspective of a native person in that time.

4. Have students discuss native people and explorers in their countries.

EXPANSION

Research Project about an American Indian Tribe
Assign higher-level students to do a research project about an American Indian tribe. Students can choose any tribe, or it might be more interesting for students to research a tribe in your area. Students can work on their own, in pairs, or as a small group. They can use the Internet, the library, a museum, and other sources to find information about the tribe, including its location, history, leaders, language, culture, and current status.

TEXT PAGES 96–101 THE COLONIES

FOCUS

TOPIC
Colonization

GRAMMAR

Past Tense: Irregular Verbs

People from England first **came** to America in the 1600s.
They **grew** tobacco.

The first colony **was** in Jamestown, Virginia.
These people **were** called colonists.

NEW VOCABULARY

because	persecution
church	Pilgrims
colonies	Plymouth, Massachusetts
colonist	political liberty
come	practice religion
create	Providence Plantation
economic opportunity	Puritans
England	religious beliefs
establish	religious freedom
followers	religious persecution
freedom	Rhode Island
grow	rights
Jamestown, Virginia	settle
leave	ship
Massachusetts Bay	speak against
Colony	system
Mayflower	tobacco
original	trade
persecute	women

GETTING READY

1. Introduce the past tense of irregular verbs.
   Write on the board:

come	came
grow	grew
be	was/were

   Read the simple and past tense forms of the verbs. Have students repeat chorally and individually.

2. Using a large classroom map of the United States or the map on text page 26, have students locate Virginia, Massachusetts, and Rhode Island.

PREVIEWING THE READING

Have students talk about the title and the pictures on pages 96–97 to establish the context of the passage. Ask some or all of the following questions:

(Page 96 top picture)

   What do you see in this picture? (Ships. / Land. / A place where people are living near the water.)

(Page 96 bottom picture)

   Where are these people standing? (On land near the ocean/water.)
   How did they get there? (By boat. / By ship.)
   What's wrong with the woman on the right? (Have students give ideas.)
   Who is standing by the tree? (A Native American. / An American Indian.)

(Page 97 top picture)

   These people are wearing similar clothing. What are they wearing?
   Why are they dressed the same? (They are part of a group.)

(Page 97 bottom left picture)

   How are these people traveling? (By canoe. / By boat.)
   Are they on the ocean? Are they coming from Europe to America? (No. They're on a river. They're going from one place to another place nearby.)

(Page 97 bottom right picture)

   What is the woman who is standing up doing? (She's speaking.)
   Who is she speaking to? (She's speaking to a group of men and women.)

READING THE PASSAGE

1. Have students read the passage silently. (If you wish, you may read the passage aloud or play the audio program as students read along silently.)

2. **Check Reading Comprehension:** Ask students a question about each line of the passage. For beginning-level students, ask these questions in the order below so that the questions follow the sequence of the passage. For higher-level students, ask the questions in random order.

   When did people from England first come to America?
   What were these people called?
   What were the original thirteen states called?

   Where was the first colony?
   When did the colonists come to Jamestown?
   Why did they come to America?
   What did the colonists in Jamestown do?

When did colonists come to Plymouth, Massachusetts?

What were these colonists called?

Why did the Pilgrims come to America?

Did they just want religious freedom? What else did they want?

What was the name of the ship they sailed to America?

What did the Puritans want?

What did they hope to create in America?

What did they establish in 1629?

Why did Roger Williams and his followers leave the Massachusetts Bay Colony?

Why did the people there persecute them?

Where did they go in 1636?

What did they establish?

Why did Anne Hutchinson and her followers leave the Massachusetts Bay Colony?

Why did the people there persecute her?

What did she speak against?

What did she also speak about?

Where did Hutchinson and her followers settle in 1638?

3. Ask students if they have any questions about the passage; check understanding of vocabulary.

4. **Choral Repetition:** Read aloud each line of the passage and have students repeat.

5. **Class Circle Reading:** Have students read the passage aloud as a class, with different students reading each line. (You can assign each line to a particular student or by seating patterns, or by letting students take turns spontaneously. In large classes, have a different group or row of students read each line.)

6. **Pair Practice:** Have students work in pairs, reading the passage to each other section by section. Circulate around the room and check students' reading and pronunciation, focusing more attention on students who need more assistance.

CHECK-UP (Pages 98–99)

VOCABULARY CHECK

1. England
2. colonies
3. colonists
4. freedom
5. opportunity
6. persecution

GRAMMAR & PRONUNCIATION CHECK: *Regular Verbs*

[t]	[d]	[ɪd]
established	called	persecuted
hoped	settled	traded
		wanted

1. hoped
2. traded
3. called
4. wanted
5. persecuted
6. settled
7. established

GRAMMAR CHECK: *Irregular Verbs*

After students fill in the blanks with the correct forms of the verbs, have them work in pairs and practice asking and answering the questions.

1. came
2. grew
3. left
4. spoke
5. went

CIVICS CHECK

Note: Encourage low beginners to practice a single answer to the question. Higher-level students can practice the multiple answers.

1. **Listening:** Have students read along silently as they listen to the question and answer(s)—presented by you, by a pair of students, or on the audio program.

2. **Choral Repetition:** Model the question and answer(s) and have the whole class repeat in unison.

3. **Choral Conversation Practice:** Divide the class in half. Have Group 1 ask the question and Group 2 give the answer(s); then reverse. (Or: You ask the question and have the whole class answer in unison; then reverse.)

4. **Pair Practice:** Have students practice the question and answer(s) in pairs.

5. **Presentation:** Call on one or two pairs of students to present the question and answer(s) to the class.

CHECK-UP (Pages 100–101)

FACT CHECK

1. Jamestown
2. Pilgrims
3. Massachusetts
4. Native Americans
5. religious freedom
6. Providence

LISTENING

Have students complete the exercises as you play the audio program or read the following:

Listen and circle the correct answer.

1. Where was the first American colony?
2. When did people from England come to the first American colony?
3. When did the Pilgrims come to America?
4. Why did the Pilgrims come to America?
5. What is the name of the colony that the Pilgrims came to?
6. What is the name of the ship that the Pilgrims sailed to America?

ANSWERS

1. a
2. b
3. b
4. a
5. b
6. a

DISCUSSION

Lead a class discussion about the reasons people come to the United States today.

YOUR IMMIGRATION STORY

Have students write the answers to these questions in the space provided. For additional speaking practice, students can discuss their answers.

INFORMATION EXCHANGE

Have the entire class practice asking the questions in the box. Then have students circulate around the room and interview seven other students, writing the information they gather in the appropriate place on the grid. (For additional speaking practice, students can later report back to the class and tell about the students they interviewed.)

ANOTHER PERSPECTIVE

Have students look again at the picture at the bottom of page 96. Ask them to imagine that they are the Native American in that picture. Have them share their thoughts and feelings as the Pilgrims land in the place where they live.

EXPANSION

Colonization and Students' Native Countries
Ask students to share what they know about the history of colonization in their native countries.

FOCUS

TOPICS

The First Thanksgiving
Thanksgiving Celebrations Today

GRAMMAR

Past Tense: Regular Verbs

The Native Americans help**ed** the Pilgrims.
The Pilgrims want**ed** to give thanks.
Many of them die**d** during the first year.
They celebrate**d** a holiday.
They invite**d** the Native Americans to a big dinner.

Past Tense: Irregular Verbs

Life **was** very difficult for the Pilgrims.
They **taught** the Pilgrims how to grow food.
The Native Americans **brought** most of the food.
The Native Americans already **had** celebrations like
    this one.

NEW VOCABULARY

believe	during	invite
bring	eat	potato
build	every	special
celebrate	fish (v.)	squash
celebration	food	teach
come together	fourth	thanks
corn	good	Thanksgiving
cranberry	holiday	turkey
difficult	house	usually
dinner	how to	

PREVIEWING THE READING

Have students talk about the title and the picture to
establish the context of the passage. Ask some or all of
the following questions:

> What people do you see in the picture? (Colonists
>   and Native Americans / American Indians.)
> What are they doing? (They're eating a meal /
>   dinner.)
> What are they eating?

READING THE PASSAGE

1. Have students read the passage silently. (If you
   wish, you may read the passage aloud or play the
   audio program as students read along silently.)

2. **Check Reading Comprehension:** Ask students
   a question about each line of the passage. For
   beginning-level students, ask these questions in
   the order below so that the questions follow the

sequence of the passage. For higher-level students,
ask the questions in random order.

> How was life for the Pilgrims in the Plymouth
>   colony?
> What happened to many of them during the first
>   year?
> Who helped the Pilgrims?
> What did the Native Americans teach the Pilgrims?
>   (3 answers)
> Why did the Pilgrims want to give thanks?
> What did the Pilgrims celebrate?
> Who did the Pilgrims invite to a big dinner?
> Who brought most of the food?
> What is this holiday in the Plymouth Colony called?
> Was it really the first Thanksgiving in America?
> What do many people believe about the
>   Jamestown colonists and Thanksgiving?
> What do others believe about the first
>   Thanksgiving holiday?
> Do Americans still celebrate Thanksgiving?
> When is Thanksgiving?
> What do families do on Thanksgiving?
> What do they usually eat?
> Why do Americans eat turkey, potatoes, corn,
>   squash, and cranberries on Thanksgiving?

3. Ask students if they have any questions about the
   passage; check understanding of vocabulary.

4. **Choral Repetition:** Read aloud each line of the
   passage and have students repeat.

5. **Class Circle Reading:** Have students read the
   passage aloud as a class, with different students
   reading each line. (You can assign each line to a
   particular student or by seating patterns, or by letting
   students take turns spontaneously. In large classes,
   have a different group or row of students read each
   line.)

6. **Pair Practice:** Have students work in pairs, reading
   the passage to each other section by section.
   Circulate around the room and check students'
   reading and pronunciation, focusing more attention
   on students who need more assistance.

EXPANSION

Thanksgiving in the Classroom

Begin preparations for a Thanksgiving celebration in
your classroom (the Civics Enrichment Project Activity on
text page 108). Have students take responsibility for
organizing the event, forming committees for different
activities, and delegating tasks. (Students will prepare
various dishes with Thanksgiving foods and share their
recipe instructions with other students in conversations
during the meal.)

CHECK-UP

VOCABULARY CHECK

1. helped
2. taught
3. celebrated
4. invited
5. came

GRAMMAR CHECK

1. came
2. come
3. have
4. had
5. ate
6. eat

DISCUSSION

Have students discuss the three topics as a class: how they celebrated holidays in their native country; how they celebrate Thanksgiving in the United States; and what it was like to adjust to life when they first arrived in the United States. Before or after students discuss as a class, you may want to have them write a composition about one of these topics. You can create a bulletin board display or publish within the school a collection of their compositions.

TEXT PAGE 104 CIVICS TEST: *TELL ME ONE REASON . . .*

FOCUS

> ### TOPIC
> Colonization
>
> ### GRAMMAR
>
> #### Question Formation
>
> Who lived in America before the Europeans arrived?
> Can you tell me who lived in America before the Europeans arrived?
>
> What is one reason colonists came to America?
> Can you tell me one reason colonists came to America?
>
> ### FUNCTIONAL INTERVIEW SKILL
>
> Recognizing different ways a question may be asked

KEY VOCABULARY

> Tell me . . .
> Can you tell me . . . ?
>
> What is one reason . . . ?
> Tell me one reason . . . .
> Give me one reason . . . .
> Can you tell me one reason . . . ?
> Can you give me one reason . . . ?
> Why did . . . ? Give me one reason.

PRACTICING THE QUESTIONS AND ANSWERS

Notes:

- Explain to students that this lesson is about the different ways the USCIS officer might ask a question. The first part of the lesson shows three different ways to ask about who lived in America before the Europeans arrived. The second part of the lesson shows six different ways to ask why colonists came to America. Practice each part of the lesson separately.

- These dialogs have blank lines and answer-choice boxes since the questions have multiple acceptable answers. Encourage low beginners to consistently practice one answer to a question so that they master it—the first answer in the text or another answer they prefer. Higher-level students can practice the multiple answers. (For this lesson, the audio offers practice with all the answers.)

1. **Setting the Scene:** Have students look at the photograph and determine who is talking: a USCIS officer and an applicant for citizenship. Establish the context: "The USCIS officer is asking about United States history."

2. **Listening:** With books closed, have students listen to the different ways to ask the question and the different answers—presented by you, by a pair of students, or on the audio program.

3. **Choral Repetition:** With books still closed, model each line and have the whole class repeat in unison.

4. **Reading:** With books open, have students follow along as two students present the questions and answers. Ask students if they have any questions and check understanding of vocabulary.

5. **Choral Conversation Practice:** Divide the class in half. Have Group 1 ask the questions and Group 2 give the answers; then reverse. (Or: You ask the questions and have the whole class answer in unison; then reverse.)

6. **Pair Practice:** Have students practice the questions and answers in pairs, taking turns being the USCIS officer and the applicant.

7. **Presentations:** Call on pairs of students to present the questions and answers to the class.

TEXT PAGE 105: SONG OF FREEDOM: AMERICA (MY COUNTRY 'TIS OF THEE)

PRACTICING THE SONG

1. **Listening to the Lyrics:** Have students listen to the lyrics of the song by playing the audio or saying the lyrics yourself.
2. **Choral Repetition:** Read aloud each line of the song and have students repeat in unison.
3. **Listening to the Song:** Have students listen to the song by playing the audio or singing it yourself.
4. **Singing Aloud:** Have students sing along as you play the audio or sing the song.

EXPANSION

> ### NEW VOCABULARY
>
> colonial fort
> holiday tradition
> homesite
> Jamestown Settlement
> living history museum
> nearby
> parade
> Plimoth Plantation
> popular
> re-creation
> settlers
> village

Discuss with students the photos of the Macy's Thanksgiving Day parade, Plimoth Plantation, Jamestown Settlement and the information in the caption for each photo.

TEXT PAGES 106–107   UNIT TEST

The end-of-unit assessment evaluates student achievement of the unit's learning objectives while developing the specific test-taking skills required for success during the USCIS English and civics exam. Students can practice and complete the tests in class or at home.

A. CIVICS

This section contains the official USCIS questions that appear in the unit. Students can practice the questions and answers outside of class on their own or with a study partner. (Since many questions have multiple acceptable answers, encourage low beginners to consistently practice a single answer to a question, while higher-level students can practice the multiple answers.) For in-class assessment, call on students to answer different questions, or observe students as they test each other through pair practice.

B. GRAMMAR

1. lived
2. came
3. have
4. wanted
5. want
6. was
7. went

C. KEY VOCABULARY

1. Thanksgiving
2. states
3. Columbus
4. American Indians
5. October
6. free
7. November

D. READING AND WRITING

This section contains the types of reading and writing questions on the USCIS test. You can assess students' reading skills by their ability to read aloud the questions. You can assess their writing skills by their ability to write the sentences from dictation. (The dictation sentences appear below, in the text on page 239, and on the audio program. Each dictation sentence is on a separate audio track so that the audio can be paused while students write.)

1. Columbus Day is in October.
2. American Indians lived here first.
3. Thanksgiving is in November.
4. People want to be free.
5. The first Thanksgiving was in November.

CIVICS ENRICHMENT

> ### PERFORMANCE-BASED ASSESSMENT
>
> These civics enrichment activities are designed to promote students' active participation in class and in the civic life of the community—through projects, issues discussions, community tasks, field trips, and Internet activities. Reproducible performance-based assessment forms for use in evaluating and documenting student participation in these activities are included in the Appendix.

CIVIC PARTICIPATION

Field Trip: Arrange for your class to visit a local supermarket. Have them talk with a supermarket employee about the products sold in the store. Have students look at the information that appears on the shelves, including unit prices, and have them learn how to compare prices of products or different sizes of the same product. Then have students talk with the manager of the supermarket. Have them tell about any foods they like that the supermarket doesn't have, and have them describe any problems they encounter when using a supermarket.

PROJECT ACTIVITY

Classroom Thanksgiving Celebration: Review with students the foods normally associated with the Thanksgiving holiday: turkey, potatoes, corn, squash, and cranberries. Have students prepare at home some dishes that use these foods—either native country recipes that use the Thanksgiving foods as ingredients, or recipes for typical American Thanksgiving dishes. If students wish to try making some typical American dishes, bring in cookbooks or prepare handouts with some recipes. (As an alternative to home preparation, if your class meets in a school that has a home economics classroom or other kitchen facilities, try to arrange permission for your class to use these facilities to prepare the foods.) During the holiday meal in class, have students share their recipe instructions. Have students take responsibility for all aspects of the holiday meal. Use the celebration as a basis for building students' skills in leadership and teamwork—key SCANS* skills useful for success in the workplace.

*Secretary's Commission on Achieving Necessary Skills

INTERNET ACTIVITY

Visiting the Plimoth Plantation colonial village: Have students go to the website of Plimoth Plantation in Massachusetts. (This is the living history museum described in a photograph caption on text page 105.) Have them click on "Features & Exhibits" and watch the multimedia program and write sentences about what they see. Students can do this Internet activity individually, in pairs, or in small groups based on the computer resources available. Make sure students have the basic skills needed to access the Internet for this activity.

TECHNOLOGY ENRICHMENT

See Appendix page 311 for additional Internet enrichment activities related to this unit.

UNIT SUMMARY

KEY VOCABULARY

Have students review the lists of words they have learned in this unit. Encourage students to get a small notebook where they can write down vocabulary that is new for them.

GRAMMAR

Have students review the lists of regular and irregular past tense verbs in this unit. Have students write sentences that use the past tense forms of these verbs.

FUNCTIONAL EXPRESSIONS

Have students review the different ways to ask questions and find where they occur in the unit. For enrichment, have students ask each other new questions using these different expressions.

UNIT REVIEW WORKSHEETS

Unit 6 Writing Practice
Unit 6 Reading Practice
Unit 6 Civics Practice

FOCUS

TOPIC
Answering Form N-400 "Part 10" questions during the USCIS interview
FUNCTIONAL INTERVIEW SKILL
Reporting information

KEY VOCABULARY

advocate (v.)	government
all	group
associated with	join
association	labor union
bad	member
change	mental health problems
church	overthrow (n.)
club	organization
Communism	parents' association
Communist	party
Communist Party	peacefully
community	people
compulsory	place
confined to a mental institution	rights
	school
country	similar
declared legally incompetent	society
	terrorism
dictator	terrorist organization
election	totalitarian party
force	very
former country	violence
foundation	within the last ___ years
freedoms	work
fund	

ROLE PLAY: Questions 7–10

Have students work in pairs and role-play interviews using questions 7–10. Have them use in their conversations some of the expressions that appear in the blue boxes on pages 216, 220, and 222 to practice asking for repetition and clarification. Have students take turns being the USCIS officer and the applicant. Then have pairs of students present their role plays to the class.

WORKSHEETS

Interview Practice Worksheets 26–28

UNIT 7

THE REVOLUTIONARY WAR
THE DECLARATION OF INDEPENDENCE

LESSONS & UNIT ACTIVITIES	OBJECTIVES	STUDENT TEXT	TEACHER'S GUIDE
Vocabulary Preview	Identifying vocabulary related to the Revolutionary War and independence	109	101
Before the Revolution	Identifying events leading up to the Revolutionary War	110–111	102–103
The Revolutionary War	Identifying reasons the colonists fought the British	112–113	104
Declaring Independence	Identifying the purpose, writer, and date of the Declaration of Independence	114–115	105–106
Document of Freedom: The Declaration of Independence	Identifying rights in the Declaration of Independence	116–117	107–108
Voice of Freedom: Thomas Jefferson	Identifying Thomas Jefferson as the writer of the Declaration of Independence; Reciting an excerpt of the Declaration of Independence	118	109–110
Holidays and History: Independence Day (The Fourth of July)	Identifying the date of Independence Day and how it is celebrated	119	111
Review	Talking Time Line: Reviewing important dates in U.S. history	120	112
Civics Test: I'm Afraid I Don't Remember	Hesitating; Saying you don't know the answer	121	112–113
Unit Test	Preparing for USCIS civics, reading, and writing test questions	122–123	113
Civics Enrichment	Getting information about local government taxes and how the money is used; Project: Time line bulletin board showing events in the history of students' countries and events in U.S. history; Internet Activity: Visiting historic Philadelphia online	124	114
The English Test (Speaking)*	Answering Form N-400 "Part 10" questions during the USCIS interview	224	115

* This interview preparation lesson is in the Appendix for students' convenience. It can be introduced in this unit and then reviewed along with the other interview preparation lessons as students get ready for their appointment at USCIS. If you prefer, you can do these lessons later in the course if that is more appropriate for the timing of your students' interviews. Interview Practice worksheets accompany these lessons.

UNIT RESOURCES

Worksheets:
Unit 7 Writing Practice
Unit 7 Reading Practice
Unit 7 Civics Practice
Interview Practice Worksheets 29–31

Audio Program:
CD 2: Tracks 26–44

RELATED PRACTICE

Foundations: Unit 10
Word by Word Basic: pages 38, 39, 152–153
Word by Word: pages 17, 80, 163
Side by Side / Side by Side Plus: Book 1, Unit 16
Side by Side Interactive CD-ROM / Side by Side TV: Level 1B, Segment 25
ExpressWays: Book 1, Unit 6

UNIT OVERVIEW

KEY VOCABULARY

READING	WRITING	PEOPLE	EVENTS	ACTIONS	
capital	be	(the) British	band concert	adopt	govern
do	capital	colonist	barbecue	announce	have
first	first	family	Boston Tea Party	become	like
George	free	friends	celebration	begin	meet
Washington	have	George Washington	fireworks	buy	merge
have	in	King	Fourth of July	carry	pay
in	Independence	leader	Independence Day	celebrate	prepare
Independence	Day	Patrick Henry	(national) holiday	complain	put
Day	is	representative	parade	control	require
is	July	Thomas Jefferson	picnic	create	say
of	of	writer	Revolutionary War	decide	sign
people	people			declare	take away
President	President	**PLACES**	**CONCEPTS**	end	tell
right	right	America	equal	fight	throw
the	the	Boston	independence	form (v.)	want (to)
United States	to	Boston Harbor	liberty	get together	win
was	United States	colony	life	give	write
what	was	country	pursuit of happiness	go	
when	Washington	Great Britain	rights		
who	Washington, D.C.	Independence Hall	self-government		
		Massachusetts	taxation without		
		Philadelphia	representation		
		United States			

GRAMMAR

PAST TENSE: REGULAR VERBS

The colonists want**ed** to be
  independent.

DID/DIDN'T

What **did** the colonists do?
The colonists **didn't** like British laws.

PAST TENSE: IRREGULAR VERBS

become – became	pay – paid
begin – began	put – put
come – came	say – said
fight – fought	throw – threw
go – went	win – won
meet – met	write – wrote

FUNCTIONAL EXPRESSIONS

SAYING YOU DON'T KNOW

Hmm. I studied that, but I don't
  remember.
I'm afraid I don't know the
  answer.

TEXT PAGE 109 VOCABULARY PREVIEW

You may want to introduce these words before beginning the unit, or you may choose to wait until they first occur in a specific lesson. If you choose to introduce them at this point, here are some suggestions:

1. Have students look at the photographs on text page 109 and identify the words they already know.

2. Present the vocabulary. Say each word and have the class repeat it chorally and individually. Check students' understanding and pronunciation of the words.

3. Practice the vocabulary as a class, in pairs, or in small groups. Have students cover the word list and look at the photographs. Practice the words in the following ways:

   • Say a word and have students tell the correct number on the photograph.
   • Give a number on a photograph and have students say the word.

FOCUS

TOPIC

Events Leading up to the Revolutionary War

GRAMMAR

Past Tense: Regular Verbs

Great Britain want**ed** to control its colonies in
   America.
They decide**d** not to buy British goods.

Past Tense: Irregular Verbs

Great Britain **put** a high tax on tea.
The colonists **were** very angry.
Some colonists **went** onto a ship.
They **threw** the tea into the water.
The colonists **met** in Philadelphia.
They **wrote** to the King of Great Britain.

Didn't

The colonists **didn't** like British laws.

KEY VOCABULARY

against	liberty
angry	meet
any	meeting
army	onto
boarding	pay
Boston	Philadelphia
Boston Harbor	prepare
Boston Tea Party	provide
British	put
buy	quartering
carry	Quartering Act
colonists	representative
complain	require
control	room
death	self-government
decide	ship
fight	taxation without
food	representation
give	tax
goods	taxes
govern	tea
Great Britain	throw
high	war
home	water
into	write
king	
law	

PREVIEWING THE READING

Have students talk about the title and the picture to
establish the context of the passage. Ask some or all of
the following questions:

(Point to the picture.)

   Who are these people? (Colonists. / American
      colonists. / Leaders.)
   Where are they? (At a meeting.)
   What do you think they're talking about? (Have
      students discuss.)

READING THE PASSAGE

Note: Point out to students the information in the
footnote on page 110 so they understand what the
country name *Great Britain* refers to.

1. Have students read the passage silently. (If you
   wish, you may read the passage aloud or play the
   audio program as students read along silently.)

2. **Check Reading Comprehension:** Ask students
   a question about each line of the passage. For
   beginning-level students, ask these questions in
   the order below so that the questions follow the
   sequence of the passage. For higher-level students,
   ask the questions in random order.

   What country wanted to control its colonies in
      America?
   How did the colonists in America feel about this?
   What did the colonists want to have?
   How did they want to govern?

   What did the colonists pay to Great Britain?
   Did the colonists have any representatives in
      Great Britain?
   What did they call this?

   How did the colonists feel about British laws?
   What did the Quartering Act require?

   What did Great Britain do in 1773?
   How did the colonists feel about this?
   What did some colonists in Boston do?
   What did the colonists do with the tea?
   What is this event called?

   Where did the colonists meet in 1774?
   What did they decide?
   Who did they write to? / What did they complain
      about?
   Who said, "Give me liberty or give me death?"
   Who did the colonists prepare to fight?
   What did they prepare for?

3. Ask students if they have any questions about the
   passage; check understanding of vocabulary.

4. **Choral Repetition:** Read aloud each line of the passage and have students repeat.

5. **Class Circle Reading:** Have students read the passage aloud as a class, with different students reading each line. (You can assign each line to a particular student or by seating patterns, or by letting students take turns spontaneously. In large classes, have a different group or row of students read each line.)

6. **Pair Practice:** Have students work in pairs, reading the passage to each other section by section. Circulate around the room and check students' reading and pronunciation, focusing more attention on students who need more assistance.

EXPANSION

Bring in a photo book about Boston that includes pictures of famous colonial sites such as Faneuil Hall, Concord, and Lexington. Share it with students and discuss what they can see if they visit there.

CHECK-UP

VOCABULARY CHECK

1. colonies
2. representatives
3. taxes
4. tea
5. boarding

BOSTON TEA PARTY GRAMMAR CHECK

After students fill in the blanks with the correct forms of the verbs, have them work in pairs and practice asking and answering the questions.

1. put
   put

2. go
   went

3. throw
   threw

CIVICS CHECK

Note: Encourage low beginners to practice a single answer to the question. Higher-level students can practice the multiple answers.

1. **Listening:** Have students read along silently as they listen to the question and answer(s)—presented by you, by a pair of students, or on the audio program.

2. **Choral Repetition:** Model the question and answer(s) and have the whole class repeat in unison.

3. **Choral Conversation Practice:** Divide the class in half. Have Group 1 ask the question and Group 2 give the answer(s); then reverse. (Or: You ask the question and have the whole class answer in unison; then reverse.)

4. **Pair Practice:** Have students practice the question and answer(s) in pairs.

5. **Presentation:** Call on one or two pairs of students to present the question and answer(s) to the class.

FOCUS

TOPIC

Reasons for the Revolutionary War

GRAMMAR

Past Tense: Regular Verbs

It end**ed** in 1783.

Past Tense: Irregular Verbs

The Revolutionary War **began** in 1775.
The American colonies **fought** Great Britain.
The colonies **won** the war.

Didn't

They **didn't** like British taxes.

NEW VOCABULARY

begin	independent
Colonial Army	leader
end	Revolutionary War
fight	win

PREVIEWING THE READING

Have students talk about the title and the illustration to establish the context of the passage. Ask some or all of the following questions:

> Who are the people in this picture? (Soldiers. / Armies. / British and Americans.)
> What are they doing? (They're fighting.)
> Which countries' flags do you see? (America and Great Britain.)
> Who is the man on the horse? (George Washington.)

READING THE PASSAGE

1. Have students read the passage silently. (If you wish, you may read the passage aloud or play the audio program as students read along silently.)

2. **Check Reading Comprehension:** Ask students a question about each line of the passage. For beginning-level students, ask these questions in the order below so that the questions follow the sequence of the passage. For higher-level students, ask the questions in random order.

> When did the Revolutionary War begin?
> When did the Revolutionary War end?
> Who did the American colonies fight against?
> Why did the colonies fight the war?
> What didn't the colonies want England to do?
> What did the colonies want?
> Who was the leader of the Colonial Army?
> Who won the war?

3. Ask students if they have any questions about the passage; check understanding of vocabulary.

4. **Choral Repetition:** Read aloud each line of the passage and have students repeat.

5. **Class Circle Reading:** Have students read the passage aloud as a class, with different students reading each line. (You can assign each line to a particular student or by seating patterns, or by letting students take turns spontaneously. In large classes, have a different group or row of students read each line.)

6. **Pair Practice:** Have students work in pairs, reading the passage to each other section by section. Circulate around the room and check students' reading and pronunciation, focusing more attention on students who need more assistance.

CHECK-UP

GRAMMAR CHECK

1. begin
   began
2. fight
   fought
3. win
   won

DID YOU UNDERSTAND?

1. We fought Great Britain during the Revolutionary War.
2. They didn't like British taxes. / They didn't like British laws. / They didn't have any representatives in Great Britain.
3. George Washington was the leader of the Colonial Army.
4. The Revolutionary War ended in 1783.

DISCUSSION

Have students list the taxes they pay. Discuss how often these taxes are paid and what the money is used for. Have students list the different services they receive that are funded through tax revenue. (Point out that the colonists did not receive any services for their tax dollars.)

EXPANSION

1. Discuss revolutions and revolutionary heroes in students' native countries.

2. Have students prepare a short report about George Washington.

3. Locate sites of important Revolutionary War battles on a map of the United States.

FOCUS

TOPIC

Writing and Adopting the Declaration of Independence

GRAMMAR

Past Tense: Regular Verbs

The colonists want**ed** to be independent.
Representatives sign**ed** the Declaration of Independence.

Past Tense: Irregular Verbs

The Revolutionary War **began** in 1775.
The colonists **met** at Independence Hall in Philadelphia.
Thomas Jefferson **wrote** the Declaration of Independence.

Didn't

The American colonists **didn't** want Great Britain to govern the colonies.

NEW VOCABULARY

adopt	declare
announce	free
Declaration of Independence	Independence Hall
	sign (v.)

PREVIEWING THE READING

Have students talk about the title and the illustration to establish the context of the passage. Ask some or all of the following questions:

Who are the people in the picture? (Colonists. / American colonists. / Leaders. / Representatives.)
Where are they? (In a large meeting room.)
What is on the table? (Documents. / Pieces of paper.)

READING THE PASSAGE

1. Have students read the passage silently. (If you wish, you may read the passage aloud or play the audio program as students read along silently.)

2. **Check Reading Comprehension:** Ask students a question about each line of the passage. For beginning-level students, ask these questions in the order below so that the questions follow the sequence of the passage. For higher-level students, ask the questions in random order.

   What didn't the American colonies want Great Britain to do?
   What did the colonists want?
   Who did the colonists want to be independent of?

   When did the Revolutionary War begin?
   Where did the colonists meet in 1776?
   What did they decide to declare?

   Who wrote the Declaration of Independence?
   What did the Declaration of Independence say?
   What did it announce?
   Who signed the Declaration of Independence?
   When was the Declaration of Independence adopted?

3. Ask students if they have any questions about the passage; check understanding of vocabulary.

4. **Choral Repetition:** Read aloud each line of the passage and have students repeat.

5. **Class Circle Reading:** Have students read the passage aloud as a class, with different students reading each line. (You can assign each line to a particular student or by seating patterns, or by letting students take turns spontaneously. In large classes, have a different group or row of students read each line.)

6. **Pair Practice:** Have students work in pairs, reading the passage to each other section by section. Circulate around the room and check students' reading and pronunciation, focusing more attention on students who need more assistance.

CHECK-UP

GRAMMAR CHECK

After students fill in the blanks with the correct forms of the verbs, have them work in pairs and practice asking and answering the questions.

1. meet
   met
2. write
   wrote
3. say
   said
4. begin
   began

CIVICS CHECK

Note: Since the first question has multiple acceptable answers, encourage low beginners to consistently practice a single answer to the question, while higher-level students can practice the multiple answers.

First, practice each question separately:

1. **Listening:** Have students read along silently as they listen to the question and answer(s)—presented by you, by a pair of students, or on the audio program.
2. **Choral Repetition:** Model the question and answer(s) and have the whole class repeat in unison.
3. **Choral Conversation Practice:** Divide the class in half. Have Group 1 ask the question and Group 2 give the answer(s); then reverse. (Or: You ask the question and have the whole class answer in unison; then reverse.)
4. **Pair Practice:** Have students practice the question and answer(s) in pairs.
5. **Presentation:** Call on one or two pairs of students to present the question and answer(s) to the class.

Then practice all the questions together:

6. **Choral Answers:** Ask any question and have students give the answer in unison. (If there are multiple answers, have them give the first answer in the text.)
7. **Pair Practice:** Have students work in pairs, taking turns asking and answering all the questions in random order.

DISCUSSION

Have students share as a class information about the history of any revolutionary wars in their countries. Have them talk about any revolutionary war heroes and discuss whether their countries are independent today.

FOCUS

TOPIC

The Declaration of Independence

GRAMMAR

Past Tense: Regular Verbs

The thirteen colonies declare**d** their independence.

NEW VOCABULARY

based on	liberty
basic	life
belief	must
create	nobody
equal	pursuit of happiness
form (v.)	take away

PREVIEWING THE READING

Have students talk about the title and the illustration to establish the context of the passage.

Ask some or all of the following questions:

What is a document? (A piece of paper with writing or information on it.)
What is the date on this document? (July 4, 1776)
What is at the bottom of the document?
   (Signatures. / Names of people who signed the document.)

READING THE PASSAGE

1. Have students read the passage silently. (If you wish, you may read the passage aloud or play the audio program as students read along silently.)

2. **Check Reading Comprehension:** Ask students a question about each line of the passage. For beginning-level students, ask these questions in the order below so that the questions follow the sequence of the passage. For higher-level students, ask the questions in random order.

   What is the Declaration of Independence?
   What does the Declaration of Independence say?
   What is the basic belief of the Declaration of Independence?

   What do people have that nobody can take away?
   What are the rights that nobody can take away?

   According to the Declaration of Independence, who can tell the government what to do?
   What must the government do?
   What can the people do if they want to?

   What did the colonies do based on these beliefs?
   When was the Declaration of Independence adopted?

3. Ask students if they have any questions about the passage; check understanding of vocabulary.

4. **Choral Repetition:** Read aloud each line of the passage and have students repeat.

5. **Class Circle Reading:** Have students read the passage aloud as a class, with different students reading each line. (You can assign each line to a particular student or by seating patterns, or by letting students take turns spontaneously. In large classes, have a different group or row of students read each line.)

6. **Pair Practice:** Have students work in pairs, reading the passage to each other section by section. Circulate around the room and check students' reading and pronunciation, focusing more attention on students who need more assistance.

CHECK-UP

VOCABULARY CHECK

1. document
2. independence
3. government
4. liberty
5. equal

LISTENING

Have students complete the exercises as you play the audio program or read the following:

Listen and circle the correct answer.

1. When did the colonists sign the Declaration of Independence?
2. Where did the colonists sign the Declaration of Independence?
3. Why did the colonists sign the Declaration of Independence?
4. Who did the colonies fight during the Revolutionary War?
5. When did the colonies fight the Revolutionary War?
6. Why did the colonies fight the Revolutionary War?

ANSWERS

1. b
2. a
3. c
4. a
5. b
6. c

CIVICS CHECK

Note: Students must give two rights when they answer this question.

1. **Listening:** Have students read along silently as they listen to the question and answers—presented by you, by a pair of students, or on the audio program.

2. **Choral Repetition:** Model the question and answers and have the whole class repeat in unison.

3. **Choral Conversation Practice:** Divide the class in half. Have Group 1 ask the question and Group 2 give the answer(s); then reverse. (Or: You ask the question and have the whole class answer in unison; then reverse.)

4. **Pair Practice:** Have students practice the question and answer(s) in pairs.

5. **Presentation:** Call on one or two pairs of students to present the question and answer(s) to the class.

EXPANSION

1. Have students look again at the illustration on page 116. Ask them what they see at the bottom of the Declaration of Independence. (Signatures.) Ask them whose signature is the largest. (John Hancock.) Explain that this is a very famous signature. Hancock signed his name very large so that the King of Great Britain could see it without his glasses. Even today the expression "put your John Hancock on this" is used to mean writing one's signature.

2. Bring in a copy of the Declaration of Independence. Affix some additional paper at the bottom and have students sign their names underneath the colonists' signatures. Display the Declaration of Independence on a bulletin board in your classroom.

(As noted in the text, this lesson is provided for enrichment and speaking practice. It is not required for the citizenship exam.)

FOCUS

TOPICS

Thomas Jefferson
The Declaration of Independence

GRAMMAR

Past Tense: Regular Verbs

The thirteen colonies adopt**ed** the Declaration of Independence.

Past Tense: Irregular Verbs

Thomas Jefferson **wrote** the Declaration of Independence.

NEW VOCABULARY

famous	words

GETTING READY

Ask students to identify the person whose face is on a nickel and a two-dollar bill (if you can find one).

PREVIEWING THE READING

Have students talk about the title and the pictures to establish the context of the passage.

Ask some or all of the following questions:

(Point to the first picture.)

Where have you seen this face before? (On a nickel coin. / On a two-dollar bill.)
Who is it? (Thomas Jefferson.)
Was he a President? (Yes. He was the third President.)

(Point to the second picture.)

This is the building you see in the picture on page 114. What is the name of this building? (Independence Hall.)
Where is this building? (In Philadelphia.)
What happened here? (The Declaration of Independence was adopted.)

READING THE PASSAGE

Note: Practice the first paragraph of the passage first. (Don't practice the excerpt of the Declaration of Independence yet.)

1. Have students read the passage silently. (If you wish, you may read the passage aloud or play the audio program as students read along silently. Stop the audio after the first paragraph.)

2. **Check Reading Comprehension:** Ask students a question about each line of the passage. For beginning-level students, ask these questions in the order below so that the questions follow the sequence of the passage. For higher-level students, ask the questions in random order.

   Who wrote the Declaration of Independence?
   Where did the thirteen colonies adopt the Declaration of Independence?
   When?

3. Ask students if they have any questions about the passage; check understanding of vocabulary.

4. **Choral Repetition:** Read aloud each line of the passage and have students repeat.

5. **Class Circle Reading:** Have students read the passage aloud as a class, with different students reading each line. (You can assign each line to a particular student or by seating patterns, or by letting students take turns spontaneously. In large classes, have a different group or row of students read each line.)

6. **Pair Practice:** Have students work in pairs, reading the passage to each other section by section. Circulate around the room and check students' reading and pronunciation, focusing more attention on students who need more assistance.

PRACTICING THE EXCERPT*

* Note: The excerpt of the Declaration of Independence is not required for the USCIS civics test. It is provided for enrichment and speaking practice.

1. **Listening:** Have students read along silently as you recite the excerpt or play the audio.

2. **Choral Repetition (line by line):** Read aloud each separate line of the excerpt as it appears in the text and have students repeat in unison.

3. **Reading:** Have students practice reading aloud the excerpt as a class, in small groups, or on their own.

4. Ask students if they understand the general meaning of the excerpt. (They do not have to know the exact meaning of unfamiliar words.)

5. **Public Speaking Practice:** Have individual students present the excerpt to the class. If you feel it is appropriate to do so, help students with their diction and projection to improve their public speaking skills in English.

6. **Reciting:** Have students memorize the excerpt and practice reciting it (without the text) as a class, in small groups, and on their own.

CIVICS CHECK

Note: Students must give *two* rights when they answer the third question.

First, practice each question separately:

1. **Listening:** Have students read along silently as they listen to the question and answer—presented by you, by a pair of students, or on the audio program.

2. **Choral Repetition:** Model the question and answer and have the whole class repeat in unison.

3. **Choral Conversation Practice:** Divide the class in half. Have Group 1 ask the question and Group 2 give the answer; then reverse. (Or: You ask the question and have the whole class answer in unison; then reverse.)

4. **Pair Practice:** Have students practice the question and answer in pairs.

5. **Presentation:** Call on one or two pairs of students to present the question and answer to the class.

Then practice all the questions together:

6. **Choral Answers:** Ask any question and have students give the answer in unison. (If there are multiple answers, have them give the first answer in the text.)

7. **Pair Practice:** Have students work in pairs, taking turns asking and answering all the questions in random order.

EXPANSION

1. **Oratorical Contest:** Have interested students memorize the excerpt or a larger portion of the Declaration of Independence and recite it for the class. Have class members vote on the best rendition, and award a prize to the winner.

2. **Independence Hall:** Bring in a photo book about Independence Hall in Philadelphia. Share it with students and discuss what they can see if they visit there.

3. **Research Project about Thomas Jefferson:** Have higher-level students prepare short oral or written reports about Thomas Jefferson. Students can work on their own, in pairs, or as a small group. Ask them to include the following information:

   When was he born?
   Where was he born?
   Where did he live?
   What did he do?
   When was he President?
   When did he die?

FOCUS

TOPIC

Independence Day (The Fourth of July)

GRAMMAR

To Be (Review)

Independence Day **is** a very happy celebration.

Simple Present Tense (Review)

Americans **celebrate** a national holiday.

Past Tense: Regular Verbs

The thirteen colonies declare**d** their independence.

NEW VOCABULARY

band concert	happy	parade
barbecue	national holiday	picnic
birthday	outside	summer
fireworks		

PREVIEWING THE READING

Have students talk about the title and the photograph to establish the context of the passage. Ask some or all of the following questions:

What are these children doing? (They're marching. / They're walking in a parade.)
Why? (It's a holiday.)
What colors and shapes do you see on their clothing? (Red, white, blue, stars, stripes.)
What are they carrying? (Flags of the United States.)
What holiday do you think this is? (The Fourth of July. / Independence Day.)

READING THE PASSAGE

1. Have students read the passage silently. (If you wish, you may read the passage aloud or play the audio program as students read along silently.)
2. **Check Reading Comprehension:** Ask students a question about each line of the passage. For beginning-level students, ask these questions in the order below so that the questions follow the sequence of the passage. For higher-level students, ask the questions in random order.

What do Americans celebrate on July 4th?
What is the holiday called?
What's another name for Independence Day?
What do Americans celebrate on this day?
Why is it the country's birthday?

What kind of celebration is Independence Day?
What do many Americans do on that day?
How do many Americans celebrate outside on that day?

What happens in many cities and towns on Independence Day?
3. Ask students if they have any questions about the passage; check understanding of vocabulary.
4. **Choral Repetition:** Read aloud each line of the passage and have students repeat.
5. **Class Circle Reading:** Have students read the passage aloud as a class, with different students reading each line. (You can assign each line to a particular student or by seating patterns, or by letting students take turns spontaneously. In large classes, have a different group or row of students read each line.)
6. **Pair Practice:** Have students work in pairs, reading the passage to each other section by section. Circulate around the room and check students' reading and pronunciation, focusing more attention on students who need more assistance.

CIVICS CHECK

1. **Listening:** Have students read along silently as they listen to the question and answer—presented by you, by a pair of students, or on the audio program.
2. **Choral Repetition:** Model the question and answer and have the whole class repeat in unison.
3. **Choral Conversation Practice:** Divide the class in half. Have Group 1 ask the question and Group 2 give the answer; then reverse. (Or: You ask the question and have the whole class answer in unison; then reverse.)
4. **Pair Practice:** Have students practice the question and answer in pairs.
5. **Presentation:** Call on one or two pairs of students to present the question and answer to the class.

DISCUSSION

Have students discuss how they celebrate Independence Day in the United States. Also have them discuss any celebrations like Independence Day in their native countries, when they occur, and how people celebrate those holidays.

EXPANSION

Have a Fourth of July picnic celebration with your class (even if it isn't the Fourth of July)! Prepare typical foods (hot dogs, hamburgers, corn on the cob, etc.), play some John Philip Sousa marches as patriotic background music, and if an outdoor picnic is possible, do some typical activities, such as a softball game, a three-legged race, a pie-eating contest, or simply toss a Frisbee around and have some fun. (Encourage students to wear red, white, and blue clothing to help set the mood.)

TEXT PAGE 120   REVIEW

TALKING TIME LINE: Important Dates in U.S. History

Have students complete the time line. Then have them work in pairs, asking and answering the questions at the bottom of the page, based on the information recorded on the time line.

1492	Columbus sailed to America.
1607	Colonists came to Jamestown, Virginia.
1620	Pilgrims came to the Plymouth Colony.
1775	The Revolutionary War began.
1776	The colonies declared their independence.
1783	The Revolutionary War ended.

TEXT PAGE 121   CIVICS TEST: *I'm Afraid I Don't Remember*

FOCUS

TOPIC

The Declaration of Independence

GRAMMAR

Past Tense: Regular Verbs

I stud**ied** that.

Past Tense: Irregular Verbs

Who **wrote** the Declaration of Independence?

To Be

What **are** two rights in the Declaration of Independence?
He **was** the third President.

FUNCTIONAL INTERVIEW SKILLS

Hesitating
Saying you don't know the answer

KEY VOCABULARY

Do you know . . . ?
Hmm.
I don't remember.
I'm afraid I don't know the answer.
I studied that.
Oh, yes.

GETTING READY

Introduce hesitating and saying you don't understand.
Point out that this dialog contains two important strategies students can use when they need time to think of an answer or when they don't know an answer. The applicant in the dialog doesn't remember who wrote the Declaration of Independence, so she says:

3rd Line B: Hmm. I studied that, but I don't remember.

The USCIS officer gives her a clue that the writer was the third President of the United States. The applicant still doesn't know the answer, so she says:

4th Line B: The third President? I'm afraid I don't know the answer.

When the applicant says the sound "Hmm" or repeats part of the question ("The third President?"), she is hesitating—she is saying something while she is thinking of how to answer. This is much better than simply being silent. Filling the thinking time with a sound or a word lets the officer know that the applicant has heard the question and is thinking about how to answer.

When the applicant says, "I don't remember" or "I'm afraid I don't know the answer," the officer knows to go on to the next question. This is much better than being silent, spending too much time thinking of an answer, or giving an answer that you know is wrong.

PRACTICING THE DIALOG

Note: This dialog has blank lines and answer-choice boxes since two questions have multiple acceptable answers. Encourage low beginners to consistently practice one answer to a question so that they master it—the first answer in the text or another answer they prefer. Higher-level students can practice the multiple answers. (The audio contains the first answer.)

1. **Setting the Scene:** Have students look at the photograph and determine who is talking: a USCIS officer and an applicant for citizenship. Establish the context: "The USCIS officer is asking about the Declaration of Independence."

2. **Listening:** With books closed, have students listen to the dialog—presented by you, by a pair of students, or on the audio program.

3. **Choral Repetition:** With books still closed, model each line and have the whole class repeat in unison.

4. **Reading:** With books open, have students follow along as two students present the dialog. Ask students if they have any questions and check understanding of vocabulary.

5. **Choral Conversation Practice:** Divide the class in half. Have Group 1 ask the questions and Group 2 give the answers; then reverse. (Or: You ask the questions and have the whole class answer in unison; then reverse.)

6. **Pair Practice:** Have students practice the dialog in pairs, taking turns being the USCIS officer and the applicant.

7. **Presentations:** Call on pairs of students to present the dialog to the class.

TEXT PAGES 122–123 UNIT TEST

The end-of-unit assessment evaluates student achievement of the unit's learning objectives while developing the specific test-taking skills required for success during the USCIS English and civics exam. Students can practice and complete the tests in class or at home.

A. CIVICS

This section contains the official USCIS questions that appear in the unit. Students can practice the questions and answers outside of class on their own or with a study partner. (Since many questions have multiple acceptable answers, encourage low beginners to consistently practice a single answer to a question, while higher-level students can practice the multiple answers.) For in-class assessment, call on students to answer different questions, or observe students as they test each other through pair practice.

B. CIVICS MATCHING

1. d
2. c
3. a
4. e
5. b

C. KEY VOCABULARY

1. taxes
2. Washington
3. Independence
4. July
5. rights
6. free
7. Independence Day

D. READING AND WRITING

This section contains the types of reading and writing questions on the USCIS test. You can assess students' reading skills by their ability to read aloud the questions. You can assess their writing skills by their ability to write the sentences from dictation. (The dictation sentences appear below, in the text on page 239, and on the audio program. Each dictation sentence is on a separate audio track so that the audio can be paused while students write.)

1. Independence Day is in July.
2. The first President of the United States was Washington.
3. Washington, D.C. is the capital of the United States.
4. Washington was the first President of the United States.
5. People have the right to be free.

CIVICS ENRICHMENT

PERFORMANCE-BASED ASSESSMENT

These civics enrichment activities are designed to promote students' active participation in class and in the civic life of the community—through projects, issues discussions, community tasks, field trips, and Internet activities. Reproducible performance-based assessment forms for use in evaluating and documenting student participation in these activities are included in the Appendix.

CIVIC PARTICIPATION

Have students brainstorm the kinds of taxes people pay to your local government, such as sales taxes, real estate taxes, and taxes on cars or other personal property. Have them discuss what the local government does with this money by brainstorming a list of all the services provided to the community. Then have students obtain information from your city hall, town hall, or other local government office about local government services and their costs. As a class, students should make a chart that shows the services and how much they cost. Have students take responsibility for all aspects of this activity, including obtaining the information and designing the chart of government services and costs. Use the activity as a basis for building students' skills in leadership, teamwork, and acquiring, evaluating, and communicating information—key SCANS* skills useful for success in the workplace.

PROJECT ACTIVITY

Time Line Bulletin Board Project: In this project, students make a large time line on a bulletin board. On the time line, they show events that happened in the history of their countries and events in U.S. history that they studied in the unit. Students should draw pictures of the events and write brief paragraphs about them to include on the bulletin board. Have students take responsibility for all aspects of this project. Have them identify the particular tasks involved in the project, who will accomplish each task, what resources are needed, and what form the final bulletin board display will take. Use the project as a basis for building students' skills in leadership, teamwork, and communicating information.

*Secretary's Commission on Achieving Necessary Skills

INTERNET ACTIVITY

Visiting historic Philadelphia online: Have students go to the indicated website and take the virtual tour or click on the following places in the Index: Betsy Ross House, First Bank of the United States, Independence Hall, and Liberty Bell. Have students write sentences about what they see and why these places are important in U.S. history. Students can do this Internet activity individually, in pairs, or in small groups based on the computer resources available. Make sure students have the basic skills needed to access the Internet.

TECHNOLOGY ENRICHMENT

See Appendix page 312 for additional Internet enrichment activities related to this chapter.

UNIT SUMMARY

KEY VOCABULARY

Have students review the lists of words they have learned in this unit. Encourage students to get a small notebook where they can write down vocabulary that is new for them.

GRAMMAR

Have students review the regular and irregular past tense verbs in this unit. Have students write sentences that use the past tense forms of these verbs.

FUNCTIONAL EXPRESSIONS

Have students review the different ways to say you don't know and find where they occur in the unit. For enrichment, have students practice new dialogs using these expressions.

UNIT REVIEW WORKSHEETS

Unit 7 Writing Practice
Unit 7 Reading Practice
Unit 7 Civics Practice

FOCUS

TOPIC
Answering Form N-400 "Part 10" questions during the USCIS interview

FUNCTIONAL INTERVIEW SKILL
Reporting information

KEY VOCABULARY

against the law	never
arrested	nonresident
associate	offense
because	officer
believe	particular
between	people
call oneself	persecute
cited	person
commit a crime	police officer
connection	political opinion
consider oneself	problem
crime	race
detained	reason
drive	religion
fail	required
federal, state, or local tax return	resident
	rights
file (v.)	send in
Germany	should
give	social group
government	tax return
group	ticket
hurt	way
law enforcement officer	wear a seat belt
membership	while
national origin	work for
Nazi	

ROLE PLAY: Questions 11–16

Have students work in pairs and role-play interviews using questions 11–16. Have them use in their conversations some of the expressions that appear in the blue boxes on pages 216, 220, and 222 to practice asking for repetition and clarification. Have students take turns being the USCIS officer and the applicant. Then have pairs of students present their role plays to the class.

WORKSHEETS

Interview Practice Worksheets 29–31

UNIT  8

THE CONSTITUTION
THE 13 ORIGINAL STATES
THE FEDERALIST PAPERS
BENJAMIN FRANKLIN

BRANCHES OF GOVERNMENT
THE BILL OF RIGHTS
GEORGE WASHINGTON

LESSONS & UNIT ACTIVITIES	OBJECTIVES	STUDENT TEXT	TEACHER'S GUIDE
Vocabulary Preview	Identifying the Constitution, the Bill of Rights, and freedoms guaranteed by the First Amendment	125	117
Document of Freedom: The Constitution	Identifying the Constitution as the supreme law of the land; Identifying what the Constitution does; Describing when and where the Constitution was written; Identifying the *Founding Fathers*	126–127	118–119
The Thirteen Original States	Naming the thirteen original states	128–129	120
Document of Freedom: The Federalist Papers	Identifying the purpose and the writers of the Federalist Papers	130–131	121–122
Profile: Benjamin Franklin	Describing things Benjamin Franklin is famous for	132–133	123–124
Review: Three Branches of Government	Describing the functions of and public officials in the three branches of government	134–137	125–127
Document of Freedom: The Bill of Rights	Identifying the Bill of Rights as the first ten amendments to the Constitution; Naming rights or freedoms from the First Amendment	138–139	128–129
Presidential Profile: George Washington	Identifying George Washington as the first President and the *Father of Our Country*	140	130
Civics Test: Let Me Think	Hesitating	141	131
Unit Test	Preparing for USCIS civics, reading, and writing test questions	142–143	132
Civics Enrichment	Discussing how people exercise their rights guaranteed by the First Amendment; Project: Making a bulletin board display about rights guaranteed by the First Amendment; Discussing limits on First Amendment rights	144	132–133
The English Test (Speaking)*	Answering Form N-400 "Part 10" questions during the USCIS interview	224	133

* This interview preparation lesson is in the Appendix for students' convenience. It can be introduced in this unit and then reviewed along with the other interview preparation lessons as students get ready for their appointment at USCIS. If you prefer, you can do these lessons later in the course if that is more appropriate for the timing of your students' interviews. Interview Practice worksheets accompany these lessons.

UNIT RESOURCES

Worksheets:
Unit 8 Writing Practice
Unit 8 Reading Practice
Unit 8 Civics Practice
Interview Practice Worksheets 32–34

Audio Program:
CD 2: Tracks 45–63

RELATED PRACTICE

Foundations: Unit 11
Word by Word Basic: pages 162–187
Word by Word: pages 86–100, 163
Side by Side / Side by Side Plus: Book 1, Unit 17
Side by Side Interactive CD-ROM / Side by Side TV: Level 1B, Segment 26
ExpressWays: Book 1, Unit 7

UNIT OVERVIEW

KEY VOCABULARY

READING	WRITING	PEOPLE	FOUNDING FATHERS	THE CONSTITUTION & BILL OF RIGHTS	ACTIONS
capital	capital	ambassador	Alexander Hamilton	addition	advise
city	Delaware	chief executive	Benjamin Franklin	amendment	appoint
dollar bill	dollar bill	citizen	Father of Our	change	approve
Father of Our	Father of Our	Commander-in-Chief	Country	Constitution	declare war
Country	Country	diplomat	George Washington	Constitutional	define
first	first	inventor	James Madison	Convention	elect
George	is	justice	John Jay	Federalist Papers	establish
Washington	New York City	lawyer	Publius	First Amendment	go to court
in	of	leader		freedom	guarantee
is	on	member	GOVERNMENT	freedom of	inaugurate
of	President	natural-born citizen	Cabinet	assembly	invent
on	state	non-citizen	Congress	freedom of	meet
state	the	person	enforce the laws	religion	protect
the	United States	police	executive branch	freedom of speech	publish
United States	was	Postmaster General	explain the laws	freedom of the	represent
was	Washington	President	federal courts	press	respect
what		representative	House of	right	serve
who		senator	Representatives	right to petition	set up
why		Speaker of the	judicial branch	the government	sign
		House of	legislative branch	supreme law of	support
		Representatives	make the laws	the land	veto
		Vice President	Senate		vote
		voter	Supreme Court		win
		voting member			write
		writer			

GRAMMAR

PAST TENSE: IRREGULAR VERBS

become – became   meet – met
give – gave   set up – set up
have – had   win – won
is/are – was/were   write – wrote

PAST TENSE: WAS/WERE

Washington **was** the first President.
There **were** thirteen original states.

FUNCTIONAL EXPRESSIONS

HESITATING

Let me see.
Let me think.
Let me think for a moment.

I know the answer.
I studied this.

TEXT PAGE 125 VOCABULARY PREVIEW

You may want to introduce these words before beginning the unit, or you may choose to wait until they first occur in a specific lesson. If you choose to introduce them at this point, here are some suggestions:

1. Have students look at the photographs on text page 125 and identify the words they already know.

2. Present the vocabulary. Say each word and have the class repeat it chorally and individually. Check students' understanding and pronunciation of the words.

3. Practice the vocabulary as a class, in pairs, or in small groups. Have students cover the word list and look at the photographs. Practice the words in the following ways:

   • Say a word and have students tell the correct number on the photograph.
   • Give a number on a photograph and have students say the word.

FOCUS

TOPIC

The Constitution

GRAMMAR

Past Tense: Regular Verbs

It establish**ed** three branches of government.
It define**d** the powers of the national government.

Past Tense: Irregular Verbs

The colonies in America **won** the Revolutionary War.
But they **had** a problem.
Representatives from the states **met** in Philadelphia.
They **wrote** the Constitution.
The Constitution **set up** the government.

Past Tense: Was/Were

There **wasn't** one strong national government.
They **were** free and independent states.

To Be

It **is** the supreme law of the land.

NEW VOCABULARY

describe	protect
establish	separate
Founding Fathers	set up
power	strong
problem	

PREVIEWING THE READING

Have students talk about the title and the illustration to establish the context of the passage. Ask some or all of the following questions:

Who are the people in this picture? (Leaders. / Representatives.)
Who is the man standing up on the right? (George Washington.)
What's he holding in his hand? (A document. / Paper.)
What document is it? (The Constitution.)
What are the people doing at this meeting? (They're writing the Constitution.)

READING THE PASSAGE

1. Have students read the passage silently. (If you wish, you may read the passage aloud or play the audio program as students read along silently.)

2. **Check Reading Comprehension:** Ask students a question about each line of the passage. For beginning-level students, ask these questions in the order below so that the questions follow the sequence of the passage. For higher-level students, ask the questions in random order.

    Who won the Revolutionary War? When?
    What did the colonies become?
    Did they have a problem?
    How many separate governments did the thirteen states have?
    Was there one strong national government?

    What happened in Philadelphia in 1787?
    What kind of meeting did they have?
    What did they write?
    What are these representatives called?

    What did the Constitution set up?
    What are the three branches of government?
    What powers did the Constitution define?
    What did the Constitution protect?

    What is the highest law in the United States?
    What is the Constitution called?

3. Ask students if they have any questions about the passage; check understanding of vocabulary.

4. **Choral Repetition:** Read aloud each line of the passage and have students repeat.

5. **Class Circle Reading:** Have students read the passage aloud as a class, with different students reading each line. (You can assign each line to a particular student or by seating patterns, or by letting students take turns spontaneously. In large classes, have a different group or row of students read each line.)

6. **Pair Practice:** Have students work in pairs, reading the passage to each other section by section. Circulate around the room and check students' reading and pronunciation, focusing more attention on students who need more assistance.

CHECK-UP

VOCABULARY CHECK

1. Constitution
2. government
3. branches
4. powers
5. Convention

GRAMMAR CHECK

1. were
2. weren't
3. was
4. wasn't

CIVICS CHECK

Note: Since some questions have multiple acceptable answers, encourage low beginners to consistently practice a single answer to a question, while higher-level students can practice the multiple answers.

First, practice each question separately:

1. **Listening:** Have students read along silently as they listen to the question and answer(s)—presented by you, by a pair of students, or on the audio program.

2. **Choral Repetition:** Model the question and answer(s) and have the whole class repeat in unison.

3. **Choral Conversation Practice:** Divide the class in half. Have Group 1 ask the question and Group 2 give the answer(s); then reverse. (Or: You ask the question and have the whole class answer in unison; then reverse.)

4. **Pair Practice:** Have students practice the question and answer(s) in pairs.

5. **Presentation:** Call on one or two pairs of students to present the question and answer(s) to the class.

Then practice all the questions together:

6. **Choral Answers:** Ask any question and have students give the answer in unison. (If there are multiple answers, have them give the first answer in the text.)

7. **Pair Practice:** Have students work in pairs, taking turns asking and answering all the questions in random order.

For more practice or for review during the next class session, do one of these activities:

LINE PRACTICE: Have students stand in two lines facing each other. Each pair of facing students should take turns asking and answering a question. After sufficient time for this practice, say "Move," and have one line of students move down one position while the other line remains in place. (The student at the end of the line moves to the beginning of the line.) In this way, new pairs are created and students practice with another partner. Continue until students have practiced all the questions.

"ROUND ROBIN": Have students circulate around the room and ask each other the questions. Students should move on to another person after they have taken turns asking and answering a question.

DISCUSSION

Have students describe their native countries' constitutions and how they are similar to and different from the U.S. Constitution.

EXPANSION

1. Bring in a copy of the U.S. Constitution. Show students the various articles of the Constitution and describe what the articles are about.

2. Have a "Constitutional Convention" in class. Have students write a constitution for the class or the school. Have them decide who should have which powers and responsibilities.

FOCUS

TOPIC

The Thirteen Original States

GRAMMAR

Past Tense: Irregular Verbs

The thirteen colonies **became** the thirteen original states.

Past Tense: Was/Were

These states **were** all on the Atlantic Coast.

KEY VOCABULARY

coast	New Jersey
Connecticut	New York
Delaware	North Carolina
Georgia	Pennsylvania
Maryland	Rhode Island
Massachusetts	South Carolina
New Hampshire	Virginia

GETTING READY

Using a large classroom map of the United States or the map on text page 26, point out the location of the thirteen colonies.

PREVIEWING THE READING

Have students talk about the title and the illustration to establish the context of the passage. Ask some or all of the following questions:

What is this a map of? (Part of the United States. / The thirteen colonies.)

What part of the United States does this map show? (The eastern part. / The states on the Atlantic Coast.)

What states do you see?

What cities are on this map?

READING THE PASSAGE

1. Have students read the passage silently. (If you wish, you may read the passage aloud or play the audio program as students read along silently.)

2. **Check Reading Comprehension:** Ask students a question about each line of the passage. For beginning-level students, ask these questions in the order below so that the questions follow the sequence of the passage. For higher-level students, ask the questions in random order.

   What did the thirteen colonies become?
   Where were these states?
   What were the thirteen original states?

3. Ask students if they have any questions about the passage; check understanding of vocabulary.

4. **Choral Repetition:** Read aloud each line of the passage and have students repeat. (Read the names of the thirteen original states one at a time, and have students repeat.)

5. **Class Circle Reading:** Have students read the passage aloud as a class, with different students reading each line. (You can assign each line to a particular student or by seating patterns, or by letting students take turns spontaneously. In large classes, have a different group or row of students read each line. During this practice, have different students read each colony name as though it were a separate line.)

6. **Pair Practice:** Have students work in pairs, reading the passage to each other line by line. (Have students read each state name as though it were a separate line.) Circulate around the room and check students' reading and pronunciation, focusing more attention on students who need more assistance.

CHECK-UP

PRACTICING THE THIRTEEN ORIGINAL STATES

Connecticut
Delaware
Georgia
Maryland
Massachusetts
New Hampshire
New Jersey
New York
North Carolina
Pennsylvania
Rhode Island
South Carolina
Virginia

QUESTIONS AND ANSWERS

This exercise offers students important practice with the multiple ways a question might be posed by the USCIS officer. First, have students repeat each question after you. Then have students practice asking and answering the questions with other students.

SOCIAL STUDIES ENRICHMENT

Have students work in small groups, in pairs, or individually as they prepare an oral presentation about one of the thirteen original states. Have students give their presentations to the class.

FOCUS

TOPIC

The *Federalist Papers*

GRAMMAR

Past Tense: Regular Verbs

Newspapers publish**ed** 85 essays.

Past Tense: Irregular Verbs

They **wrote** the *Federalist Papers*.

Passive Voice

The Constitution **was written** in 1787.
These essays **were called** the *Federalist Papers*.

NEW VOCABULARY

convince	newspaper	support
essay	passage	voter
Federalist Papers	publish	writer

PREVIEWING THE READING

Have students look at the illustration. Explain that this is the cover of an important document in U.S. history. Have them read the complete title: "The Federalist: A Collection of Essays, written in favour of the New Constitution, as agreed upon by the Federal Convention, September 17, 1787."

Ask: What was the purpose of this document?
(To support the new Constitution.)

Then tell students that the three pictures at the bottom of the page are portraits of the three writers of these essays. Have them practice the names of the three writers.

READING THE PASSAGE

1. Have students read the passage silently. (If you wish, you may read the passage aloud or play the audio program as students read along silently.)

2. **Check Reading Comprehension:** Ask students a question about each line of the passage. For beginning-level students, ask these questions in the order below so that the questions follow the sequence of the passage. For higher-level students, ask the questions in random order.

    What did voters in the thirteen original states have to do after the Constitution was written in 1787?
    What did newspapers in New York publish in 1787 and 1788?

What were these essays called?
Why were they written?

Who wrote the *Federalist Papers*?
Did they give their names as the writers of the essays?
What is the name of the writer on every one of the *Federalist Papers*?

3. Ask students if they have any questions about the passage; check understanding of vocabulary.

4. **Choral Repetition:** Read aloud each line of the passage and have students repeat.

5. **Class Circle Reading:** Have students read the passage aloud as a class, with different students reading each line. (You can assign each line to a particular student or by seating patterns, or by letting students take turns spontaneously. In large classes, have a different group or row of students read each line.)

6. **Pair Practice:** Have students work in pairs, reading the passage to each other section by section. Circulate around the room and check students' reading and pronunciation, focusing more attention on students who need more assistance.

CHECK-UP

VOCABULARY CHECK

1. written
2. Convention
3. Papers
4. approve
5. writers
6. published
7. Publius

CIVICS CHECK

Note: Since some questions have multiple acceptable answers, encourage low beginners to consistently practice a single answer to a question, while higher-level students can practice the multiple answers.

First, practice each question separately:

1. **Listening:** Have students read along silently as they listen to the question and answer(s)—presented by you, by a pair of students, or on the audio program.

2. **Choral Repetition:** Model the question and answer(s) and have the whole class repeat in unison.

3. **Choral Conversation Practice:** Divide the class in half. Have Group 1 ask the question and Group 2 give the answer(s); then reverse. (Or: You ask the question and have the whole class answer in unison; then reverse.)

4. **Pair Practice:** Have students practice the question and answer(s) in pairs.

5. **Presentation:** Call on one or two pairs of students to present the question and answer(s) to the class.

Then practice all the questions together:

6. **Choral Answers:** Ask any question and have students give the answer in unison. (If there are multiple answers, have them give the first answer in the text.)

7. **Pair Practice:** Have students work in pairs, taking turns asking and answering all the questions in random order.

For more practice or for review during the next class session, do one of these activities:

LINE PRACTICE: Have students stand in two lines facing each other. Each pair of facing students should take turns asking and answering a question. After sufficient time for this practice, say "Move," and have one line of students move down one position while the other line remains in place. (The student at the end of the line moves to the beginning of the line.) In this way, new pairs are created and students practice with another partner. Continue until students have practiced all the questions.

"ROUND ROBIN": Have students circulate around the room and ask each other the questions. Students should move on to another person after they have taken turns asking and answering a question.

FOCUS

TOPIC

Benjamin Franklin

GRAMMAR

Past Tense: Regular Verbs

He invent**ed** the lightning rod.
He figure**d** out routes for delivering the mail.

Past Tense: Was/Were

He **was** a U.S. diplomat.

NEW VOCABULARY

Ambassador	inventor
bifocals	lenses
book	library
cartoon	lightning rod
deliver the mail	oldest
diplomat	*Poor Richard's Almanack*
eyeglasses	popular
famous	Postmaster General
far	route
figure out	saying
Franklin stove	short
free	start
near	support
interesting	unity
invent	yearly

PREVIEWING THE READING

Have students talk about the title and the pictures to establish the context of the passage. Ask some or all of the following questions:

(Point to the top illustration.)

This is a portrait of a famous Founding Father. What's his name? (Benjamin Franklin.)

(Point to the bottom left illustration.)

What is this? (A cartoon.)
What do you see in the cartoon? (A snake, and below it, the words "Join, or Die.")
The snake is in pieces. What do you see next to each piece? (Letters.)
What do the letters stand for? What do they mean? (They are abbreviations for the thirteen original states.)

From left to right, what are the states in this illustration of the snake?

(S.C. = South Carolina)
(N.C. = North Carolina)
(V. = Virginia)
(M. = Maryland)
(P. = Pennsylvania)
(N.J. = New Jersey)
(N.Y. = New York)
(N.E. = New England = the states of Connecticut, Rhode Island, Massachusetts, New Hampshire)

Which of the thirteen original states *aren't* in the cartoon? (Georgia and Delaware)

(Point to the bottom right illustration.)

This is the cover of a small book that Benjamin Franklin published every year. What year is this book about? (1733.)
What is the book called? (An *Almanack*.)

READING THE PASSAGE

1. Have students read the passage silently. (If you wish, you may read the passage aloud or play the audio program as students read along silently.)

2. **Check Reading Comprehension:** Ask students a question about each section of the passage. For beginning-level students, ask these questions in the order below so that the questions follow the sequence of the passage. For higher-level students, ask the questions in random order.

    Who was famous for many things?
    Compare Benjamin Franklin with the other members of the Constitutional Convention.
    What position/job did he have as a U.S. diplomat? Where?
    What did he invent?
    What did he do as the first Postmaster General of the United States?
    What kind of libraries did he start?
    What was the name of his popular yearly book?

3. Ask students if they have any questions about the passage; check understanding of vocabulary.

4. **Choral Repetition:** Read aloud each line of the passage and have students repeat.

5. **Class Circle Reading:** Have students read the passage aloud as a class, with different students reading each line. (You can assign each line to a particular student or by seating patterns, or by letting students take turns spontaneously. In large classes, have a different group or row of students read each line.)

6. **Pair Practice:** Have students work in pairs, reading the passage to each other line by line. Circulate around the room and check students' reading and pronunciation, focusing more attention on students who need more assistance.

CHECK-UP

VOCABULARY CHECK

1. diplomat
2. Father
3. Convention
4. Postmaster
5. writer
6. libraries
7. stove

CIVICS CHECK

Note: Since this question has multiple acceptable answers, encourage low beginners to consistently practice a single answer to the question, while higher-level students can practice the multiple answers.

1. **Listening:** Have students read along silently as they listen to the question and answer(s)—presented by you, by a pair of students, or on the audio program.

2. **Choral Repetition:** Model the question and answer(s) and have the whole class repeat in unison.

3. **Choral Conversation Practice:** Divide the class in half. Have Group 1 ask the question and Group 2 give the answer(s); then reverse. (Or: You ask the question and have the whole class answer in unison; then reverse.)

4. **Pair Practice:** Have students practice the question and answer(s) in pairs.

5. **Presentation:** Call on one or two pairs of students to present the question and answer(s) to the class.

BENJAMIN FRANKLIN'S SAYINGS

Explain to students that Benjamin Franklin wrote many popular *sayings* in his *Poor Richard's Almanack*. Point out that these sayings were short sentences that gave advice—that told people how to live or what to do. Have students first work in pairs or small groups to discuss what they think each of these sayings means. Ask them to write down a sentence that gives the advice using different words. Then have them share and discuss as a class.

FOCUS

TOPIC
Branches of Government

GRAMMAR

Past Tense: Regular Verbs

The Constitution establish**ed** three branches of government.

Past Tense: Irregular Verbs

The Constitution **gave** the rules for the three branches of government.

Simple Present Tense

The legislative branch make**s** the federal laws.

To Be

The President **is** the Commander-in-Chief.

Have/Has

Some states **have** more people.
The Congress **has** two parts.

Must

The President **must** be age 35 or older.

NEW VOCABULARY

age	inaugurate
at least	natural-born citizen
certain	requirement

PREVIEWING THE READING

(This reading passage has an introductory section followed by four major sections, each accompanied by one or more photographs. You may want to treat each section as a separate passage, previewing and reading one passage before going on to the next.)

Have students talk about the title and the photographs to establish the context of the passage. Ask some or all of the following questions:

(Point to the photograph on page 134.)

Who are these people? (U.S. representatives.)
Where are they? (In the U.S. House of Representatives.)
What do they do? (They make the laws of the United States.)

(Point to the top left photograph on page 135.)

What is this building? (The White House.)
Who lives and works there? (The President.)
Where is it? (In Washington, D.C.)

(Point to the top right photograph on page 135.)

Who is this? (The President.)
Where does he live and work? (In the White House.)
What does he do? (He enforces the laws of the United States.)

(Point to the top photograph on page 136.)

Who is this man? (President Lyndon B. Johnson.)
Who is the woman standing next to him? (Jacqueline Kennedy, the wife of President John F. Kennedy.)
What is he doing? (He's raising his right hand. / He's taking the oath of office.)
Why? What happened? (President Kennedy was assassinated.)
Where are these people in this photograph? (They're on an airplane flying from Dallas, Texas, to Washington, D.C.)
When did this happen? (On November 22, 1963.)

(Point to the bottom left photograph on page 136.)

What building is this? (The Supreme Court building.)
Where is it located? (In Washington, D.C.)

(Point to the bottom right photograph on page 136.)

Who are these people? (The Supreme Court justices.)
What do they do? (They explain the laws of the United States.)

READING THE PASSAGE

1. Have students read the passage silently. (If you wish, you may read the passage aloud or play the audio program as students read along silently.)

2. **Check Reading Comprehension:** Ask students a question about each line of the passage. For beginning-level students, ask these questions in the order below, so that the questions follow the sequence of the passage. For higher-level students, ask the questions in random order.

Page 134 (Introductory section):

How many branches of government did the Constitution establish? What are they?
What did the Constitution give the rules for?

Page 134 (Main section):

What does the legislative branch do?
What is the legislative branch called?
What are the two parts of Congress?
Where does the Congress meet?

How many U.S. senators are there?
How many U.S. senators are there from each state?
Who does a U.S. senator represent?
For how long do we elect a U.S. senator?

How many voting members does the House of Representatives have?

Do all states have the same number of representatives?

Why?

Do some states have more people?

Which states have more representatives?

For how long do we elect a U.S. representative?

What does the Constitution give to the Congress?

Name one important power of Congress.

Page 135:

What does the executive branch do?

Who works in the executive branch?

Who is in charge of the executive branch?

Who is the chief executive of the United States?

Who is the Commander-in-Chief of the military?

Why does the President sign bills?

What else does the President do with bills?

Who does the President appoint?

What does the Cabinet do?

Can any person become President?

What kind of citizen must the President be?

How old must the President be?

How long must the President live in the United States before becoming President?

Page 136 (top):

How long is the President's term?

For how long do the American people elect a President?

How many terms can the President serve?

When do Americans vote for the President?

When is the President inaugurated?

If the President can no longer serve, who becomes the President?

If both the President and the Vice President can no longer serve, who becomes the President?

Page 136 (bottom):

What does the judicial branch do?

What is the judicial branch of the government?

What is the highest court in the United States?

How many justices are there on the Supreme Court?

Who appoints them? Who approves them?

How long do they serve?

3. Ask students if they have any questions about the passage; check understanding of vocabulary.

4. **Choral Repetition:** Read aloud each line of the passage and have students repeat.

5. **Class Circle Reading:** Have students read the passage aloud as a class, with different students reading each line. (You can assign each line to a particular student or by seating patterns, or by letting students take turns spontaneously. In large classes,

have a different group or row of students read each line.)

6. **Pair Practice:** Have students work in pairs, reading the passage to each other section by section. Circulate around the room and check students' reading and pronunciation, focusing more attention on students who need more assistance.

CHECK-UP (Page 137)

QUESTIONS AND ANSWERS: *System of Government Review*

This activity reviews key USCIS civics test questions related to the U.S. system of government. Have students practice with a partner, taking turns asking and answering the questions. Then have them write the answers on a separate sheet of paper. Many of the questions have multiple acceptable answers, and some questions require students to name public officials. For reference, the complete official USCIS questions and answers can be found in the textbook on Appendix pages 229–231. Here is a correlation of the questions in this activity to the USCIS question numbers:

Activity Question Number	USCIS Question Number	Activity Question Number	USCIS Question Number
1	13	14	27
2	15	15	28
3	16	16	29
4	17	17	30
5	18	18	31
6	19	19	32
7	20	20	33
8	21	21	34
9	22	22	35
10	23	23	37
11	24	24	38
12	25	25	39
13	26	26	40

ANSWERS

1. Congress. / Legislative. / President. / Executive. / The courts. / Judicial.
2. The President.
3. Congress. / Senate and House of Representatives./ The (U.S. or national) legislature.
4. The Senate and House (of Representatives).
5. One hundred (100).
6. Six (6).
7. (Name of one of your state's U.S. senators.)
8. Four hundred thirty-five (435).
9. Two (2).
10. (Name of your U.S. Representative.)

11. All people of the state.
12. Because of the state's population. / Because they have more people. / Because some states have more people.
13. Four (4).
14. November.
15. Barack Obama. / Obama.
16. Joe Biden. / Joseph R. Biden, Jr. / Biden.
17. The Vice President.
18. The Speaker of the House.
19. The President.
20. The President.
21. The President.
22. Advises the President.
23. Reviews laws. / Explains laws. / Resolves disputes (disagreements). / Decides if a law goes against the Constitution.
24. The Supreme Court.
25. Nine (9).
26. John Roberts. / John G. Roberts, Jr.

FOCUS

TOPIC
The Bill of Rights

GRAMMAR

Simple Present Tense

The First Amendment guarantee**s** freedom of speech.

Have/Has

They **have** the right to go to court.
The Constitution **has** 27 amendments.

NEW VOCABULARY

accuse	non-citizen
add	person
crime	police
fair	quick
lawyer	trial

PREVIEWING THE READING

Have students talk about the title and the illustration to establish the context of the passage.

Ask some or all of the following questions:

Q What are rights? (Freedoms. / The freedom to do things.)
Q What is an example of a right? (Various answers.)
Q What is this document? (The Bill of Rights.)
Q What is it part of? (The Constitution. / It's the first ten amendments to the Constitution.)

READING THE PASSAGE

1. Have students read the passage silently. (If you wish, you may read the passage aloud or play the audio program as students read along silently.)

2. **Check Reading Comprehension:** Ask students a question about each line of the passage. For beginning-level students, ask these questions in the order below, so that the questions follow the sequence of the passage. For higher-level students, ask the questions in random order.

   Can the people of the United States change the Constitution?
   What is a change to the Constitution called?
   What is an amendment?
   How many amendments does the Constitution have?

What do we call the first ten amendments?
When were these ten amendments added to the Constitution?
What does the Bill of Rights protect?
Whose rights are guaranteed by the Constitution and the Bill of Rights?

Finish these sentences:

Americans can say what they want to because the First Amendment guarantees _____. (freedom of speech)
Americans can write what they want to because the First Amendment guarantees _____. (freedom of the press)
Americans can worship as they want to because the First Amendment guarantees _____. (freedom of religion.)
Americans can meet together as they want to because the First Amendment guarantees _____. (freedom of assembly)
Americans can ask the government to do something, or not do something, because the First Amendment guarantees _____. (the right to petition the government)
Does the Bill of Rights guarantee the rights of people who are accused of crimes?
What rights do people accused of crimes have?
Where else does the Bill of Rights protect people?
What do police need before they can go into a person's home?

3. Ask students if they have any questions about the passage; check understanding of vocabulary.

4. **Choral Repetition:** Read aloud each line of the passage and have students repeat.

5. **Class Circle Reading:** Have students read the passage aloud as a class, with different students reading each line. (You can assign each line to a particular student or by seating patterns, or by letting students take turns spontaneously. In large classes, have a different group or row of students read each line.)

6. **Pair Practice:** Have students work in pairs, reading the passage to each other section by section. Circulate around the room and check students' reading and pronunciation, focusing more attention on students who need more assistance.

CHECK-UP

MATCHING

1. c
2. d
3. b
4. e
5. a

CIVICS CHECK

Note: Since some questions have multiple acceptable answers, encourage low beginners to consistently practice a single answer to a question, while higher-level students can practice the multiple answers.

First, practice each question separately:

1. **Listening:** Have students read along silently as they listen to the question and answer(s)—presented by you, by a pair of students, or on the audio program.

2. **Choral Repetition:** Model the question and answer(s) and have the whole class repeat in unison.

3. **Choral Conversation Practice:** Divide the class in half. Have Group 1 ask the question and Group 2 give the answer(s); then reverse. (Or: You ask the question and have the whole class answer in unison; then reverse.)

4. **Pair Practice:** Have students practice the question and answer(s) in pairs.

5. **Presentation:** Call on one or two pairs of students to present the question and answer(s) to the class.

Then practice all the questions together:

6. **Choral Answers:** Ask any question and have students give the answer in unison. (If there are multiple answers, have them give the first answer in the text.)

7. **Pair Practice:** Have students work in pairs, taking turns asking and answering all the questions in random order.

For more practice or for review during the next class session, do one of these activities:

LINE PRACTICE: Have students stand in two lines facing each other. Each pair of facing students should take turns asking and answering a question. After sufficient time for this practice, say "Move," and have one line of students move down one position while the other line remains in place. (The student at the end of the line moves to the beginning of the line.) In this way, new pairs are created and students practice with another partner. Continue until students have practiced all the questions.

"ROUND ROBIN": Have students circulate around the room and ask each other the questions. Students should move on to another person after they have taken turns asking and answering a question.

DISCUSSION

Have students discuss these topics first in pairs or small groups, and then as a class.

1. Have students discuss the importance of the Bill of Rights in their everyday lives. What can they do in the United States because of the freedoms guaranteed by the Bill of Rights?

2. Have students discuss examples from current events of particular rights and freedoms that are not allowed elsewhere in the world.

FOCUS

TOPIC
George Washington

GRAMMAR

Past Tense: Was/Were

He **was** an excellent leader.

Past Tense: Regular Verbs

The American people respect**ed** him very much.
He serv**ed** two terms.

Past Tense: Irregular Verbs

At this meeting the representatives **wrote** the Constitution.
In 1789 George Washington **became** the first President of the United States.

NEW VOCABULARY

dollar bill	respect

PREVIEWING THE READING

Have students talk about the title and the photograph to establish the context of the passage.

Ask some or all of the following questions:

Who is this a portrait of? (George Washington.)
What do you know about him? (He was the first President. / He was the leader of the Colonial Army. / etc.)
What places in the United States are named after George Washington? (Washington, D.C. / The state of Washington.)
What money (coins or bills) have his picture? (The quarter. / The dollar bill.)

READING THE PASSAGE

1. Have students read the passage silently.

2. **Check Reading Comprehension:** Ask students a question about each line of the passage. For beginning-level students, ask these questions in the order below, so that the questions follow the sequence of the passage. For higher-level students, ask the questions in random order.

   Who was the leader of the Colonial Army during the Revolutionary War?
   Was he a good leader?
   How did the American people feel about him?
   What was George Washington the leader of in 1787?
   What happened at this meeting?
   When did George Washington become the first President of the United States?

How many terms did he serve?
Was George Washington an important leader in American history?
Where is his picture?
What do Americans call him?

3. Ask students if they have any questions about the passage; check understanding of vocabulary.

4. **Choral Repetition:** Read aloud each line of the passage and have students repeat.

5. **Class Circle Reading:** Have students read the passage aloud as a class, with different students reading each line. (You can assign each line to a particular student or by seating patterns, or by letting students take turns spontaneously. In large classes, have a different group or row of students read each line.)

6. **Pair Practice:** Have students work in pairs, reading the passage to each other section by section. Circulate around the room and check students' reading and pronunciation, focusing more attention on students who need more assistance.

CIVICS CHECK

Practice each question separately:

1. **Listening:** Have students read along silently as they listen to the question and answer—presented by you, by a pair of students, or on the audio program.

2. **Choral Repetition:** Model the question and answer and have the whole class repeat in unison.

3. **Choral Conversation Practice:** Divide the class in half. Have Group 1 ask the question and Group 2 give the answer; then reverse. (Or: You ask the question and have the whole class answer in unison; then reverse.)

4. **Pair Practice:** Have students practice the question and answer in pairs.

5. **Presentation:** Call on one or two pairs of students to present the question and answer to the class.

EXPANSION

1. Bring in a picture book about Washington, D.C. Share it with students, pointing out the Washington Monument, the Jefferson Memorial, the U.S. Capitol, and the Supreme Court building. Discuss with students what they can see if they visit the nation's capital.

2. Have students prepare short oral or written reports on George Washington. Ask them to include the following information:

When was he born?	What did he do?
Where was he born?	When was he President?
Where did he live?	When did he die?

FOCUS

TOPICS

The Constitution
Benjamin Franklin
The Federalist Papers

GRAMMAR

WH-Questions

What is an amendment?

To Be

What **is** an amendment?
He **was** a U.S. diplomat.

FUNCTIONAL INTERVIEW SKILL

Hesitating

KEY VOCABULARY

I know the answer.
I studied this.
Let me see.
Let me think.
Let me think for a moment.

GETTING READY

Practicing how to hesitate to fill time.

Point out that these three dialogs contain an important strategy (hesitating) that students can use when they need time to think of an answer. As a class, have students read the information in the blue box. Then have them look at the three dialogs and identify how the applicant uses hesitating to fill time.

1st dialog: The applicant repeats two words in the question ("An amendment?"), says an expression to fill time ("Let me see."), and answers with a full sentence and puts the answer at the end ("An amendment is _____.").

2nd dialog: The applicant repeats two words in the question ("Benjamin Franklin?"), says two expressions to fill time ("Let me think. I know the answer."), and then answers the question.

3rd dialog: The applicant restates the question ("One of the writers of the *Federalist Papers*?"), says two expressions to fill time ("I studied this. Let me think for a moment."), and answers with a full sentence and puts the answer at the end ("One of the writers of the Federalist Papers was _____.")

If you wish, you can have students count the number of seconds the applicant hesitates in the third dialog to demonstrate how much thinking time the applicant gains by using this strategy.

PRACTICING THE DIALOG

Notes:

- There are three short dialogs. Lower-level students should practice each dialog separately. Higher-level students can practice the dialogs either separately or together.

- These dialogs have blank lines and answer-choice boxes since the questions have multiple acceptable answers. Encourage low beginners to consistently practice one answer to a question so that they master it—the first answer in the text or another answer they prefer. Higher-level students can practice the multiple answers. (The audio contains the first answer.)

1. **Setting the Scene:** Establish the context: "The USCIS officer is asking a citizenship applicant some civics questions."

2. **Listening:** With books closed, have students listen to the dialog—presented by you, by a pair of students, or on the audio program.

3. **Choral Repetition:** With books still closed, model each line and have the whole class repeat in unison.

4. **Reading:** With books open, have students follow along as two students present the dialog. Ask students if they have any questions and check understanding of vocabulary.

5. **Choral Conversation Practice:** Divide the class in half. Have Group 1 ask the questions and Group 2 give the answers; then reverse. (Or: You ask the questions and have the whole class answer in unison; then reverse.)

6. **Pair Practice:** Have students practice the dialog in pairs, taking turns being the USCIS officer and the applicant.

7. **Presentations:** Call on pairs of students to present the dialog to the class.

The end-of-unit assessment evaluates student achievement of the unit's learning objectives while developing the specific test-taking skills required for success during the USCIS English and civics exam. Students can practice and complete the tests in class or at home.

A. CIVICS

This section contains the official USCIS questions that appear in the unit. Students can practice the questions and answers outside of class on their own or with a study partner. (Since many questions have multiple acceptable answers, encourage low beginners to consistently practice a single answer to a question, while higher-level students can practice the multiple answers.) For in-class assessment, call on students to answer different questions, or observe students as they test each other through pair practice.

B. KEY VOCABULARY

1. President
2. dollar bill
3. Delaware
4. Senators
5. freedom of speech
6. Father of Our Country
7. New York City

C. READING AND WRITING

This section contains the types of reading and writing questions on the USCIS test. You can assess students' reading skills by their ability to read aloud the questions. You can assess their writing skills by their ability to write the sentences from dictation. (The dictation sentences appear below, in the text on page 239, and on the audio program. Each dictation sentence is on a separate audio track so that the audio can be paused while students write.)

1. Washington was the Father of Our Country.
2. President Washington is on the dollar bill.
3. Washington was the first President of the United States.
4. Delaware was the first state.
5. New York City was the first capital of the United States.

TEXT PAGE 144

CIVICS ENRICHMENT

PERFORMANCE-BASED ASSESSMENT

These civics enrichment activities are designed to promote students' active participation in class and in the civic life of the community—through projects, issues discussions, community tasks, field trips, and Internet activities. Reproducible performance-based assessment forms for use in evaluating and documenting student participation in these activities are included in the Appendix.

CIVIC PARTICIPATION

Review with students the rights guaranteed by the First Amendment, and have students discuss how people in your community exercise these rights. Have them brainstorm as a class examples of freedom of speech, freedom of the press, freedom of religion, freedom of assembly, and the right to petition the government. This discussion serves as preparation for the project activity that follows.

PROJECT ACTIVITY

First Amendment Bulletin Board Project: In this project, students create a bulletin board display about rights guaranteed by the First Amendment. They cut out newspaper headlines and photographs that are examples of these rights and display them on the bulletin board. They should also write brief paragraphs about the different rights and the examples they find. Have students take responsibility for all aspects of this project. Have them identify the particular tasks involved in the project, who will accomplish each task, what resources are needed, and what form the final bulletin board display will take. Use the project as a basis for building students' skills in leadership, teamwork, and communicating information—key SCANS* skills useful for success in the workplace.

*Secretary's Commission on Achieving Necessary Skills

COMMUNITY ISSUES

Problem-Posing Discussion: Have students discuss limits on the rights guaranteed by the First Amendment. Point out the examples given in the text: a person can't shout "Fire!" in a movie theater; in some cities young people can't be in large groups in public places. Have students give examples of limits on the rights guaranteed by the First Amendment, and have them share their opinions about these limits.

TECHNOLOGY ENRICHMENT

See Appendix page 312 for Internet enrichment activities related to this unit.

UNIT SUMMARY

KEY VOCABULARY

Have students review the lists of words they have learned in this unit. Encourage students to get a small notebook where they can write down vocabulary that is new for them.

GRAMMAR

Have students review the list of irregular past tense verbs in this unit. Have students write sentences that use the past tense forms of these verbs.

FUNCTIONAL EXPRESSIONS

Have students review the different ways to hesitate and find where they occur in the unit. For enrichment, have students ask each other new questions using these different expressions.

UNIT REVIEW WORKSHEETS

Unit 8 Writing Practice
Unit 8 Reading Practice
Unit 8 Civics Practice

TEXT PAGE 224 (QUESTIONS 17–20) THE ENGLISH TEST (SPEAKING)

FOCUS

TOPIC

Answering Form N-400 "Part 10" questions during the USCIS interview

FUNCTIONAL INTERVIEW SKILL

Reporting information

KEY VOCABULARY

accused of	found guilty
against the law	happened
alternative sentencing program	paroled
	placed in a program
charged with	placed on probation
commit a crime	receive a suspended
commit an offense	sentence
convicted of a crime	rehabilitative program
convicted of an offense	

ROLE PLAY: Questions 17–20

Have students work in pairs and role-play interviews using questions 17–20. Have them use in their conversations some of the expressions that appear in the blue boxes on pages 216, 220, and 222 to practice asking for repetition and clarification. Have students take turns being the USCIS officer and the applicant. Then have pairs of students present their role plays to the class.

WORKSHEETS

Interview Practice Worksheets 32–34

UNIT 9

THE WAR OF 1812
THE NATIONAL ANTHEM
EXPANSION
WARS IN THE 1800s

THE CIVIL WAR
ABRAHAM LINCOLN
AMENDMENTS

LESSONS & UNIT ACTIVITIES	OBJECTIVES	STUDENT TEXT	TEACHER'S GUIDE
Vocabulary Preview	Identifying vocabulary related to the War of 1812, the Civil War, and Abraham Lincoln	145	135
The War of 1812	Identifying the War of 1812	146	136
Song of Freedom: The Star-Spangled Banner (The National Anthem)	Identifying the national anthem	147	137
Expansion & Wars in the 1800s	Describing how the nation expanded during the 1800s; Identifying wars fought by the U.S. in the 1800s	148–149	138–139
The Civil War	Identifying the Civil War; Describing problems that led to the Civil War	150–151	140–141
Presidential Profile: Abraham Lincoln	Describing the importance of Abraham Lincoln; Describing the result of the Emancipation Proclamation	152–154	142–143
Voice of Freedom: Lincoln's Gettysburg Address	Identifying Lincoln's speech at the Gettysburg National Cemetery; Reciting excerpts of Lincoln's Gettysburg Address	155	144
Amendments to the Constitution	Identifying amendments to the Constitution; Identifying the Bill of Rights as the first ten amendments; Naming rights or freedoms from the First Amendment; Identifying other amendments; Describing amendments about who can vote; Describing the importance of Susan B. Anthony	156–159	145–146
Review	Talking Time Line: Reviewing important dates in U.S. history	160	146
Civics Test: Did You Say the 1800s?	Asking for repetition; Asking for clarification	161	147
Unit Test	Preparing for USCIS civics, reading, and writing test questions	162–163	148
Civics Enrichment	Examining a copy of the Constitution and discussing ideas for a new amendment; Debate Activity: Debating the voting age in the United States; Internet Activity: Visiting historic places online	164	148–149
The English Test (Speaking)*	Answering Form N-400 "Part 10" questions during the USCIS interview	224	149

* This interview preparation lesson is in the Appendix for students' convenience. It can be introduced in this unit and then reviewed along with the other interview preparation lessons as students get ready for their appointment at USCIS. If you prefer, you can do these lessons later in the course if that is more appropriate for the timing of your students' interviews. Interview Practice worksheets accompany these lessons.

UNIT RESOURCES

Worksheets:
Unit 9 Writing Practice
Unit 9 Reading Practice
Unit 9 Civics Practice
Interview Practice Worksheets 35–37

Audio Program:
CD 2: Tracks 64–71
CD 3: Tracks 1–10

RELATED PRACTICE

Foundations: Unit 12
Word by Word Basic: pages 35, 156–161, 188–191, 244–245
Word by Word: pages 15, 82–85, 101–104, 162, 163
Side by Side / Side by Side Plus: Book 2, Unit 1
Side by Side Interactive CD-ROM / Side by Side TV: Level 2A, Segments 27, 28
ExpressWays: Book 1, Unit 7

UNIT OVERVIEW

KEY VOCABULARY

READING	WRITING	PEOPLE	PLACES/GEOGRAPHY	OTHER WORDS
Abraham Lincoln	Abraham Lincoln	Abraham Lincoln	Africa	civil rights
Bill of Rights	Alaska	Blacks	Alaska	Confederacy
can	can	(the) British	Arlington, Virginia	Confederate states
for	citizens	citizens	Baltimore Harbor	economic reasons
in	Civil War	firefighter	border	factory
is	during	Francis Scott Key	California	farm products
largest	February	George Washington	Florida	federal laws
one	for	leader	France	freedoms
President	freedom of speech	slave	Gettysburg National Cemetery	land
Presidents' Day	have	soldier	Great Britain	national anthem
right	in	Susan B. Anthony	Hawaii	national election
state	is	women	Lincoln Memorial	native country
the	largest		Louisiana Territory	plantation
United States	of	**EVENTS**	Mexico	property
vote	one	Battle of Gettysburg	Mississippi River	rights
was	people	Civil War	(the) North	slavery
what	President	Emancipation Proclamation	Oregon	*Star-Spangled Banner*
when	Presidents' Day	Gettysburg Address	Pacific Ocean	state laws
who	right	Mexican-American War	Pentagon	states' rights
	state	Presidents' Day	Russia	taxes
	the	Revolutionary War	(the) South	territory
	United States	September 11, 2001	Spain	treaty
	vote	Spanish-American War	Texas	Union
	was	terrorist attack	United States	women's rights
		War Between the States	western border	women's suffrage
		War of 1812		

GRAMMAR

PAST TENSE: IRREGULAR VERBS

become – became	have – had	sell – sold
begin – began	lead – led	speak – spoke
buy – bought	leave – left	win – won
fight – fought	make – made	write – wrote
give – gave	say – said	

FUNCTIONAL EXPRESSIONS

ASKING FOR REPETITION

I'm not sure I heard the question correctly.
I'm not sure I heard that correctly.
Could you repeat the question, please?

CLARIFYING

Did you say . . . ?

INDICATING UNDERSTANDING

I understand.

TEXT PAGE 145 VOCABULARY PREVIEW

You may want to introduce these words before beginning the unit, or you may choose to wait until they first occur in a specific lesson. If you choose to introduce them at this point, here are some suggestions:

1. Have students look at the photographs on text page 145 and identify the words they already know.

2. Present the vocabulary. Say each word and have the class repeat it chorally and individually. Check students' understanding and pronunciation of the words.

3. Practice the vocabulary as a class, in pairs, or in small groups. Have students cover the word list and look at the photographs. Practice the words in the following ways:

   • Say a word and have students tell the correct number on the photograph.
   • Give a number on a photograph and have students say the word.

TEXT PAGE 146 THE WAR OF 1812

FOCUS

TOPICS

The War of 1812
The National Anthem

GRAMMAR

Past Tense: Regular Verbs

During the war, the British burn**ed** the White House.

Past Tense: Irregular Verbs

The United States and Great Britain **fought** against each other.
The Americans **won** the battle.
Francis Scott Key **wrote** about this.

NEW VOCABULARY

attack	fort
Baltimore Harbor	national anthem
battle	*Star-Spangled Banner*
burn (v.)	War of 1812
each other	watch (v.)
fight	win

PREVIEWING THE READING

Have students talk about the title and the illustrations to establish the context of the passage.

Ask some or all of the following questions:

(Point to the top picture.)

What's happening in this picture? (A building is burning. / Soldiers are marching. / Soldiers are fighting.)
The scene in this picture is in Washington, D.C. What building is burning? (The White House.)

(Point to the bottom left picture and its caption.)

What do you see in the picture? (Boats. / Water. / Bombs exploding.)
Where is this happening? (On the water. / Near Fort McHenry.)

(Point to the bottom right picture and its caption.)

This picture shows the same place as the picture on the left, but it's the next morning. What do you see at Fort McHenry? (The U.S. flag.)

READING THE PASSAGE

1. Have students read the passage silently. (If you wish, you may read the passage aloud or play the audio program as students read along silently.)

2. **Check Reading Comprehension:** Ask students a question about each line of the passage. For beginning-level students, ask these questions in the order below so that the questions follow the sequence of the passage. For higher-level students, ask the questions in random order.

   Which countries fought against each other in the War of 1812?
   During the war, what did the British burn?
   What did they attack in Baltimore Harbor?
   Who watched the battle?
   What did he watch at the fort?
   What happened the next morning?
   Who won the battle?
   What did Francis Scott Key do?
   What is the national anthem of the United States?

3. Ask students if they have any questions about the passage; check understanding of vocabulary.

4. **Choral Repetition:** Read aloud each line of the passage and have students repeat.

5. **Class Circle Reading:** Have students read the passage aloud as a class, with different students reading each line. (You can assign each line to a particular student or by seating patterns, or by letting students take turns spontaneously. In large classes, have a different group or row of students read each line.)

6. **Pair Practice:** Have students work in pairs, reading the passage to each other section by section. Circulate around the room and check students' reading and pronunciation, focusing more attention on students who need more assistance.

TEXT PAGE 147 THE *STAR-SPANGLED BANNER* (THE NATIONAL ANTHEM)

FOCUS

TOPIC
The National Anthem

GRAMMAR

Past Tense: Irregular Verbs
Francis Scott Key **wrote** this song.

PREVIEWING THE NATIONAL ANTHEM

Have students read as a class the first two lines that introduce the national anthem. Ask the following questions:

What is the name of the national anthem?
Who wrote this song? What is the song about?

PRACTICING THE NATIONAL ANTHEM*

*Note: The *Star-Spangled Banner* is not required for the USCIS civics test. It is provided for enrichment and speaking practice.

1. **Listening to the Lyrics:** Have students listen to the lyrics of the song by playing the audio or saying the lyrics yourself.

2. **Choral Repetition:** Read aloud each line of the song and have students repeat in unison.

3. **Listening to the Song:** Have students listen to the song by playing the audio or singing it yourself.

4. **Singing Aloud:** Have students sing along as you play the audio or sing the song.

YOUR NATIVE COUNTRY'S NATIONAL ANTHEM

Have students discuss their native countries' national anthems and then sing them for the class.

EXPANSION

1. Discuss with students the photo (and caption) of the flag being displayed by firefighters standing on the roof of the Pentagon after the terrorist attack on September 11, 2001. Explain to students that Arlington, Virginia, is next to Washington, D.C. Have them locate Washington, D.C., on a map of the United States. Ask students if they know why the Pentagon building is important. (It is the headquarters of the U.S. military.)

2. Point out the photo (and caption) of the original *Star-Spangled Banner* flag. Have students visit the website of the National Museum of American History in Washington, D.C., to learn about the flag and how the museum has preserved it.

TEXT PAGES 148–149 EXPANSION & WARS IN THE 1800s

FOCUS

TOPICS

Expansion
Wars in the 1800s

GRAMMAR

Past Tense: Regular Verbs

The United States expand**ed** to the Pacific Ocean.

Past Tense: Irregular Verbs

It **bought** Florida from Spain.
This **led** to the Mexican-American War.
Russia **sold** Alaska to the United States.
Hawaii **became** a territory.
The United States and Spain **fought** the Spanish-American War.

Ordinal Numbers

Alaska and Hawaii are the **49th** and **50th** states of the Union.

NEW VOCABULARY

after	Oregon country
annex (v.)	Philippines
buy	receive
Colorado	region
control (v.)	Russia
Cuba	sell
expand	Spain
farm	Spanish-American War
farm products	transport
Florida	treaty
France	Union
Hawaii	use
land	Utah
Louisiana Territory	western border
Mexican-American War	Wyoming
Nevada	

PREVIEWING THE READING

Have students talk about the title and the map to establish the context of the passage. Ask some or all of the following questions:

> What is this a map of? (The United States.)
> What do the dates mean? (The years when different areas became part of the country.)
> Where is our state located?

Have students look at the map on page 148 and a current map of the United States showing geographical features. Ask:

> What was the western border of the United States in 1783? (The Mississippi River.)

READING THE PASSAGE

1. Have students read the passage silently. (If you wish, you may read the passage aloud or play the audio program as students read along silently.)

2. **Check Reading Comprehension:** Ask students a question about each line of the passage. For beginning-level students, ask these questions in the order below so that the questions follow the sequence of the passage. For higher-level students, ask the questions in random order.

> Where did the United States expand to in the 1800s?
> Why did Americans want more land?
> What did they want to use the Mississippi River for?
> Where was the western border of the United States after the Revolutionary War?
> How did the United States expand to the Louisiana Territory?
> How did the United States expand into Florida?
> How did it expand into Texas?
> What did this lead to?
> How did the United States expand to the Oregon country?
> Which states became part of the United States after the Mexican-American War ended in 1848?
> How did Alaska become part of the United States?
> What area became a territory of the United States in 1898?
> What are the 49th and 50th states of the Union?
> Which countries fought the Spanish-American War in 1898?
> What did the United States control after that war?

3. Ask students if they have any questions about the passage; check understanding of vocabulary.

4. **Choral Repetition:** Read aloud each line of the passage and have students repeat.

5. **Class Circle Reading:** Have students read the passage aloud as a class, with different students reading each line. (You can assign each line to a particular student or by seating patterns, or by letting students take turns spontaneously. In large classes, have a different group or row of students read each line.)

6. **Pair Practice:** Have students work in pairs, reading the passage to each other section by section. Circulate around the room and check students' reading and pronunciation, focusing more attention on students who need more assistance.

CHECK-UP

FACT CHECK

1. Louisiana
2. Florida
3. California
4. Alaska
5. Oregon
6. Hawaii

CIVICS CHECK

Note: Since some questions have multiple acceptable answers, encourage low beginners to consistently practice a single answer to a question, while higher-level students can practice the multiple answers.

First, practice each question separately:

1. **Listening:** Have students read along silently as they listen to the question and answer(s)—presented by you, by a pair of students, or on the audio program.
2. **Choral Repetition:** Model the question and answer(s) and have the whole class repeat in unison.
3. **Choral Conversation Practice:** Divide the class in half. Have Group 1 ask the question and Group 2 give the answer(s); then reverse. (Or: You ask the question and have the whole class answer in unison; then reverse.)
4. **Pair Practice:** Have students practice the question and answer(s) in pairs.
5. **Presentation:** Call on one or two pairs of students to present the question and answer(s) to the class.

Then practice all the questions together:

6. **Choral Answers:** Ask any question and have students give the answer in unison. (If there are multiple answers, have them give the first answer in the text.)
7. **Pair Practice:** Have students work in pairs, taking turns asking and answering all the questions in random order.

YOUR STATE

Have students answer with the appropriate information.

EXPANSION

1. Bring in a current map of the United States. Have students identify in which territories current states are located. (For example, Washington in the Oregon country; California in the Mexican Cession.)
2. If you have students from Mexico in your class, have them discuss the Texas Annexation and the Mexican Cession. Ask them what they learned about this when they studied history in school in Mexico. How did their country react at that time? How do people in their country feel today about what happened? How would the United States be different today if this had not happened?

FOCUS

TOPIC

The Civil War

GRAMMAR

Past Tense: Regular Verbs

The Northern states want**ed** to end the system of slavery.

Past Tense: Irregular Verbs

The North and the South **fought** the Civil War from 1861 to 1865.

The owners **bought** and **sold** them like property.

They **left** the Union and **became** the Confederate states.

NEW VOCABULARY

Africa	owner
Civil War	plantation
Confederacy	powerful
Confederate states	property
disagree	reason
economic	secede
expensive	slavery
factory	state laws
farm products	states' rights
federal laws	Union
overseas	War between the States

PREVIEWING THE READING

(This reading passage has four sections, each introduced by a photograph. You may want to treat each section as a separate passage, previewing and reading one section before going on to the next.)

Have students talk about the title and the photographs to establish the context of the passage.

Ask some or all of the following questions:

Page 150 (top):

   What's happening in this picture? (Soldiers are fighting. / Armies are fighting. / It's a war. / It's a battle.)
   What kinds of flags do you see? (Two flags that look like the U.S. flag, and one flag on the left that looks different.)
   The people fighting in both armies are Americans. They are fighting against each other. What kind of war is this called? (A civil war.)

Page 150 (bottom):

   Who are these people? (Slaves.)
   Where are they? (On a farm. / In a field.)
   What are they doing? (Working on a farm. / Picking cotton.)
   Where are they from? (Africa.)

Page 151 (top):

   (Point to the picture on the left.)
   What do you see in the picture? (A factory.)
   Do you think this is in the North or the South? (The North.)
   What kind of jobs do people have in this place? (Have students list types of factory jobs.)

   (Point to the picture on the right.)
   What do you see in the picture? (A farm.)
   Do you think this is in the North or the South? (The South.)
   What kind of jobs do people have in this place? (Farming jobs.)

Page 151 (bottom):

   What are the people in this picture doing? (They're arguing. / They're fighting.)
   What do you think they're arguing/fighting about? (Various answers.)

READING THE PASSAGE

1. Have students read the passage silently. (If you wish, you may read the passage aloud or play the audio program as students read along silently.)

2. **Check Reading Comprehension:** Ask students a question about each line of the passage. For beginning-level students, ask these questions in the order below so that the questions follow the sequence of the passage. For higher-level students, ask the questions in random order.

   What was the Civil War?
   What is the Civil War also called?
   When did the North and the South fight the Civil War?
   What were the Northern states also called?
   What were the Southern states also called?
   What was one main problem that led to the Civil War?
   What happened to people from Africa?
   Did slaves have any rights or freedoms?
   What did their owners do to them?
   Why did the Southern states say they needed slaves?
   What did the Northern states want to do?

What other reasons were there for the Civil War?
What did the North have?
What did the South have?
What did the North and the South disagree about?
What did these taxes do to the North and South?

What was another problem that led to the Civil War?
What did the Southern states believe about state and federal laws?
What did the Northern states believe about state and federal laws?
What happened in 1860 and 1861?
What did eleven Southern states do when they left the Union?
When did the Civil War begin?
What happened in 1865?

3. Ask students if they have any questions about the passage; check understanding of vocabulary.

4. **Choral Repetition:** Read aloud each line of the passage and have students repeat.

5. **Class Circle Reading:** Have students read the passage aloud as a class, with different students reading each line. (You can assign each line to a particular student or by seating patterns, or by letting students take turns spontaneously. In large classes, have a different group or row of students read each line.)

6. **Pair Practice:** Have students work in pairs, reading the passage to each other section by section. Circulate around the room and check students' reading and pronunciation, focusing more attention on students who need more assistance.

EXPANSION

1. Have students discuss civil wars in their native countries. What were the causes? the key people and events? the outcomes?

2. Have students discuss differences between how African-American people came to the United States and how people from other countries came as immigrants. Ask them what it would have been like to live as a slave before the Civil War.

FOCUS

TOPICS

Abraham Lincoln
The Civil War

GRAMMAR

Past Tense: Regular Verbs

Lincoln want**ed** to save the Union.

Past Tense: Irregular Verbs

He **led** the United States during the Civil War.
In 1865 the North **won** the Civil War.

Ordinal Numbers

Abraham Lincoln was the **sixteenth** President of the
United States.

NEW VOCABULARY

assassinate	preserve
Emancipation Proclamation	Presidents' Day
free (v.)	save
great	sixteenth
honor	stay together

PREVIEWING THE READING

Have students talk about the title and the photographs
to establish the context of the passage.

Ask some or all of the following questions:

(Page 152 top)

> Who is this a portrait of? (Abraham Lincoln.)
> What do you know about him? (Various answers.)

(Page 152 bottom left)

> This is a photograph of Abraham Lincoln. Where
>   is he in this photograph? (Antietam, Maryland—
>   pronounced "An–tee–tum")
> What year is it? (1862)
> What war was happening when this photograph was
>   taken? (The Civil War.)
> What do you see in the photograph? (A tent and two
>   men/soldiers.)
> Tell students that Antietam, Maryland, was the scene
>   of a famous battle during the Civil War.

(Page 152 bottom right)

> What is this? (A statue/monument.)
> Who is it? (President Lincoln.)
> What's it called? (The Lincoln Memorial.)
> Where is it? (Washington, D.C.)

READING THE PASSAGE

1. Have students read the passage silently. (If you
   wish, you may read the passage aloud or play the
   audio program as students read along silently.)

2. **Check Reading Comprehension:** Ask students
   a question about each line of the passage. For
   beginning-level students, ask these questions in
   the order below so that the questions follow the
   sequence of the passage. For higher-level students,
   ask the questions in random order.

   > Who was the sixteenth President of the United
   >   States?
   > Who led the United States during the Civil War?
   > Who was the leader of the Northern states during
   >   the Civil War?
   > What did Lincoln want to save?
   > What did he want the Northern and Southern
   >   states to do?

   > How did Lincoln feel about slavery?
   > What did he sign in 1863?
   > What did this document do?

   > Which side won the Civil War? When?
   > What happened five days after the war ended?

   > What kind of president was Abraham Lincoln?
   > What did he preserve?
   > When do Americans celebrate Presidents' Day?
   > Who do Americans honor on this national holiday?

3. Ask students if they have any questions about the
   passage; check understanding of vocabulary.

4. **Choral Repetition:** Read aloud each line of the
   passage and have students repeat.

5. **Class Circle Reading:** Have students read the
   passage aloud as a class, with different students
   reading each line. (You can assign each line to a
   particular student or by seating patterns, or by letting
   students take turns spontaneously. In large classes,
   have a different group or row of students read each
   line.)

6. **Pair Practice:** Have students work in pairs, reading
   the passage to each other section by section.
   Circulate around the room and check students'
   reading and pronunciation, focusing more attention
   on students who need more assistance.

EXPANSION

1. Bring in a picture book about Washington, D.C. Point
   out the Lincoln Memorial and Ford's Theatre (site of
   Lincoln's assassination.)

2. Ask students: What money (coins or bills) have a
   picture of Abraham Lincoln? (The penny. / The five-
   dollar bill.)

3. Have students prepare short oral or written reports on Abraham Lincoln. Ask them to include the following information:

When was he born?
Where was he born?
Where did he live?
What did he do?
When was he President?
When did he die?

CHECK-UP (Pages 153–154)

VOCABULARY CHECK

1. slavery
2. Confederacy
3. plantations
4. rights
5. Union

FACT CHECK

1. in factories
2. Southern
3. Emancipation Proclamation
4. federal, state
5. 1865

THE ANSWER IS "ABRAHAM LINCOLN!"

1. Abraham Lincoln.
2. Abraham Lincoln.
3. Abraham Lincoln.
4. Abraham Lincoln.
5. Abraham Lincoln.

MATCHING: *Expressions*

1. c
2. a
3. b

MATCHING: *Reasons for the Civil War*

1. b
2. c
3. a

CIVICS CHECK

Note: Since many questions have multiple acceptable answers, encourage low beginners to consistently practice a single answer to a question, while higher-level students can practice the multiple answers.

First, practice each question separately:

1. **Listening:** Have students read along silently as they listen to the question and answer(s)—presented by you, by a pair of students, or on the audio program.
2. **Choral Repetition:** Model the question and answer(s) and have the whole class repeat in unison.

3. **Choral Conversation Practice:** Divide the class in half. Have Group 1 ask the question and Group 2 give the answer(s); then reverse. (Or: You ask the question and have the whole class answer in unison; then reverse.)
4. **Pair Practice:** Have students practice the question and answer(s) in pairs.
5. **Presentation:** Call on one or two pairs of students to present the question and answer(s) to the class.

Then practice all the questions together:

6. **Choral Answers:** Ask any question and have students give the answer in unison. (If there are multiple answers, have them give the first answer in the text.)
7. **Pair Practice:** Have students work in pairs, taking turns asking and answering all the questions in random order.

For more practice or for review during the next class session, do one of these activities:

LINE PRACTICE: Have students stand in two lines facing each other. Each pair of facing students should take turns asking and answering a question. After sufficient time for this practice, say "Move," and have one line of students move down one position while the other line remains in place. (The student at the end of the line moves to the beginning of the line.) In this way, new pairs are created and students practice with another partner. Continue until students have practiced all the questions.

"ROUND ROBIN": Have students circulate around the room and ask each other the questions. Students should move on to another person after they have taken turns asking and answering a question.

(As noted in the text, this lesson is provided for enrichment and speaking practice. It is not required for the citizenship exam.)

FOCUS

TOPICS

Abraham Lincoln   Lincoln's Gettysburg Address

GRAMMAR

Past Tense: Irregular Verbs

He **gave** his most famous speech in Gettysburg, Pennsylvania.

He **spoke** at the dedication of the Gettysburg National Cemetery.

NEW VOCABULARY

cemetery	Gettysburg	soldier	speech
dedication	nation	speaker	voice

GETTING READY

Bring in a map of the United States and have students locate Pennsylvania and Gettysburg.

PREVIEWING THE READING

Have students talk about the title and the illustration to establish the context of the passage.

Ask some or all of the following questions:

Who is this man? (Abraham Lincoln.)

What's he doing? (He's speaking. / He's giving a speech.)

Where's Gettysburg? (In Pennsylvania.)

The word *address* has two meanings. It means the location of a place. What's another meaning of *address*? (A speech.)

READING THE PASSAGE

Note: Practice the first two sections of the passage first. (Don't practice the excerpt of Lincoln's Gettysburg Address yet.)

1. Have students read the passage silently. (If you wish, you may read the passage aloud or play the audio program as students read along silently.)

2. **Check Reading Comprehension:** Ask students questions about each line of the passage. For beginning-level students, ask these questions in the order below so that the questions follow the sequence of the passage. For higher-level students, ask the questions in random order.

    Was Abraham Lincoln a good speaker?

    Where did he give his most famous speech? When?

    What event did he speak at?

What happened there four months before this speech?

What is Lincoln's speech called?

3. Ask students if they have any questions about the passage; check understanding of vocabulary.

4. **Choral Repetition:** Read aloud each line of the passage and have students repeat.

5. **Class Circle Reading:** Have students read the passage aloud as a class, with different students reading each line. (You can assign each line to a particular student or by seating patterns, or by letting students take turns spontaneously. In large classes, have a different group or row of students read each line.)

6. **Pair Practice:** Have students work in pairs, reading the passage to each other section by section. Circulate around the room and check students' reading and pronunciation, focusing more attention on students who need more assistance.

PRACTICING THE EXCERPT*

* Note: The excerpt of Lincoln's Gettysburg Address is not required for the USCIS civics test. It is provided for enrichment and speaking practice.

1. **Listening:** Have students read along silently as you recite the excerpt or play the audio.

2. **Choral Repetition (line by line):** Read aloud each separate line of the excerpt as it appears in the text and have students repeat in unison.

3. **Reading:** Have students practice reading aloud the excerpt as a class, in small groups, or on their own.

4. Ask students if they understand the general meaning of the excerpt. (They do not have to know the exact meaning of unfamiliar words.)

5. **Public Speaking Practice:** Have individual students present the excerpt to the class. If you feel it is appropriate to do so, help students with their diction and projection to improve their public speaking skills.

6. **Reciting:** Have students memorize the excerpt and practice reciting it (without the text) as a class, in small groups, and on their own.

EXPANSION

1. **Oratorical Contest:** Have interested students memorize the excerpt or a larger portion of Lincoln's Gettysburg Address and recite it for the class. Have class members vote on the best rendition, and award a prize to the winner.

2. **Gettysburg National Cemetery:** Bring in a picture book about Gettysburg National Cemetery or the Battle of Gettysburg. Share it with students and tell them how great the loss of life was during that battle. Mention that the battlefield area is preserved and is a major tourist attraction in Pennsylvania.

TEXT PAGES 156–159 AMENDMENTS TO THE CONSTITUTION

FOCUS

TOPICS
Amendments
The Bill of Rights
Susan B. Anthony

GRAMMAR

Past Tense: Regular Verbs

The 13th Amendment end**ed** slavery.

Past Tense: Irregular Verbs

The 14th Amendment **made** all Blacks citizens of the United States.
The 19th Amendment **gave** women the right to vote.

Can

Americans **can** say what they want to.

Ordinal Numbers

The **13th** Amendment ended slavery.

NEW VOCABULARY

Blacks	poll tax
civil rights leader	right to vote
income taxes	soon
national election	women's rights
organization	women's suffrage

PREVIEWING THE READING

Have students talk about what they see in the photographs so that they understand the information about amendments to the Constitution. Students' ability to describe the photographs will depend on their language skill level.

(Page 156 top, from left to right)

People speaking at a public meeting (Freedom of speech)
Newspapers (Freedom of the press)
People worshipping/praying (Freedom of religion)

(Page 156 bottom left)

People demonstrating / People meeting together to support an issue (Freedom of assembly)

(Page 156 bottom right)

A person signing a document/petition (The right to petition the government)

(Page 157 top left)

Blacks/African-Americans registering to vote

(Page 157 top right)

People supporting the right to vote for women

READING THE PASSAGE

1. Have students read the passage silently. (If you wish, you may read the passage aloud or play the audio program as students read along silently.)

2. **Check Reading Comprehension:** Ask students a question about each line of the passage. For beginning-level students, ask these questions in the order below so that the questions follow the sequence of the passage. For higher-level students, ask the questions in random order.

   What is an amendment?
   What does *amendment* mean?
   How many amendments does the Constitution have?
   What do we call the first ten amendments to the Constitution?
   What does the Bill of Rights do?
   Which amendment gives Americans many important rights and freedoms?
   What is one right or freedom from the First Amendment?
   What is another right or freedom from the First Amendment? (Ask this four times to elicit answers about all the rights described in the passage.)
   What does freedom of speech mean?
   What does freedom of the press mean?
   What does freedom of religion mean?
   What does freedom of assembly mean?
   What is the right to petition the government?
   Are other amendments to the Constitution important?
   How many amendments were there soon after the Civil War?
   What did the 13th Amendment do?
   Which amendment made all Blacks citizens of the United States?
   What did the 15th Amendment do?
   Which amendment established income taxes? In what year?
   Which amendment gave women the right to vote? In what year?
   What did the 24th Amendment do? In what year?
   What did the 26th Amendment do? In what year?
   How old do citizens have to be to vote for President?

3. Ask students if they have any questions about the passage; check understanding of vocabulary.

4. **Choral Repetition:** Read aloud each line of the passage and have the students repeat.

5. **Class Circle Reading:** Have students read the passage aloud as a class, with different students

reading each line. (You can assign each line to a particular student or by seating patterns, or by letting students take turns spontaneously. In large classes, have a different group or row of students read each line.)

6. **Pair Practice:** Have students work in pairs, reading the passage to each other section by section. Circulate around the room and check students' reading and pronunciation, focusing more attention on students who need more assistance.

EXPANSION

Have students look at the photograph of Susan B. Anthony and Elizabeth Cady Stanton and the caption at the bottom of text page 157. Have them calculate how many years it took from the beginning of their women's suffrage organization in 1869 until the 19th Amendment was passed in 1920. (51/52 years.) Have students discuss if women have the right to vote in their native countries, and if so, when they got the right to vote.

CHECK-UP (Pages 158–159)

ORDINAL NUMBERS
1. 16th
2. 1st
3. 49th
4. 50th
5. 18th
6. 19th

MATCHING
1. c
2. a
3. d
4. b

VOCABULARY CHECK
1. slavery
2. women
3. income
4. age
5. right
6. poll

CIVICS CHECK

Note: Since many questions have multiple acceptable answers, encourage low beginners to consistently practice a single answer to a question, while higher-level students can practice the multiple answers.

First, practice each question separately:

1. **Listening:** Have students read along silently as they listen to the question and answer(s)—presented by you, by a pair of students, or on the audio program.

2. **Choral Repetition:** Model the question and answer(s) and have the whole class repeat in unison.

3. **Choral Conversation Practice:** Divide the class in half. Have Group 1 ask the question and Group 2 give the answer(s); then reverse. (Or: You ask the question and have the whole class answer in unison; then reverse.)

4. **Pair Practice:** Have students practice the question and answer(s) in pairs.

5. **Presentation:** Call on one or two pairs of students to present the question and answer(s) to the class.

Then practice all the questions together:

6. **Choral Answers:** Ask any question and have students give the answer in unison. (If there are multiple answers, have them give the first answer in the text.)

7. **Pair Practice:** Have students work in pairs, taking turns asking and answering all the questions in random order.

For more practice or for review during the next class session, do one of these activities:

LINE PRACTICE: Have students stand in two lines facing each other. Each pair of facing students should take turns asking and answering a question. After sufficient time for this practice, say "Move," and have one line of students move down one position while the other line remains in place. (The student at the end of the line moves to the beginning of the line.) In this way, new pairs are created and students practice with another partner. Continue until students have practiced all the questions.

"ROUND ROBIN": Have students circulate around the room and ask each other the questions. Students should move on to another person after they have taken turns asking and answering a question.

TEXT PAGE 160 REVIEW

TALKING TIME LINE: Important Dates in U.S. History

Have students complete the time line. Then have them work in pairs, asking and answering the questions at the bottom of the page, based on the information recorded on the time line.

1787	Representatives wrote the Constitution.
1791	The Bill of Rights was added to the Constitution.
1803	The United States bought the Louisiana Territory.
1861	The Civil War began.
1863	President Lincoln signed the Emancipation Proclamation.
1865	The Civil War ended.
1920	Women got the right to vote.

FOCUS

TOPICS

Susan B. Anthony
Wars in the 1800s
The First Amendment

GRAMMAR

WH-Questions

What did Susan B. Anthony do?

To Be

What **is** one right or freedom from the First Amendment?

FUNCTIONAL INTERVIEW SKILLS

Asking for repetition
Asking for clarification

KEY VOCABULARY

Certainly.
Could you repeat the question, please?
Did you say . . . ?
I'm not sure I heard the question correctly.
I'm sorry.
I understand.
That's a different question.
What was the person's name?

GETTING READY

Practicing how to ask for repetition and clarification.
Point out that these three dialogs contain important strategies that students can use when they need to hear *part* of a question again. Asking about part of a question can be more helpful than asking the officer to repeat the entire question because it focuses on the specific thing the student needs to understand. As a class, have students read the information in the blue box. Then have them look at the three dialogs and identify how the applicant asks about a specific part of a question.

> 1st dialog: The applicant needs to hear the name in the question again. ("I'm sorry. What was the person's name?")

> 2nd dialog: The applicant wants to be sure the officer is asking about the 1800s (not the 1900s, which is a different civics question). ("Did you say the 1800s?")

3rd dialog: The applicant has heard the words "right or freedom," but isn't sure what the officer is asking about. There are civics questions about rights or freedoms in the First Amendment and in the Declaration of Independence, and the applicant doesn't know which question the officer has asked. ("I'm sorry. I'm not sure I heard the question correctly. Did you say the Declaration of Independence?") The officer says that wasn't the question, the applicant asks for repetition, and the officer repeats the question.

PRACTICING THE DIALOG

Notes:

- There are three short dialogs. Lower-level students should practice each dialog separately. Higher-level students can practice the dialogs either separately or together.

- These dialogs have blank lines and answer-choice boxes since the questions have multiple acceptable answers. Encourage low beginners to consistently practice one answer to a question so that they master it—the first answer in the text or another answer they prefer. Higher-level students can practice the multiple answers. (The audio contains the first answer.)

1. **Setting the Scene:** Establish the context: "The USCIS officer is asking a citizenship applicant some civics questions."

2. **Listening:** With books closed, have students listen to the dialog—presented by you, by a pair of students, or on the audio program.

3. **Choral Repetition:** With books still closed, model each line and have the whole class repeat in unison.

4. **Reading:** With books open, have students follow along as two students present the dialog. Ask students if they have any questions and check understanding of vocabulary.

5. **Choral Conversation Practice:** Divide the class in half. Have Group 1 ask the questions and Group 2 give the answers; then reverse. (Or: You ask the questions and have the whole class answer in unison; then reverse.)

6. **Pair Practice:** Have students practice the dialog in pairs, taking turns being the USCIS officer and the applicant.

7. **Presentations:** Call on pairs of students to present the dialog to the class.

The end-of-unit assessment evaluates student achievement of the unit's learning objectives while developing the specific test-taking skills required for success during the USCIS English and civics exam. Students can practice and complete the tests in class or at home.

A. CIVICS

This section contains the official USCIS questions that appear in the unit. Students can practice the questions and answers outside of class on their own or with a study partner. (Since many questions have multiple acceptable answers, encourage low beginners to consistently practice a single answer to a question, while higher-level students can practice the multiple answers.) For in-class assessment, call on students to answer different questions, or observe students as they test each other through pair practice.

B. KEY VOCABULARY

1. flag
2. Alaska
3. North
4. South

C. READING AND WRITING

This section contains the types of reading and writing questions on the USCIS test. You can assess students' reading skills by their ability to read aloud the questions. You can assess their writing skills by their ability to write the sentences from dictation. (The dictation sentences appear below, in the text on page 239, and on the audio program. Each dictation sentence is on a separate audio track so that the audio can be paused while students write.)

1. Presidents' Day is in February.
2. Abraham Lincoln was the President during the Civil War.
3. One right people have is freedom of speech.
4. Citizens of the United States can vote for the President.
5. Alaska is the largest state in the United States.

TEXT PAGE 164

CIVICS ENRICHMENT

> ### PERFORMANCE-BASED ASSESSMENT
>
> These civics enrichment activities are designed to promote students' active participation in class and in the civic life of the community—through projects, issues discussions, community tasks, field trips, and Internet activities. Reproducible performance-based assessment forms for use in evaluating and documenting student participation in these activities are included in the Appendix.

CIVIC PARTICIPATION

Review with students the rights guaranteed by the 1st Amendment, and have students discuss how people in your community exercise these rights. Have them brainstorm as a class examples of freedom of speech, freedom of the press, freedom of religion, and freedom of assembly. This discussion serves as preparation for the project activity that follows.

CIVIC PARTICIPATION

Bring to class copies of the U.S. Constitution. In small groups, have students look at the Constitution and find the amendments that they studied in this unit. Then have each group discuss ideas for a new amendment to the Constitution and write a proposed amendment. Groups should present their new amendments to the entire class and give reasons why they think their amendments are important.

DEBATE ACTIVITY

Have students participate in a classroom debate about the voting age in the United States. Divide the class into two teams, or have students choose their teams based on the position they want to take. Each team should take one of these positions:

  a) The minimum voting age in the United States should be eighteen, as it is now.

  b) The minimum voting age should be twenty-one.

INTERNET ACTIVITY

Have students go to the websites listed in the text for the Fort McHenry National Monument in Maryland, the Gettysburg National Military Park in Pennsylvania, and the Lincoln Memorial in Washington, D.C. Have them take the virtual tours, browse the websites for additional information about the locations, and write sentences about what they see and the information they find. Students can do this Internet activity individually, in pairs, or in small groups based on the computer resources available. Make sure students have the basic skills needed to access the Internet.

TECHNOLOGY ENRICHMENT

See Appendix page 312 for additional Internet enrichment activities related to this chapter.

UNIT SUMMARY

KEY VOCABULARY

Have students review the lists of words they have learned in this unit. Encourage students to get a small notebook where they can write down vocabulary that is new for them.

GRAMMAR

Have students review the list of irregular past tense verbs in this unit. Have students write sentences that use the past tense forms of these verbs.

FUNCTIONAL EXPRESSIONS

Have students review the different functional expressions and find where they occur in the unit. For enrichment, have students practice new dialogs using these different expressions.

UNIT REVIEW WORKSHEETS

Unit 9 Writing Practice
Unit 9 Reading Practice
Unit 9 Civics Practice

TEXT PAGE 224 (QUESTIONS 21–22E) THE ENGLISH TEST (SPEAKING)

FOCUS

TOPIC
Answering Form N-400 "Part 10" questions during the USCIS interview

FUNCTIONAL INTERVIEW SKILLS
Reporting information

KEY VOCABULARY

at the same time	married
body	narcotics
bring into the country	pay/paid for sex
come into the country	permission
controlled substances	prison
drink alcohol	procure anyone for
enter the United States	prostitution
illegally	prostitute
found guilty	rarely
habitual drunkard	sell/sold
help	smuggle
husband	try
illegal drugs	wife
jail	without permission

ROLE PLAY: Questions 21–22e

Have students work in pairs and role-play interviews using questions 21–22e. Have them use in their conversations some of the expressions that appear in the blue boxes on pages 216, 220, and 222 to practice asking for repetition and clarification. Have students take turns being the USCIS officer and the applicant. Then have pairs of students present their role plays to the class.

WORKSHEETS

Interview Practice Worksheets 35–37

UNIT 10

**INDUSTRIAL REVOLUTION
LABOR MOVEMENT
IMMIGRATION**

**20th-CENTURY HISTORY
CIVIL RIGHTS MOVEMENT
SEPTEMBER 11, 2001**

LESSONS & UNIT ACTIVITIES	OBJECTIVES	STUDENT TEXT	TEACHER'S GUIDE
Vocabulary Preview	Identifying vocabulary related to U.S. history	165	151
The Industrial Revolution	Describing the importance of the Industrial Revolution; Identifying inventors and their inventions	166	152
The Labor Movement	Describing working conditions that led to the creation of the labor movement; Identifying Labor Day as a national holiday celebrating workers	167	153
A Nation of Immigrants	Describing immigration in U.S. history; Describing reasons immigrants come to the United States	168–169	154
20th-Century History	Identifying key events and wars in the 1900s: World War I, the Depression, Franklin Delano Roosevelt's presidency, World War II, the United Nations, the Cold War, the Korean War, the Vietnam War, the Persian Gulf War	170–175	155–158
The Civil Rights Movement	Describing the civil rights movement; Identifying Martin Luther King, Jr. as the leader of the civil rights movement	176	159
Voice of Freedom: Martin Luther King, Jr.	Reciting an excerpt of Martin Luther King, Jr.'s *I Have a Dream* speech	177	160
September 11, 2001	Describing the terrorist attack on the U.S. on September 11, 2001	178–179	161–162
Review	Talking Time Line: Reviewing important dates in U.S. history	180	162
Civics Test: I'm Not Sure I Heard Correctly	Asking for clarification; Hesitating	181	163
Unit Test	Preparing for USCIS civics, reading, and writing test questions	182–183	164
Civics Enrichment	Internet Activity: Using online information to learn about inventors Alexander Graham Bell, Thomas Edison, and Benjamin Franklin; Internet Activity: Visiting Ellis Island online; Debate Activity: Debating about civil rights in the U.S. today	184	164–165
The English Test (Speaking)*	Answering Form N-400 "Part 10" questions during the USCIS interview	224–225	165

* This interview preparation lesson is in the Appendix for students' convenience. It can be introduced in this unit and then reviewed along with the other interview preparation lessons as students get ready for their appointment at USCIS. If you prefer, you can do these lessons later in the course if that is more appropriate for the timing of your students' interviews. Interview Practice worksheets accompany these lessons.

UNIT RESOURCES

Worksheets:
Unit 10 Writing Practice
Unit 10 Reading Practice
Unit 10 Civics Practice
Interview Practice Worksheets 38–40

Audio Program:
CD 3: Tracks 11–30

RELATED PRACTICE

Foundations: Unit 13
Word by Word Basic: pages 204–215
Word by Word: pages 112–117, 163
Side by Side / Side by Side Plus: Book 2, Unit 2
Side by Side Interactive CD-ROM / Side by Side TV: Level 2A, Segments 29, 30
ExpressWays: Book 1, Unit 8

UNIT OVERVIEW

KEY VOCABULARY

READING	WRITING	PEOPLE	EVENTS/HISTORICAL PERIODS	PLACES/GEOGRAPHY	OTHER WORDS
can	and	American	civil rights movement	Afghanistan	Allied Nations
citizens	be	Blacks	Cold War	Arlington, Virginia	atomic bomb
come	can	Dwight D.	Great Depression	Austria-Hungary	civil rights
do	citizens	Eisenhower	Industrial Revolution	Europe	coalition forces
for	come	factory worker	Korean War	France	communist
have	for	farmer	Labor Day	Germany	democratic
in	free	Franklin D.	March on Washington	Hawaii	discrimination
is	freedom of	Roosevelt	national holiday	Hiroshima	equal rights
Labor Day	speech	general	New Deal	Iraq	equality
name	have	George H.W.	Operation Desert	Italy	factory
of	in	Bush	Storm	Japan	farmland
one	is	immigrant	Persian Gulf War	Kuwait	immigration
people	Labor Day	(the) Japanese	September 11, 2001	Lincoln Memorial	invention
right	of	leader	Vietnam War	Nagasaki	labor movement
the	people	Native	war	New Jersey	labor union
to	President	American	World War I	New York City	military forces
United States	Senators	President	World War II	Pearl Harbor	native country
vote	September	Martin Luther		Pennsylvania	political system
what	the	King, Jr.	**INVENTIONS**	Pentagon	racial discrimination
when	to	terrorist	cotton gin	Russia	railroad
who	United States	troops	light bulb	Soviet Union	Social Security system
why	vote	worker	phonograph	United Kingdom	stock market
			sewing machine	United Nations	terrorism
			telephone	United States	terrorist organization
			typewriter	Washington, D.C.	union
				World Trade Center	United Nations (UN)

GRAMMAR

PAST TENSE: IRREGULAR VERBS

become – became	get hurt – got hurt	lead – led
begin – began	give – gave	lose – lost
break up – broke up	go – went	make – made
build – built	grow – grew	send – sent
come – came	have – had	shoot – shot
fight – fought		

FUNCTIONAL EXPRESSIONS

CLARIFYING

Excuse me. Did you say ____?
I'm not sure I heard correctly.
    Did you say ____ or ____?

INDICATING UNDERSTANDING

I understand.

HESITATING

. . . hmm . . .
I know *there's one
    more country.*
Oh yes.

TEXT PAGE 165 VOCABULARY PREVIEW

You may want to introduce these words before beginning the unit, or you may choose to wait until they first occur in a specific lesson. If you choose to introduce them at this point, here are some suggestions:

1. Have students look at the photographs on text page 165 and identify the words they already know.

2. Present the vocabulary. Say each word and have the class repeat it chorally and individually. Check students' understanding and pronunciation of the words.

3. Practice the vocabulary as a class, in pairs, or in small groups. Have students cover the word list and look at the photographs. Practice the words in the following ways:

   • Say a word and have students tell the correct number on the photograph.
   • Give a number on a photograph and have students say the word.

FOCUS

TOPICS

The Industrial Revolution
Inventors and Inventions

GRAMMAR

Past Tense: Regular Verbs

In the 1790s the first factories open**ed** in the United
States.

Past Tense: Irregular Verbs

The railroads **went** across the country.
The cities **grew** larger.
People **came** from the farms to work in the factories.

Past Tense: Was/Were

The first Americans **were** farmers.

NEW VOCABULARY

across	invent	produce (v.)
clothing	invention	railroad
cotton gin	light bulb	sewing
fast	machine	machine
immigrant	open	typewriter
industrial revolution	phonograph	

PREVIEWING THE READING

Have students talk about the title and the photographs
to establish the context of the passage. Ask some or all
of the following questions:

> What inventions do you see in the photographs?
> (The cotton gin, the phonograph, the sewing
> machine, the telephone.)
> Why were these inventions important? (Various
> answers.)

READING THE PASSAGE

1. Have students read the passage silently. (If you
   wish, you may read the passage aloud or play the
   audio program as students read along silently.)
2. **Check Reading Comprehension:** Ask students
   a question about each line of the passage. For
   beginning-level students, ask these questions in
   the order below so that the questions follow the
   sequence of the passage. For higher-level students,
   ask the questions in random order.

   > What work did the first Americans do?
   > When did the first factories open in the United
   > States?
   > What were two important inventions?
   > What did the United States do with these
   > machines?

> What else did Americans invent?
> Where did the railroads go?
> Where were the factories? / What happened to
> the cities?
> Where did people come from to work in the
> factories?

3. Ask students if they have any questions about the
   passage; check understanding of vocabulary.
4. **Choral Repetition:** Read aloud each line of the
   passage and have students repeat.
5. **Class Circle Reading:** Have students read the
   passage aloud as a class, with different students
   reading each line. (You can assign each line to a
   particular student or by seating patterns, or by letting
   students take turns spontaneously. In large classes,
   have a different group or row of students read each
   line.)
6. **Pair Practice:** Have students work in pairs, reading
   the passage to each other section by section.
   Circulate around the room and check students'
   reading and pronunciation, focusing more attention
   on students who need more assistance.

EXPANSION

1. The Most Important Invention

Have students look at the photographs and captions.
Practice the names of the inventions and their
inventors. Then have students discuss which of
these inventions they think is the most important—
the cotton gin, the phonograph, the light bulb, the
sewing machine, or the telephone. If you wish, break
up the class into five groups, assign an invention to
each group, and have group members prepare and
offer a class presentation about why their invention
is the most important.

2. Farming and Industry in Students' Countries

Have students share information about whether
their home town in their native country had farms or
industry, or both. Have them discuss the importance
of farming and/or industry in their native country.
Have them describe their countries' most important
farm and industry products.

3. Research Project about an Inventor and Invention

You may want to assign higher-level students to do
a research project about one of the inventors and
inventions in this lesson. Students can work on
their own, in pairs, or as a small group. They can
use the Internet, the library, and other resources to
find information about the inventor's life, how the
invention was developed, and the importance of the
invention. Have students prepare a presentation for
the class.

TEXT PAGE 167 THE LABOR MOVEMENT

FOCUS

TOPICS
The Labor Movement
Labor Day

GRAMMAR

Past Tense: Regular Verbs

They usually work**ed** twelve hours a day.

Past Tense: Irregular Verbs

Factory workers **had** a difficult life.
Many workers **got** hurt.
Workers **began** to come together in groups.
These unions **fought** for better hours.

NEW VOCABULARY

belong	get hurt	parade
better	group	pay
celebrate	labor conditions	safe
clothing worker	Labor Day	union
come together	labor movement	worker
demonstrate	labor union	workplace
form (v.)	low	

PREVIEWING THE READING

Have students talk about the title and the photographs to establish the context of the passage. Ask some or all of the following questions:

(Top left photograph)

Where are these women working? (In a factory.)
What are they making? (Clothing material. / Fabric.)

(Top right photograph)

Where are these children working? (In a factory.)
How old do you think they are? (Have students discuss.)
What are they doing? (They're cleaning the machine.)
What's your opinion about this work? (It's dangerous. / The children can get hurt.)

(Bottom left photograph)

What kind of workers do you see? (Clothing workers. / Ladies tailors.)
What are they doing? (They're picketing. / They're striking.)
Why? (They're demonstrating for better labor conditions.)

(Bottom right photograph)

This is a "float" in a parade. Who do you see on the float? (Women workers.)
Look at the sign on their float. What kind of work do they do? (They are typographers.)

Explain to students that typographers composed the pages of text for newspapers, for signs, and other printed documents.

Ask students if there is a Labor Day parade in their community.

READING THE PASSAGE

1. Have students read the passage silently. (If you wish, you may read the passage aloud or play the audio program as students read along silently.)

2. **Check Reading Comprehension:** Ask students a question about each line of the passage. For beginning-level students, ask these questions in the order below so that the questions follow the sequence of the passage. For higher-level students, ask the questions in random order.

   What kind of life did factory workers have?
   How many hours a day did they usually work?
   How was their pay?
   Why did many workers get hurt?
   What did workers begin to do?
   What were the workers' groups called?
   What did the unions fight for?
   Do people still belong to unions today?

   When do Americans celebrate Labor Day?
   What does this national holiday celebrate?

3. Ask students if they have any questions about the passage; check understanding of vocabulary.

4. **Choral Repetition:** Read aloud each line of the passage and have students repeat.

5. **Class Circle Reading:** Have students read the passage aloud as a class, with different students reading each line. (You can assign each line to a particular student or by seating patterns, or by letting students take turns spontaneously. In large classes, have a different group or row of students read each line.)

6. **Pair Practice:** Have students work in pairs, reading the passage to each other section by section. Circulate around the room and check students' reading and pronunciation, focusing more attention on students who need more assistance.

EXPANSION

1. Have students discuss a current strike or labor problem. What group of workers is on strike or is having a labor problem? Why?

2. Have students discuss Labor Day celebrations in their native countries: if they occur, when they occur, and how the holiday is celebrated.

3. Have students discuss what they can do if there are unsafe conditions at a workplace and the employer refuses to take care of them.

FOCUS

TOPIC

Immigration

GRAMMAR

Past Tense: Regular Verbs

America need**ed** farmers and workers.

Past Tense: Irregular Verbs

In the 1800s America **grew** very quickly.
The Industrial Revolution **built** new factories.
Immigrants **came** from many countries.
The United States **began** to limit immigration.
The government **made** many laws.

NEW VOCABULARY

allow	continue	difficult	farmland	quickly
build	dangerous	except	limit	stop

PREVIEWING THE READING

Have students talk about the title and the photograph to establish the context of the passage. Ask some or all of the following questions:

> Who are the people in the photograph?
> (Immigrants.)
> Where do you think they are from? (Various
> answers.)
> What is the man carrying? (A suitcase.)
> Where are they going? Why? (Various answers.)

READING THE PASSAGE

1. Have students read the passage silently. (If you wish, you may read the passage aloud or play the audio program as students read along silently.)

2. **Check Reading Comprehension:** Ask students a question about each line of the passage. For beginning-level students, ask these questions in the order below so that the questions follow the sequence of the passage. For higher-level students, ask the questions in random order.

> When did America grow quickly?
> What did expansion and the industrial revolution do?
> What did America need as it grew?
> Who came from many countries?
> Where did they work?
> What did immigrants help build?
> When did the United States begin to limit immigration?
> What kind of laws did the government make?
> When did a new immigration law change this?

> What did the new law allow?
> Do immigrants continue to come to the United States?
> Why do immigrants come here? Give two reasons.
> Why is the United States called "a nation of immigrants?"

3. Ask students if they have any questions about the passage; check understanding of vocabulary.

4. **Choral Repetition:** Read aloud each line of the passage and have students repeat.

5. **Class Circle Reading:** Have students read the passage aloud as a class, with different students reading each line. (You can assign each line to a particular student or by seating patterns, or by letting students take turns spontaneously. In large classes, have a different group or row of students read each line.)

6. **Pair Practice:** Have students work in pairs, reading the passage to each other section by section. Circulate around the room and check students' reading and pronunciation, focusing more attention on students who need more assistance.

CHECK-UP

VOCABULARY CHECK

1. sewing machine
2. labor unions
3. immigrants
4. laws
5. clothing
6. holiday

DID YOU UNDERSTAND?

1. The cotton gin. / The sewing machine. / The telephone. / The typewriter. / The phonograph. / The light bulb.
2. They formed labor unions to fight for better hours, better pay, and safer workplaces.
3. The United States needed farmers and workers.

DISCUSSION

Have students discuss these questions in pairs or small groups and then share as a class.

EXPANSION

1. **Imagining Immigration a Century Ago**
   Have students imagine they are immigrants in the photograph on page 168. Have them describe what they are thinking and feeling, and have them imagine what their life will be like when they arrive in the United States in the early 1900s.

2. **Immigrant Interviews**
   Have students interview older immigrants who arrived in the U.S. many years ago. (Senior citizen programs in many communities will gladly assist with this activity.) Have students report on the people they interviewed: when and why they came, where they settled, their life in the United States, etc.

FOCUS

TOPICS

World War I
The Depression
Franklin Delano Roosevelt
World War II
The United Nations
The Cold War, the Korean War, and the Vietnam War
The Persian Gulf War

GRAMMAR

Past Tense: Regular Verbs

The United States enter**ed** World War II in 1941.

Past Tense: Irregular Verbs

World War I **began** in 1914.
They **fought** Japan, Germany, and Italy.
The United States **became** a great world power.
The Depression **had** many causes.
Workers **lost** their jobs.
The government **made** jobs for people.
They **built** roads, parks, bridges, and buildings.
The government **gave** people loans.
The United States and the Allied nations **won** the war.
The Soviet Union **broke** up into independent states.
The Iraqi forces **left** Kuwait.

NEW VOCABULARY

PAGE 170:

Austria-Hungary	Great Depression
bank	job
borrow	lose
century	money
close (v.)	salary
collapse	stock market
cut	United Kingdom
Depression	world power
economy	World War I
Germany	

PAGE 171:

Allied forces	later
Allied nations	loan (n.)
atomic bomb	make jobs
bomb (v.)	Nagasaki
bridge	New Deal
building	park
drop (v.)	Pearl Harbor
Hiroshima	plan (n.)
home	road
Italy	Social Security system
Japan	World War II
keep	

PAGE 172:

assistance	independent states
break up	international
Cold War	keep peace
Communism	Korean War
communist	main concern
Communist forces	organization
compete	peace
directly	political system
discuss	provide
economic aid	United Nations (UN)
education program	Vietnam War
health program	world problems

PAGE 173:

coalition forces	Operation Desert Storm
Iraq	Persian Gulf War
Iraqi forces	quickly
Kuwait	

Note: Text pages 170–173 contain seven separate passages. Cover each passage separately, using the usual teaching steps.

WORLD WAR I

PREVIEWING THE READING

Have students talk about the title and the photograph to establish the context of the passage.

Ask: What do you see in the photograph? (Soldiers. / A battle. / A war.)

READING THE PASSAGE

1. Have students read the passage silently. (If you wish, you may read the passage aloud or play the audio program as students read along silently.)

2. **Check Reading Comprehension:** Ask students a question about each line of the passage. For beginning-level students, ask these questions in the order below so that the questions follow the sequence of the passage. For higher-level students, ask the questions in random order.

   When did World War I begin?
   Who fought in the war?
   When did the United States enter the war? /
      Who did the United States help?
   Who was the President during World War I?
   When did the war end?
   What did the United States become after the war?

3. Ask students if they have any questions about the passage; check understanding of vocabulary.

4. **Choral Repetition:** Read aloud each line of the passage and have students repeat.

5. **Class Circle Reading:** Have students read the passage aloud as a class, with different students reading each line. (You can assign each line to a particular student or by seating patterns, or by letting students take turns spontaneously. In large classes, have a different group or row of students read each line.)

6. **Pair Practice:** Have students work in pairs, reading the passage to each other. Circulate around the room and check students' reading and pronunciation, focusing more attention on students who need more assistance.

EXPANSION

Have students discuss their own countries' roles in World War I.

THE DEPRESSION

PREVIEWING THE READING

Have students talk about the title and the photographs to establish the context of the passage. Ask some or all of the following questions:

(The first photograph)

What does the entire sign say? (Free soup, coffee, and doughnuts for the unemployed.)

Why are these people standing in line? (They're waiting for food. / They're hungry.)

(The second photograph)

What does the sign on the right say? (Why can't you give my dad a job?)

What are these children thinking? How are they feeling? (Various answers.)

READING THE PASSAGE

Follow the usual teaching steps. Check reading comprehension with these questions:

When was there a Great Depression?
What happened to the American economy?

Name one cause of the Depression.
Name a second cause of the Depression.
Name a third cause of the Depression.

What kind of time was it in the United States during the Depression?
What happened at that time?

EXPANSION

Have students discuss a current or past time in their native country when the economy was bad. Have them discuss the causes and effects.

FRANKLIN DELANO ROOSEVELT

PREVIEWING THE READING

Have students talk about the title and the photographs to establish the context of the passage.
Ask some or all of the following questions:

(The first photograph)

Who is this man? (President Franklin D. Roosevelt)

(The second photograph)

What are the people doing in this photograph? (They're working on a road. / They're building a road.)

What does the sign say? What government program is paying the people to do this work? (The USA Work Program.) (Explain to higher-level students that WPA stands for the *Works Progress Administration*.)

READING THE PASSAGE

Follow the usual teaching steps. Check reading comprehension with these questions:

Who was the President from 1933 to 1945?
Did Roosevelt become the President during good times in the United States?
What was the New Deal?
What did the government do for people who had no work?
What kind of work did the people do in these jobs?
Why did the government give people loans?
What system began at this time?

Who was the President during World War II?
How long did he serve?
When did he die?

EXPANSION

Have students discuss important leaders in their own countries during times of crisis. Have them describe their countries' problems at those times and how the leader helped the country.

WORLD WAR II

PREVIEWING THE READING

Have students talk about the title and the photograph to establish the context of the passage.
Ask some or all of the following questions:

Who are these people? (Soldiers. / The army.)
Who is talking with them? (A general. / A military leader. / General Dwight D. Eisenhower.)

READING THE PASSAGE

Follow the usual teaching steps. Check reading comprehension with these questions:

When did World War II begin?

Which countries were called the Allied Nations?
Who did the Allied nations fight?
When did the United States enter World War II?
What did the United States do in 1945?
Who won the war? When?

Who was the leader of the Allied forces in Europe during World War II?
What did he later become?

EXPANSION

Have students discuss their own countries' roles in World War II.

THE UNITED NATIONS (THE UN)

PREVIEWING THE READING

Have students talk about the title and the photograph to establish the context of the passage. Ask some or all of the following questions:

What is this building? (The United Nations building.)
Where is it? (In New York City.)
Who works there? (People from many countries. / People from all over the world. / Diplomats.)

READING THE PASSAGE

Follow the usual teaching steps. Check reading comprehension with these questions:

What international organization did many countries form after World War II?
What is it also called?
What happens at the United Nations?
Does the United Nations help some countries? How?

EXPANSION

1. Have students discuss the role of the United Nations in their native countries.

2. Have students discuss whether the United Nations is an effective organization, giving reasons for their answers.

THE COLD WAR, THE KOREAN WAR, AND THE VIETNAM WAR

PREVIEWING THE READING

Have students talk about the title and the photographs to establish the context of the passage. Ask some or all of the following questions:

(The first photograph)
The first photograph shows the Berlin Wall. What did this wall separate? (It separated Communist-controlled East Berlin from the rest of the city of Berlin.)
What happened to this wall in 1989 and 1990? (People took down the wall.)

(The second photograph)
What do you see in the second photograph? (Soldiers. / A helicopter.)
Where is this? (Vietnam. / Southeast Asia.)

READING THE PASSAGE

Follow the usual teaching steps. Check reading comprehension with these questions:

Which two countries became major world powers after World War II?
Did they have the same political systems?
Which system is democratic, and which was communist?
How did they compete?
What was this called?
During the Cold War, what was the main concern of the United States?

How many times did the United States fight Communist forces after World War II?
When did the United States fight in the Korean War?
What war did the United States fight in from 1964 to 1973?
When did the Cold War end?

EXPANSION

1. Have students discuss current relations between Russia and the United States.

2. Have students discuss the involvement of foreign powers in their native countries.

THE PERSIAN GULF WAR

PREVIEWING THE READING

Have students talk about the title and the photograph to establish the context of the passage. Ask some or all of the following questions:

Who do you see in the photograph? (Soldiers. / The army.)
What do you see behind them? (A tank.)
What kind of land is this? (Desert.)
What country do you think they are in? (Iraq. / Kuwait. / Other Middle Eastern country.)

READING THE PASSAGE

Follow the usual teaching steps. Check reading comprehension with these questions:

When did the Persian Gulf War begin?
When did the United States enter the war?
Who were the coalition forces?
When did the war end?

Who was the President during the Persian Gulf War?
In the United States, what was the Persian Gulf War also called?

EXPANSION

Have students discuss their own countries' roles, if any, in the Persian Gulf War.

WARS FOUGHT BY THE UNITED STATES IN THE 1900s

Have students review the information in the photographs and captions. This general information about wars fought by the United States in the 1900s is required in one of the official USCIS civics questions on the citizenship exam.

CHECK-UP (Pages 174–175)

VOCABULARY CHECK

1. United Nations
2. World War I
3. New Deal
4. Depression
5. Cold War

DID YOU UNDERSTAND?

1. The American economy collapsed. Factories and farms produced too much. / After World War I, countries in Europe didn't have money to buy American goods. / Many people borrowed too much money.
2. President Franklin D. Roosevelt's plan to help the country.
3. After the Japanese bombed Pearl Harbor in 1941.
4. The American system is democratic, and the Soviet system was communist.
5. The United Nations, an international organization.
6. After Iraq invaded Kuwait in 1990.

FACT CHECK

1. Vietnam
2. Social Security
3. Depression
4. Japan
5. communist

MATCHING: Presidents and Events

1. c
2. d
3. a
4. b

LISTENING

Have students complete the exercises as you play the audio program or read the following:

Listen and circle the correct answer.

1. Who was the President during World War II?
2. Who was the President during World War I?
3. Who did the United States fight during World War II?
4. What new international organization was formed after World War II?
5. What was the main concern of the United States during the Cold War?
6. Who was a general before he was President?

ANSWERS

1. b
2. a
3. a
4. b
5. b
6. a

CIVICS CHECK

Note: Since the first question has multiple acceptable answers, encourage low beginners to consistently practice a single answer to this question, while higher-level students can practice the multiple answers.

First, practice each question separately:

1. **Listening:** Have students read along silently as they listen to the question and answer(s)—presented by you, by a pair of students, or on the audio program.
2. **Choral Repetition:** Model the question and answer(s) and have the whole class repeat in unison.
3. **Choral Conversation Practice:** Divide the class in half. Have Group 1 ask the question and Group 2 give the answer(s); then reverse. (Or: You ask the question and have the whole class answer in unison; then reverse.)
4. **Pair Practice:** Have students practice the question and answer(s) in pairs.
5. **Presentation:** Call on one or two pairs of students to present the question and answer(s) to the class.

Then practice all the questions together:

6. **Choral Answers:** Ask any question and have students give the answer in unison. (If there are multiple answers, have them give the first answer in the text.)
7. **Pair Practice:** Have students work in pairs, taking turns asking and answering all the questions in random order.

For more practice or for review during the next class session, do one of these activities:

LINE PRACTICE: Have students stand in two lines facing each other. Each pair of facing students should take turns asking and answering a question. After sufficient time for this practice, say "Move," and have one line of students move down one position while the other line remains in place. (The student at the end of the line moves to the beginning of the line.) In this way, new pairs are created and students practice with another partner. Continue until students have practiced all the questions.

"ROUND ROBIN": Have students circulate around the room and ask each other the questions. Students should move on to another person after they have taken turns asking and answering a question.

FOCUS

TOPICS

The Civil Rights Movement
Martin Luther King, Jr.

GRAMMAR

Past Tense: Regular Verbs

It work**ed** for equal rights for all Americans.

Past Tense: Irregular Verbs

He **fought** for civil rights.
He **led** protests against discrimination.
The nation **lost** a great leader.

NEW VOCABULARY

civil rights	March on Washington
civil rights movement	protest (n.)
demonstration	racial discrimination
discrimination	remember
equality	shoot
equal rights	support
kill	thousand

PREVIEWING THE READING

Have students talk about the title and the photograph to establish the context of the passage.

Ask some or all of the following questions:

Who is the man in the center of this photograph? (Martin Luther King, Jr.)
What does the sign say? ("We want to sit down like anyone else.")
What is the sign asking for? (Equal rights.)

READING THE PASSAGE

1. Have students read the passage silently. (If you wish, you may read the passage aloud or play the audio program as students read along silently.)

2. **Check Reading Comprehension:** Ask students a question about each line of the passage. For beginning-level students, ask these questions in the order below so that the questions follow the sequence of the passage. For higher-level students, ask the questions in random order.

   What movement worked to end racial discrimination against Blacks during the 1950s and 1960s?
   Whose equal rights did this movement work for?
   Who was the most famous leader of the civil rights movement?
   What did he fight for?
   What did he work for?
   What did he lead protests against?
   What did he do in 1963?
   What was this called?
   What happened to Martin Luther King, Jr., in 1968?
   What did the nation lose?
   How does the United States remember Martin Luther King, Jr.?

3. Ask students if they have any questions about the passage; check understanding of vocabulary.

4. **Choral Repetition:** Read aloud each line of the passage and have students repeat.

5. **Class Circle Reading:** Have students read the passage aloud as a class, with different students reading each line. (You can assign each line to a particular student or by seating patterns, or by letting students take turns spontaneously. In large classes, have a different group or row of students read each line.)

6. **Pair Practice:** Have students work in pairs, reading the passage to each other section by section. Circulate around the room and check students' reading and pronunciation, focusing more attention on students who need more assistance.

(As noted in the text, this lesson is provided for enrichment and speaking practice. It is not required for the citizenship exam.)

FOCUS

TOPICS

The Civil Rights Movement
Martin Luther King, Jr.

GRAMMAR

Future: Will

One day this nation **will** rise up.

Must

If America is to be a great nation this **must** become true.

NEW VOCABULARY

beautiful
part
powerful

READING THE PASSAGE

Note: Practice the introductory section first. (Don't practice the excerpt of the speech yet.)

1. Have students read the introductory sentences silently. (If you wish, you may read the sentences aloud or play the audio program as students read along silently.)

2. **Check Reading Comprehension:** Ask students questions about the introduction.

   What year was the March on Washington?
   Who gave a speech there? Where?
   What is this speech called?

PRACTICING THE EXCERPT*

* Note: The excerpt of the "I Have a Dream" speech is not required for the USCIS civics test. It is provided for enrichment and speaking practice.

1. **Listening:** Have students read along silently as you recite the excerpt or play the audio.

2. **Choral Repetition (sentence by sentence):** Read aloud each sentence of the excerpt and have students repeat in unison.

3. **Reading:** Have students practice reading aloud the excerpt as a class, in small groups, or on their own.

4. Ask students if they understand the general meaning of the excerpt. (They do not have to know the exact meaning of unfamiliar words.)

5. **Public Speaking Practice:** Have individual students present the excerpt to the class. If you feel it is appropriate to do so, help students with their diction and projection to improve their public speaking skills in English.

6. **Reciting:** Have students memorize the excerpt and practice reciting it (without the text) as a class, in small groups, and on their own.

EXPANSION

1. Oratorical Contest

Have interested students memorize the excerpt or a larger portion of Martin Luther King, Jr.'s, speech and recite it for the class. Have class members vote on the best rendition, and award a prize to the winner.

2. Students' Dreams

Have students share their own dreams of what kind of nation or what kind of world there should be.

FOCUS

TOPIC

September 11, 2001

GRAMMAR

Past Tense: Regular Verbs

Terrorists attack**ed** the United States.

Past Tense: Irregular Verbs

He **sent** American troops there.

NEW VOCABULARY

Afghanistan	Pentagon
air attack	responsible
airplane	terrorism
attack (v.)	terrorist
collapse	terrorist organization
crash (v.)	twin towers
headquarters	victim
hijack	World Trade Center
order (v.)	

PREVIEWING THE READING

Have students talk about the title and the television images to establish the context of the passage. Ask some or all of the following questions:

What do you see on the TV screen on the left? Where is this? When did this happen? (The attack on the World Trade Center in New York City on September 11, 2001.)

What do you see on the TV screen on the right? Where is this? When did this happen? (The attack on the Pentagon in Arlington, Virginia—near Washington, D.C.—on September 11, 2001.)

READING THE PASSAGE

1. Have students read the passage silently. (If you wish, you may read the passage aloud or play the audio program as students read along silently.)

2. **Check Reading Comprehension:** Ask students a question about each line of the passage. For beginning-level students, ask these questions in the order below so that the questions follow the sequence of the passage. For higher-level students, ask the questions in random order.

What happened on the morning of September 11, 2001?

From where did terrorists hijack four airplanes?

Where did the hijackers crash two planes in New York City?

What happened to both towers of the World Trade Center?

Where did one plane crash in Virginia?

Where did the fourth plane crash?

How many people died?

How many countries were they from?

Who were most of the victims?

What did the U.S. government ask other nations to do?

What did President Bush order?

Where did he send American troops?

3. Ask students if they have any questions about the passage; check understanding of vocabulary.

(Note: Given the content of this reading passage, please refrain from the usual Choral Repetition practice.)

4. **Class Circle Reading:** Have students read the passage aloud as a class, with different students reading each line. (You can assign each line to a particular student or by seating patterns, or by letting students take turns spontaneously. In large classes, have a different group or row of students read each line.)

5. **Pair Practice:** Have students work in pairs, reading the passage to each other section by section. Circulate around the room and check students' reading and pronunciation, focusing more attention on students who need more assistance.

EXPANSION

1. If you saved newspapers or magazine articles covering the events of September 11, 2001, bring them to class to share with students.

2. Have students discuss if they think the United States or the world changed on that day, and in what ways.

3. Encourage students to share any personal stories about their reaction to the events or experiences they had related to the events. (Students commonly share feelings ranging from fear and concern to pride and identification with the United States. Their experiences might include accounts of economic difficulties or discrimination after the events, or accounts of community commemorations they attended or other events that helped make them feel a part of the community.)

CHECK-UP

VOCABULARY CHECK

1. discrimination
2. equality
3. holiday
4. demonstration
5. speech

CIVICS CHECK

Note: Since the second question has multiple acceptable answers, encourage low beginners to consistently practice a single answer to this question, while higher-level students can practice both answers.

First, practice each question separately:

1. **Listening:** Have students read along silently as they listen to the question and answer(s)—presented by you, by a pair of students, or on the audio program.
2. **Choral Repetition:** Model the question and answer(s) and have the whole class repeat in unison.
3. **Choral Conversation Practice:** Divide the class in half. Have Group 1 ask the question and Group 2 give the answer(s); then reverse. (Or: You ask the question and have the whole class answer in unison; then reverse.)

4. **Pair Practice:** Have students practice the question and answer(s) in pairs.
5. **Presentation:** Call on one or two pairs of students to present the question and answer(s) to the class.

Then practice all the questions together:

6. **Choral Answers:** Ask any question and have students give the answer in unison. (If there are multiple answers, have them give the first answer in the text.)
7. **Pair Practice:** Have students work in pairs, taking turns asking and answering all the questions in random order.

DISCUSSION

Have students discuss these questions in pairs or small groups and then share as a class. Have them talk about fair housing, equality in opportunities for education and employment, and other aspects of equal rights.

TEXT PAGE 180   REVIEW

TALKING TIME LINE: Important Dates in U.S. History

Have students complete the time line. Then have them work in pairs, asking and answering the questions at the end of the exercise based on the information recorded on the time line.

1917	The United States entered World War I.
1929	The Great Depression began in the United States.
1941	Japan bombed Pearl Harbor.
1945	World War II ended.
1953	The Korean War ended.
1963	Martin Luther King, Jr., led a civil rights march in Washington.
1968	Martin Luther King, Jr., was killed.
2001	Terrorists attacked the United States.

FOCUS

TOPIC

20th-Century History

GRAMMAR

WH-Questions

Who was President during World War II?

FUNCTIONAL INTERVIEW SKILLS

Asking for clarification

Hesitating

KEY VOCABULARY

Did you say . . . ?	I understand.
Excuse me.	Oh yes.
. . . hmm . . .	That's correct.
I'm not sure I heard correctly.	

GETTING READY

1. Practicing how to ask for clarification.

Point out that these three dialogs contain an important strategy that students can use when they need to confirm part of what they think they heard in a question. Confirming the precise information needed can be more helpful than asking the officer to repeat the entire question because it focuses on the specific thing the student needs to clarify. This is especially important because several USCIS civics questions are very similar to other civics questions.

As a class, have students look at the three dialogs and identify how the applicant confirms part of a question.

> 1st dialog: The officer said "World War I," but the applicant thinks the officer said "World War II." So the applicant asks: "Excuse me. Did you say World War II?"

> 2nd dialog: The officer said "the 1900s," but the applicant isn't sure if the officer said "the 1800s" or "the 1900s." So the applicant says: "I'm not sure I heard correctly. Did you say the 1800s or the 1900s?"

> 3rd dialog: The officer said "World War II." The applicant thinks the officer said that but isn't sure. So the applicant says those words as a question: "World War II?"

2. Practicing how to hesitate to fill time.

Point out that the third dialog contains an important strategy (hesitating) that students can use when they need time to think of an answer. The applicant

remembers two of the countries the United States fought in World War II but doesn't remember the third. The applicant fills the thinking time by saying: "and . . . hmm . . . I know there's one more country. Oh yes." Then the applicant gives the answer. Explain to students that it is much better to fill the thinking time with words than to be silent.

PRACTICING THE DIALOG

Notes:

- There are three short dialogs. Lower-level students should practice each dialog separately. Higher-level students can practice the dialogs either separately or together.

- The second dialog has an answer-choice box with multiple acceptable answers. (The first and third dialogs require all answers in the box.) Encourage low beginners to consistently practice one answer to the question so that they master it—the first answer in the text or another answer they prefer. Higher-level students can practice the multiple answers. (The audio contains the first answer.)

1. **Setting the Scene:** Establish the context: "The USCIS officer is asking a citizenship applicant some civics questions."

2. **Listening:** With books closed, have students listen to the dialog—presented by you, by a pair of students, or on the audio program.

3. **Choral Repetition:** With books still closed, model each line and have the whole class repeat in unison.

4. **Reading:** With books open, have students follow along as two students present the dialog. Ask students if they have any questions and check understanding of vocabulary.

5. **Choral Conversation Practice:** Divide the class in half. Have Group 1 ask the questions and Group 2 give the answers; then reverse. (Or: You ask the questions and have the whole class answer in unison; then reverse.)

6. **Pair Practice:** Have students practice the dialog in pairs, taking turns being the USCIS officer and the applicant.

7. **Presentations:** Call on pairs of students to present the dialog to the class.

The end-of-unit assessment evaluates student achievement of the unit's learning objectives while developing the specific test-taking skills required for success during the USCIS English and civics exam. Students can practice and complete the tests in class or at home.

A. CIVICS

This section contains the official USCIS questions that appear in the unit. Students can practice the questions and answers outside of class on their own or with a study partner. (Since many questions have multiple acceptable answers, encourage low beginners to consistently practice a single answer to a question, while higher-level students can practice the multiple answers.) For in-class assessment, call on students to answer different questions, or observe students as they test each other through pair practice.

B. CIVICS MATCHING

1. c
2. b
3. e
4. a
5. d

C. KEY VOCABULARY

1. people
2. Labor Day
3. come
4. rights
5. Washington
6. September
7. United States

D. READING AND WRITING

This section contains the types of reading and writing questions on the USCIS test. You can assess students' reading skills by their ability to read aloud the questions. You can assess their writing skills by their ability to write the sentences from dictation. (The dictation sentences appear below, in the text on page 239, and on the audio program. Each dictation sentence is on a separate audio track so that the audio can be paused while students write.)

1. Labor Day is in September.
2. People come to the United States to be free.
3. People in the United States have freedom of speech.
4. Citizens can vote for the President of the United States.
5. Citizens can vote for Senators and the President.

TEXT PAGE 184

CIVICS ENRICHMENT

PERFORMANCE-BASED ASSESSMENT

These civics enrichment activities are designed to promote students' active participation in class and in the civic life of the community—through projects, issues discussions, community tasks, field trips, and Internet activities. Reproducible performance-based assessment forms for use in evaluating and documenting student participation in these activities are included in the Appendix.

INTERNET ACTIVITY

Have students go to the Franklin Institute website pages listed in the text to learn about inventors Alexander Graham Bell, Thomas Edison, and Benjamin Franklin. Have students write sentences about the information they find. Students can do this Internet activity individually, in pairs, or in small groups based on the computer resources available. Make sure students have the basic skills needed to access the Internet.

INTERNET ACTIVITY

Have students visit the National Park Service website for the Ellis Island immigration station. Have them watch the slideshow and view photos of the historic site.

DEBATE ACTIVITY

Have students participate in a classroom debate about civil rights in the United States today. Divide the class into two teams, or have students choose their teams based on the position they want to take. Each team should take one of these positions:

a) The election of President Obama shows that discrimination in the U.S. has ended.

b) Despite the election of President Obama, discrimination in the U.S. continues today.

TECHNOLOGY ENRICHMENT

See Appendix page 312 for additional Internet enrichment activities related to this chapter.

UNIT SUMMARY

KEY VOCABULARY

Have students review the lists of words they have learned in this unit. Encourage students to get a small notebook where they can write down vocabulary that is new for them.

GRAMMAR

Have students review the list of irregular past tense verbs in this unit. Have students write sentences that use the past tense forms of these verbs.

FUNCTIONAL EXPRESSIONS

Have students review the functional expressions and find where they occur in the unit. For enrichment, have students practice new conversations using these different expressions.

UNIT REVIEW WORKSHEETS

Unit 10 Writing Practice
Unit 10 Reading Practice
Unit 10 Civics Practice

TEXT PAGES 224–225 (QUESTIONS 22F–25) THE ENGLISH TEST (SPEAKING)

FOCUS

TOPIC

Answering Form N-400 "Part 10" questions during the USCIS interview

FUNCTIONAL INTERVIEW SKILLS

Reporting information

KEY VOCABULARY

against the law	illegal gambling
alimony	immigration benefit
apply	income
children	leave
dependents	lie
deportation	official (n.)
deported from	ordered
excluded from	pay alimony
exclusion	prevent
fail to	provide money
former wife	receive income
gain admission	removal
gain entry	removed from
gamble illegally	support your dependents
gamble money	tell/told the truth
give false information	U.S. Government official
give misleading information	way

ROLE PLAY: Questions 22f–25

Have students work in pairs and role-play interviews using questions 22f–25. Have them use in their conversations some of the expressions that appear in the blue boxes on pages 216, 220, and 222 to practice asking for repetition and clarification. Have students take turns being the USCIS officer and the applicant. Then have pairs of students present their role plays to the class.

WORKSHEETS

Interview Practice Worksheets 38–40

LESSONS & UNIT ACTIVITIES	OBJECTIVES	STUDENT TEXT	TEACHER'S GUIDE
Vocabulary Preview	Identifying vocabulary related to national holidays	185	167
National Holidays	Identifying national holidays, what they celebrate, and when they occur; Reviewing months of the year	186–187	168–169
Presidential Profiles	Describing the importance of key Presidents in U.S. history	188–195	170–173
Unit Test	Preparing for USCIS civics, reading, and writing test questions	196–197	174
Civics Enrichment	Discussing students' favorite U.S. national holidays and how they celebrate; Internet Activity: Using the White House website to search for information about U.S. Presidents; Biography Project: Writing a short biography of a U.S. President	198	174
The English Test (Speaking)*	Answering Form N-400 "Part 10" questions during the USCIS interview	225	175

* This interview preparation lesson is in the Appendix for students' convenience. It can be introduced in this unit and then reviewed along with the other interview preparation lessons as students get ready for their appointment at USCIS. If you prefer, you can do these lessons later in the course if that is more appropriate for the timing of your students' interviews. Interview Practice worksheets accompany these lessons.

UNIT RESOURCES

Worksheets:
Unit 11 Writing Practice
Unit 11 Reading Practice
Unit 11 Civics Practice
Interview Practice Worksheets 41–43

Audio Program:
CD 3: Tracks 31–46

RELATED PRACTICE

Foundations: Unit 14
Word by Word Basic: pages 40, 246–247
Word by Word: pages 18, 163, 164
Side by Side / Side by Side Plus: Book 2, Units 3, 4
Side by Side Interactive CD-ROM / Side by Side TV: Level 2A, Segments 31–34
ExpressWays: Book 1, Unit 8

KEY VOCABULARY

READING/WRITING: HOLIDAYS	PRESIDENTS	PEOPLE	NATIONAL HOLIDAYS	EVENTS/HISTORICAL PERIODS
Presidents' Day	John Adams	actor	Christmas	Civil War
Memorial Day	George H.W. Bush	civil rights leader	Columbus Day	Great Depression
Flag Day	George W. Bush	Founding Father	Flag Day	Great Society
Independence Day	Jimmy Carter	general	Independence Day	programs
Labor Day	Bill Clinton	leader	Labor Day	impeachment trial
Columbus Day	Dwight D. Eisenhower	member	Martin Luther King, Jr. Day	New Deal
Thanksgiving	Gerald Ford	men	Memorial Day	Operation Desert Storm
	Thomas Jefferson	poor people	New Year's Day	Persian Gulf War
MONTHS	Lyndon B. Johnson	President	Presidents' Day	recession
February	John F. Kennedy	Secretary of State	Thanksgiving Day	Revolutionary War
May	Abraham Lincoln	senior citizens	Veterans Day	September 11, 2001
June	James Madison	slave		Vietnam War
July	Richard Nixon	soldier	**PLACES/GEOGRAPHY**	War on Terrorism
September	Barack Obama	terrorist	Afghanistan	Watergate
October	Ronald Reagan	troops	Bosnia	World War I
November	Franklin D. Roosevelt	U.S. senator	China	World War II
	George Washington	Vice President	Europe	
OTHER	Woodrow Wilson	volunteer (n.)	France	**DOCUMENTS**
in		women	Illinois	Bill of Rights
is		worker	Iraq	Constitution
when		writer	Kosovo	Declaration of Independence
			Louisiana Territory	Emancipation Proclamation
			Middle East	Federalist Papers
			Somalia	
			Soviet Union	
			Vietnam	

GRAMMAR

PAST TENSE: IRREGULAR VERBS

become – became	do – did	is/are – was/were	spend – spent
begin – began	get – got	lead – led	take – took
buy – bought	give – gave	send – sent	write – wrote

TEXT PAGE 185 VOCABULARY PREVIEW

You may want to introduce the names of these holidays before beginning the unit, or you may choose to wait until they first occur in a specific lesson. If you choose to introduce them at this point, here are some suggestions:

1. Have students look at the photographs on text page 185 and identify the holidays they already know.

2. Present the vocabulary. Say each holiday name and have the class repeat it chorally and individually. Check students' understanding and pronunciation of the words.

3. Practice the vocabulary as a class, in pairs, or in small groups. Have students cover the word list and look at the photographs. Practice the words in the following ways:

   • Say a holiday name and have students tell the correct number on the photograph.
   • Give a number on a photograph and have students say the holiday name.

FOCUS

TOPICS

National Holidays
Months of the Year

GRAMMAR

To Be

New Year's Day **is** on January 1st.

Simple Present Tense

We remember the important civil rights leader.
This holiday celebrate**s** the workers of the United
    States.

KEY VOCABULARY

Christmas	January	birthday
Columbus Day	February	celebrate
Flag Day	May	civil rights leader
Fourth of July	June	colonies
Independence Day	July	declare
Labor Day	September	Flag Resolution
Martin Luther King,	October	gave their lives
Jr. Day	November	holiday
Memorial Day	December	honor (v.)
New Year's Day		independence
Presidents' Day		remember
Thanksgiving Day		serve
Veterans Day		service
		U.S. military
		worker

PREVIEWING THE READING

Have students talk about what they see in the
photographs to preview the holiday celebrations.
Students' ability to describe the photographs will
depend on their language skill level.

(From left to right and top to bottom)

A building sign that says "Happy New Year" (in Times
    Square, New York City)
Martin Luther King, Jr. at the March on Washington
Presidents George Washington and Abraham Lincoln
Graves at a national cemetery
Children wearing red, white, and blue clothing
    marching in a parade
Members of a labor union marching in a parade
A parade float with Christopher Columbus at a ship's
    wheel
Old soldiers (veterans) marching in a parade
A man carving a turkey for the family's holiday meal
A family opening presents at their Christmas tree

READING THE PASSAGE

Note: In this lesson the passage consists of the
captions for all the photographs. Students should look
at the photographs and captions from left to right and
from top to bottom in order to learn about the holidays
in chronological order.

1. Have students read the passage silently. (If you
    wish, you may read the passage aloud or play the
    audio program as students read along silently.)

2. **Check Reading Comprehension:** Ask students
    a question about each line of the passage. For
    beginning-level students, ask these questions in
    the order below so that the questions follow the
    sequence of the passage. For higher-level students,
    ask the questions in random order.

    When is New Year's Day?
    When is Martin Luther King, Jr. Day? / Who do we
        remember on this holiday?
    When is Presidents' Day? / Who does this holiday
        celebrate?
    When is Memorial Day? / Who do we honor on
        this day?
    What is Independence Day also called? / What
        does it celebrate?
    When is Labor Day? / What does this holiday
        celebrate?
    What national holiday is in October?
    When is Veterans Day? / What does this holiday
        honor?
    When is Thanksgiving Day?
    When is Christmas?

3. Ask students if they have any questions about the
    passage; check understanding of vocabulary.

4. **Choral Repetition:** Read aloud each line of the
    passage and have students repeat.

5. **Class Circle Reading:** Have students read the
    passage aloud as a class, with different students
    reading each line. (You can assign each line to a
    particular student or by seating patterns, or by letting
    students take turns spontaneously. In large classes,
    have a different group or row of students read each
    line.)

6. **Pair Practice:** Have students work in pairs, reading
    the passage to each other line by line. Circulate
    around the room and check students' reading and
    pronunciation, focusing more attention on students
    who need more assistance.

CHECK-UP

WRITING CHECK I

1. September
2. October
3. February
4. November
5. May
6. July
7. June

WRITING CHECK II

1. Presidents' Day
2. Memorial Day
3. Flag Day
4. Independence Day
5. Labor Day
6. Columbus Day
7. Thanksgiving

CIVICS CHECK

Note: Since the second question asks students to name two U.S. holidays but has multiple acceptable answers, encourage low beginners to choose two holidays and consistently practice them as their answer. Higher-level students can practice using all the holidays.

Practice each question separately:

1. **Listening:** Have students read along silently as they listen to the question and answer(s)—presented by you, by a pair of students, or on the audio program.
2. **Choral Repetition:** Model the question and answer(s) and have the whole class repeat in unison.
3. **Choral Conversation Practice:** Divide the class in half. Have Group 1 ask the question and Group 2 give the answer(s); then reverse. (Or: You ask the question and have the whole class answer in unison; then reverse.)
4. **Pair Practice:** Have students practice the question and answer(s) in pairs.
5. **Presentation:** Call on one or two pairs of students to present the question and answer(s) to the class.

EXPANSION

Have students discuss how these national holidays are celebrated in their communities. Then have them share about how their families celebrate any of these holidays.

FOCUS

TOPIC
Presidents of the United States

GRAMMAR

Past Tense: Regular Verbs

He work**ed** for civil rights.
He serve**d** two terms.

Past Tense: Irregular Verbs

George Washington **became** the first President.
He **wrote** the Declaration of Independence.
The United States **bought** the Louisiana Territory.
He **led** the United States during the Civil War.
Women **got** the right to vote.
He **began** the interstate highway system.
He **sent** soldiers to Vietnam.
He **spent** more money on the military.
The Senate **had** an impeachment trial.
President Obama **took** office.

Passive Voice

Lincoln **was assassinated**.
His plan to help the country **was called** the *New Deal*.
Important civil rights laws **were passed**.
He **was impeached** by the House of Representatives.
President Clinton **was acquitted**.
The weapons **weren't found**.
Income taxes **were cut**.
Schools **were required** to test students.

NEW VOCABULARY

PAGE 188:

adoption	presidency
exactly	Secretary of State
organize support	

PAGE 189:

League of Nations

PAGE 190:

developing countries	satellite
interstate highway	space
system	space race
launch (v.)	*Sputnik*
Peace Corps	volunteer (n.)

PAGE 191:

administration	Medicare
civil rights laws	poor people
Great Society programs	relations
health-care program	resign
improve	senior citizens
Medicaid	

PAGE 192:

actor	national politics
aspect	policy
business	politics
enter	recession
experience	reduce
foreign countries	regulate
"great communicator"	role
human rights	social services
lower (v.)	spend money
Middle East	troops

PAGE 193:

acquitted	personal scandal
Afghanistan	police department
Bosnia	political scandal
controversial	raise (v.)
decision	reform (v.)
education system	remove
eliminate	require
impeach	responsible
impeachment trial	Somalia
improve	son
increase (v.)	stay in office
invade	terrorist organization
Kosovo	test (v.)
local	"War on Terrorism"
long	weapons of mass
national debt	destruction
peace-keeping mission	welfare system

PAGE 194:

create	low income
Democratic Party	plan (v.)
energy policy	reduce
health care	Republican Party
increase (v.)	take office
lose jobs	wealthy

Note: Text pages 188–194 contain 18 separate passages. Cover each passage separately, using the usual teaching steps.

PREVIEWING THE READINGS

Have students look at the photographs and practice the names of the Presidents profiled on pages 188–194. Have them cover the caption at the bottom of page 194 and name each of the Presidents in this historic photograph.

READING EACH PASSAGE

1. Have students read the passage silently. (If you wish, you may read the passage aloud or play the audio program as students read along silently.)

2. **Check Reading Comprehension:** Ask students a question about each line of the passage. For beginning-level students, ask the questions in order so that the questions follow the sequence of the passage. For higher-level students, ask the questions in random order. (The questions for each passage appear in the next section.)

3. Ask students if they have any questions about the passage; check understanding of vocabulary.

4. **Choral Repetition:** Read aloud each line of the passage and have students repeat.

5. **Class Circle Reading:** Have students read the passage aloud as a class, with different students reading each line. (You can assign each line to a particular student or by seating patterns, or by letting students take turns spontaneously. In large classes, have a different group or row of students read each line.)

6. **Pair Practice:** Have students work in pairs, reading the passage to each other. Circulate around the room and check students' reading and pronunciation, focusing more attention on students who need more assistance.

CHECKING READING COMPREHENSION

PAGE 188:

GEORGE WASHINGTON

What did George Washington become in 1789?
What was he during the Revolutionary War?
What was he the leader of in 1787?
How many terms did he serve as President?
What do we call him?

JOHN ADAMS

Who was the second President?
When did he serve as President?
What was he before that?
Was Adams a Founding Father?
What did he write before the Revolutionary War?
What did he help the colonies do?
What did he organize support for?

THOMAS JEFFERSON

Who was the third President?
When did he serve as President?
Was Jefferson a Founding Father?
What did he write?
Who was the first Secretary of State?
What did the United States buy during his presidency?

When did Thomas Jefferson die? / He died exactly 50 years after what event?
Who died on the same day just a few hours later?

PAGE 189:

JAMES MADISON

Who was the fourth President?
When did he serve as President?
Was Madison a Founding Father?
What did he write?
What did the *Federalist Papers* support?
What did he also write?

ABRAHAM LINCOLN

Who was the sixteenth President?
When did he serve as President?
During what war did he lead the United States?
What did he save?
What did he sign?
What did this document do?
What happened five days after the Civil War ended?

WOODROW WILSON

Who was the 28th President?
When did he serve as President?
During what war was he the President?
What organization did he work to create?
Who got the right to vote during his time in office?

PAGE 190:

FRANKLIN D. ROOSEVELT

Who was the 32nd President?
When did he serve as President?
Who was the President during the Great Depression?
What was the *New Deal*?
During what war was he the President?
When did he die?

DWIGHT D. EISENHOWER

Who was the 34th President?
When did he serve as President?
What was he before he was President?
What was he during World War II?
What did he begin?
What did the Soviet Union do during his time in office?
Which countries were in the "space race?"

JOHN F. KENNEDY

Who was the 35th President?
When did he serve as President?
What did he work for?
Who did he want to help?
What program did he begin to help in developing countries?
Where did he send soldiers?
What program did he expand?
What happened in 1963?

PAGE 191:

LYNDON B. JOHNSON

Who was the 36th President?
When did he become President?
Until what year did he serve as President?
What did his *Great Society* programs do?
What is Medicaid?
What is Medicare?
What laws were passed during Johnson's administration?
What war expanded during his time in office?

RICHARD NIXON

Who was the 37th President?
When did he serve as President?
What country did he begin relations with?
What country did he improve relations with?
What did he end?
Why did he resign?

GERALD FORD

Who was the 38th President?
Was he elected?
When did he become President?
Until what year did he serve as President?
How was the economy during his time in office?

PAGE 192:

JAMES EARL (JIMMY) CARTER

Who was the 39th President?
When did he serve as President?
What did he work for?
For which part of the world did he work for peace?
Did he have experience in national politics?
How was the economy during his time in office?

RONALD REAGAN

Who was the 40th President?
When did he serve as President?
What did he do?
What happened to the role of the federal government during his time in office?
How was the economy during his two terms?
What did Ronald Reagan do before he entered politics?
What was he called?

GEORGE H.W. BUSH

Who was the 41st President?
When did he serve as President?
What did he do before that?
What did he do with many of the Reagan policies?
Where did he send troops in 1991?
How was the economy during his time in office?

PAGE 193:

WILLIAM J. (BILL) CLINTON

Who was the 42nd President?
When did he serve as President?
What did he do to taxes, the welfare system, and the national debt?
What did he increase federal money for?
Where did he send troops, and why?
What kind of scandals was he involved in?
In what year was he impeached by the House of Representatives?
What happened in the Senate a year later?
Did President Clinton stay in office?

GEORGE W. BUSH

Who was the 43rd President?
Who is his father?
When did George W. Bush serve as President?
What happened on September 11, 2001?
What did President Bush declare?
Where did he send U.S. troops in 2001, and why?
Where did he send U.S. troops in 2003, and why?
What was the country's opinion about the decision to invade Iraq?
What happened to income taxes during his time in office? / What were schools required to do?
What happened to the U.S. economy in the last year of the Bush presidency?

PAGE 194:

BARACK H. OBAMA

Who is the 44th President?
When did he become President?
Why was his election historic?
What did he do before he became President?
Where was the United States at war as President Obama took office?
How was the U.S. economy as he took office?
What does President Obama plan to do with U.S. troops in Iraq and Afghanistan?
What does he plan to use government money to do?
What does he want to do with health care and the country's energy policy?
What does he plan to do with taxes?
What is the political party of the President now?
What are the two major political parties in the United States?

CIVICS CHECK (Page 195)

Note: Since some questions have multiple acceptable answers, encourage low beginners to consistently practice a single answer to a question, while higher-level students can practice the multiple answers.

First, practice each question separately:

1. **Listening:** Have students read along silently as they listen to the question and answer(s)—presented by you, by a pair of students, or on the audio program.
2. **Choral Repetition:** Model the question and answer(s) and have the whole class repeat in unison.
3. **Choral Conversation Practice:** Divide the class in half. Have Group 1 ask the question and Group 2 give the answer(s); then reverse. (Or: You ask the question and have the whole class answer in unison; then reverse.)
4. **Pair Practice:** Have students practice the question and answer(s) in pairs.
5. **Presentation:** Call on one or two pairs of students to present the question and answer(s) to the class.

Then practice all the questions together:

6. **Choral Answers:** Ask any question and have students give the answer in unison. (If there are multiple answers, have them give the first answer in the text.)
7. **Pair Practice:** Have students work in pairs, taking turns asking and answering all the questions in random order.

For more practice or for review during the next class session, do one of these activities:

LINE PRACTICE: Have students stand in two lines facing each other. Each pair of facing students should take turns asking and answering a question. After sufficient time for this practice, say "Move," and have one line of students move down one position while the other line remains in place. (The student at the end of the line moves to the beginning of the line.) In this way, new pairs are created and students practice with another partner. Continue until students have practiced all the questions.

"ROUND ROBIN": Have students circulate around the room and ask each other the questions. Students should move on to another person after they have taken turns asking and answering a question.

EXPANSION

1. Have students discuss who their favorite U.S. President is and give reasons for their answers.
2. Have students discuss whether they think the President today is doing a good job and give reasons for their answers.

The end-of-unit assessment evaluates student achievement of the unit's learning objectives while developing the specific test-taking skills required for success during the USCIS English and civics exam. Students can practice and complete the tests in class or at home.

A. CIVICS

This section contains the official USCIS questions that appear in the unit. Students can practice the questions and answers outside of class on their own or with a study partner. (Since many questions have multiple acceptable answers, encourage low beginners to consistently practice a single answer to a question, while higher-level students can practice the multiple answers.) For in-class assessment, call on students to answer different questions, or observe students as they test each other through pair practice.

B. KEY VOCABULARY

1. February
2. September
3. November
4. July
5. June

C. READING AND WRITING

This section contains the types of reading and writing questions on the USCIS test. You can assess students' reading skills by their ability to read aloud the questions. You can assess their writing skills by their ability to write the sentences from dictation. (The dictation sentences appear below, in the text on page 239, and on the audio program. Each dictation sentence is on a separate audio track so that the audio can be paused while students write.)

1. Memorial Day is in May.
2. Independence Day is in July.
3. Thanksgiving is in November.
4. Columbus Day is in October.
5. Flag Day is in June.

TEXT PAGE 198

CIVICS ENRICHMENT

These civics enrichment activities are designed to promote students' active participation in class and in the civic life of the community—through projects, issues discussions, community tasks, field trips, and Internet activities. Reproducible performance-based assessment forms for use in evaluating and documenting student participation in these activities are included in the Appendix.

CIVIC PARTICIPATION

Have students discuss their favorite national holidays in the United States, the reason they like them, and how they celebrate.

INTERNET ACTIVITY

Have students use the White House website to see a slideshow about the Presidents and to get information about specific Presidents.

PROJECT

Have students write a short biography about a President. They can use the Internet, the library, and other resources to find information about the President's birthplace, childhood years, family, education, political career, and major accomplishments and events during the President's time in office.

TECHNOLOGY ENRICHMENT

See Appendix page 312 for additional Internet enrichment activities related to this unit.

UNIT SUMMARY

KEY VOCABULARY

Have students review the lists of words they have learned in this unit. Encourage students to get a small notebook where they can write down vocabulary that is new for them.

GRAMMAR

Have students review the list of irregular past tense verbs in this unit. Have students write sentences that use the past tense forms of these verbs.

UNIT REVIEW WORKSHEETS

Unit 11 Writing Practice
Unit 11 Reading Practice
Unit 11 Civics Practice

FOCUS

TOPIC

Answering Form N-400 "Part 10" questions during the USCIS interview

FUNCTIONAL INTERVIEW SKILLS

Reporting information

KEY VOCABULARY

age	leave/left
any kind of	letter
application file	local
ask to be excused from	military service
	never
avoid	online
because of	post office
beliefs	religion
between	register
country	resident
desert (v.)	run/ran away
drafted into the U.S. Armed Forces	Selective Service board
	Selective Service System
during	serve
exemption	U.S. Armed Forces
high school	U.S. military

ROLE PLAY: Questions 29–33

Have students work in pairs and role-play interviews using questions 29–33. Have them use in their conversations some of the expressions that appear in the blue boxes on pages 216, 220, and 222 to practice asking for repetition and clarification. Have students take turns being the USCIS officer and the applicant. Then have pairs of students present their role plays to the class.

WORKSHEETS

Interview Practice Worksheets 41–43

UNIT 12

	CITIZENS' RIGHTS		THE OATH OF
	CITIZENS' RESPONSIBILITIES		ALLEGIANCE
	PARTICIPATING IN OUR DEMOCRACY		

LESSONS & UNIT ACTIVITIES	OBJECTIVES	STUDENT TEXT	TEACHER'S GUIDE
Vocabulary Preview	Identifying vocabulary related to civic rights and responsibilities	199	177
Citizens' Rights	Identifying rights of everyone living in the United States; Identifying rights only for United States citizens; Identifying the minimum voting age; Naming the two major political parties	200–201	178–179
Citizens' Responsibilities	Identifying responsibilities of everyone living in the United States; Identifying responsibilities only for United States citizens; Describing the Selective Service system registration requirement	202–203	180–181
Participating in Our Democracy	Describing ways that Americans can participate in their democracy	204–205	182–183
The Oath of Allegiance	Describing promises one makes when becoming a United States citizen; Reciting the Oath of Allegiance	206–207	184–185
Civics Test: Rights and Responsibilities	Answering questions about civic rights and responsibilities and participating in our democracy; Asking for clarification; Hesitating; Asking for repetition	208	186–187
Unit Test	Preparing for USCIS civics, reading, and writing test questions	209–211	187
Civics Enrichment	Discussing Election Day in the community; Discussing rights and responsibilities and how these are different for citizens and non-citizens; Debate Activity: Debating whether non-citizens should have the right to vote in local elections	212	188
The English Test (Speaking)*	Answering Form N-400 "Part 10" questions during the USCIS interview	225	189

* This interview preparation lesson is in the Appendix for students' convenience. It can be introduced in this unit and then reviewed along with the other interview preparation lessons as students get ready for their appointment at USCIS. If you prefer, you can do these lessons later in the course if that is more appropriate for the timing of your students' interviews. Interview Practice worksheets accompany these lessons.

UNIT RESOURCES

Worksheets:
Unit 12 Writing Practice
Unit 12 Reading Practice
Unit 12 Civics Practice
Interview Practice Worksheets 44–46

Audio Program:
CD 3: Tracks 47–62

RELATED PRACTICE

Foundations: Unit 15
Word by Word Basic: pages 154–155
Word by Word: pages 160–161
Side by Side / Side by Side Plus: Book 2, Units 5, 11
Side by Side Interactive CD-ROM / Side by Side TV: Levels 2A & 2B, Segments 35, 36, 47, 48
ExpressWays: Book 1, Unit 8

UNIT OVERVIEW

KEY VOCABULARY

READING	WRITING	RIGHTS	PARTICIPATING IN OUR DEMOCRACY

READING
can
citizens
do
elects
for
government
have
in
is
of
one
pay
people
President
right
the
to
United States
vote
what
who

WRITING
and
can
citizens
Congress
elect
for
have
in
of
pay
people
President
right
taxes
the
to
United States
vote

RIGHTS
freedom of assembly
freedom of expression
freedom of speech
freedom of worship
freedom to petition the government
right to bear arms
right to run for federal office
right to vote

RESPONSIBILITIES
obey the law
pay taxes
register for the Selective Service
rule of law
serve on a jury
vote

PARTICIPATING IN OUR DEMOCRACY
call your senators and representatives
give an elected official your opinion on an issue
help with a campaign
join a civic group
join a political party
publicly support or oppose an issue or policy
run for office
vote
write to a newspaper

OATH OF ALLEGIANCE
be loyal to the United States
defend the Constitution and laws of the United States
do important work for the nation if needed
give up loyalty to other countries
obey the laws of the United States
recite an oath of allegiance
serve in the U.S. military if needed
serve the nation if needed

GRAMMAR

CAN
Citizens **can** vote for President.

SHOULD
People **should** obey the law.

MUST
All men **must** register for the Selective Service.

WILL
I **will** support and defend the Constitution.

FUNCTIONAL EXPRESSIONS

CLARIFYING
Did you say ___?
I'm sorry. Did you say ___ or ___?

ASKING FOR REPETITION
Could you please repeat the question?

HESITATING
Let me see.
Let me think for a moment.

TEXT PAGE 199 VOCABULARY PREVIEW

You may want to introduce these words and phrases before beginning the unit, or you may choose to wait until they first occur in a specific lesson. If you choose to introduce them at this point, here are some suggestions:

1. Have students look at the photographs on text page 199 and identify the words and phrases they already know.

2. Present the vocabulary. Say each word or phrase and have the class repeat it chorally and individually. Check students' understanding and pronunciation of the words and phrases.

3. Practice the vocabulary as a class, in pairs, or in small groups. Have students cover the word list and look at the photographs. Practice the words and phrases in the following ways:

   • Say a word or phrase and have students tell the correct number on the photograph.
   • Give a number on a photograph and have students say the word or phrase.

FOCUS

TOPICS

Citizens' and Non-Citizens' Rights
The Minimum Voting Age
The Two Major Political Parties

GRAMMAR

Can

Citizens **can** vote for President.

NEW VOCABULARY

freedom of expression
right to bear arms
run for federal office

PREVIEWING THE READING

Have students talk about what they see in the photographs to preview the context of the passage. Students' ability to describe the photographs will depend on their language skill level.

(Page 200 top, from left to right)

People speaking at a public meeting
People demonstrating / People meeting together to support an issue
People worshipping/praying

(Page 200 middle left)

A person signing a document/petition

(Page 200 middle right)

A person hunting with a rifle/gun

(Page 200 bottom left)

People voting

(Page 200 bottom right)

Barack Obama campaigning for the presidency

READING THE PASSAGE

Note: The captions under the photographs are part of the passage.

1. Have students read the passage silently. (If you wish, you may read the passage aloud or play the audio program as students read along silently.)

2. **Check Reading Comprehension:** Ask students a question about each line of the passage. For beginning-level students, ask these questions in the order below, so that the questions follow the sequence of the passage. For higher-level students, ask the questions in random order.

What does everyone living in the United States have?
What are five rights of everyone living in the United States? (Answer consists of captions for the top and middle photographs.)
Name two rights only for United States citizens. (Answer consists of captions for the bottom photographs.)
How old do citizens have to be to vote for President?
Which candidates for President do citizens usually choose between?
What are the two major political parties in the United States?

3. Ask students if they have any questions about the passage; check understanding of vocabulary.

4. **Choral Repetition:** Read aloud each line of the passage and each photograph caption and have students repeat.

5. **Class Circle Reading:** Have students read the passage aloud as a class, with different students reading each line and photograph caption. (You can assign each line or caption to a particular student or by seating patterns, or by letting students take turns spontaneously. In large classes, have a different group or row of students read each line or caption.)

6. **Pair Practice:** Have students work in pairs, reading the passage to each other. Circulate around the room and check students' reading and pronunciation, focusing more attention on students who need more assistance.

CHECK-UP

WHOSE RIGHTS?

1. everyone
2. everyone
3. citizens
4. everyone
5. everyone
6. citizens

MATCHING

1. e
2. d
3. a
4. c
5. b

CIVICS CHECK

Note: Since some questions have multiple acceptable answers, encourage low beginners to consistently practice a single answer to a question, while higher-level students can practice the multiple answers.

First, practice each question separately:

1. **Listening:** Have students read along silently as they listen to the question and answer(s)—presented by you, by a pair of students, or on the audio program.

2. **Choral Repetition:** Model the question and answer(s) and have the whole class repeat in unison.

3. **Choral Conversation Practice:** Divide the class in half. Have Group 1 ask the question and Group 2 give the answer(s); then reverse. (Or: You ask the question and have the whole class answer in unison; then reverse.)

4. **Pair Practice:** Have students practice the question and answer(s) in pairs.

5. **Presentation:** Call on one or two pairs of students to present the question and answer(s) to the class.

Then practice all the questions together:

6. **Choral Answers:** Ask any question and have students give the answer in unison. (If there are multiple answers, have them give the first answer in the text.)

7. **Pair Practice:** Have students work in pairs, taking turns asking and answering all the questions in random order.

For more practice or for review during the next class session, do one of these activities:

LINE PRACTICE: Have students stand in two lines facing each other. Each pair of facing students should take turns asking and answering a question. After sufficient time for this practice, say "Move," and have one line of students move down one position while the other line remains in place. (The student at the end of the line moves to the beginning of the line.) In this way, new pairs are created and students practice with another partner. Continue until students have practiced all the questions.

"ROUND ROBIN": Have students circulate around the room and ask each other the questions. Students should move on to another person after they have taken turns asking and answering a question.

EXPANSION

1. Have students discuss how they feel on Election Day when they cannot vote. How will they feel different when they become citizens and they can vote?

2. Invite a member of the League of Women Voters or a similar organization to speak to the class about voting and the election process.

FOCUS

TOPICS

Citizens' and Non-Citizens' Responsibilities
Selective Service System Registration

GRAMMAR

Should

People **should** obey the law.

Must

Everyone **must** follow the law.

NEW VOCABULARY

above the law	register
county	responsibilities
federal income tax forms	Selective Service
follow the law	serve in the military
local income taxes	serve on a jury
obey the law	state income taxes
pay income taxes	

PREVIEWING THE READING

Have students talk about what they see in the photographs to preview the context of the passage. Students' ability to describe the photographs will depend on their language skill level.

(Page 200 top left)

A police officer talking to a driver / A driver broke a law and a police officer stopped him

(Page 200 top right)

A federal income tax form

(Page 200 bottom left to right)

A young man filling out a form / A young man who is between ages 18 and 25 registering for the Selective Service (Ask students if they recognize the poster shown with this illustration.)

A courtroom / A trial / A judge and jury (and lawyer and witness) in a courtroom

A person voting at a voting machine

READING THE PASSAGE

Note: Make sure students understand the Selective Service registration age requirement. Men who are present in the country when they become age 18 should register at that time. Men who are older than age 18 when they enter the U.S. must register BEFORE their 26th birthday, which means while they are age 25 at the latest. One of the official USCIS civics test

answers related to this is misleading as it gives the age requirement as "between 18 and 26."

1. Have students read the passage silently. (If you wish, you may read the passage aloud or play the audio program as students read along silently.)

2. **Check Reading Comprehension:** Ask students a question about each line of the passage. For beginning-level students, ask these questions in the order below, so that the questions follow the sequence of the passage. For higher-level students, ask the questions in random order.

   People in the United States have rights, but what do they also have?
   What should people obey?
   What is a basic principle of American democracy?
   What is the "rule of law"?
   Who must follow the law?
   Who is above the law?

   What should people in the United States pay?
   What should they send in and pay?
   When is the last day you can send in federal income tax forms?
   What do people in many states also pay?
   What do people in some cities and counties also pay?

   What must men in the United States do if they are needed?
   What must all men in the United States do at age eighteen?
   What must men who are older than age eighteen when they enter the United States do before their 26th birthday?

   Are all responsibilities for both citizens and non-citizens?
   What should citizens serve on?
   When should citizens vote?

3. Ask students if they have any questions about the passage; check understanding of vocabulary.

4. **Choral Repetition:** Read aloud each line of the passage and have students repeat.

5. **Class Circle Reading:** Have students read the passage aloud as a class, with different students reading each line. (You can assign each line to a particular student or by seating patterns, or by letting students take turns spontaneously. In large classes, have a different group or row of students read each line or caption.)

6. **Pair Practice:** Have students work in pairs, reading the passage to each other section by section. Circulate around the room and check students' reading and pronunciation, focusing more attention on students who need more assistance.

CHECK-UP

VOCABULARY CHECK

1. law
2. jury
3. taxes
4. register
5. vote

CIVICS CHECK

Note: Since some questions have multiple acceptable answers, encourage low beginners to consistently practice a single answer to a question, while higher-level students can practice the multiple answers.

First, practice each question separately:

1. **Listening:** Have students read along silently as they listen to the question and answer(s)—presented by you, by a pair of students, or on the audio program.
2. **Choral Repetition:** Model the question and answer(s) and have the whole class repeat in unison.
3. **Choral Conversation Practice:** Divide the class in half. Have Group 1 ask the question and Group 2 give the answer(s); then reverse. (Or: You ask the question and have the whole class answer in unison; then reverse.)
4. **Pair Practice:** Have students practice the question and answer(s) in pairs.
5. **Presentation:** Call on one or two pairs of students to present the question and answer(s) to the class.

Then practice all the questions together:

6. **Choral Answers:** Ask any question and have students give the answer in unison. (If there are multiple answers, have them give the first answer in the text.)
7. **Pair Practice:** Have students work in pairs, taking turns asking and answering all the questions in random order.

For more practice or for review during the next class session, do one of these activities:

LINE PRACTICE: Have students stand in two lines facing each other. Each pair of facing students should take turns asking and answering a question. After sufficient time for this practice, say "Move," and have one line of students move down one position while the other line remains in place. (The student at the end of the line moves to the beginning of the line.) In this way, new pairs are created and students practice with another partner. Continue until students have practiced all the questions.

"ROUND ROBIN": Have students circulate around the room and ask each other the questions. Students should move on to another person after they have taken turns asking and answering a question.

DISCUSSION

Have students discuss these questions in pairs or small groups and then share as a class.

FOCUS

TOPIC	GRAMMAR
Participating in Our Democracy	**Can** You **can** vote.

NEW VOCABULARY

campaign (n.)	issue	policy
civic group	join	run for office
democracy	oppose	support
give your opinion	participate	

PREVIEWING THE READING

Have students talk about what they see in the photographs to preview the context of the passage. Students' ability to describe the photographs will depend on their language skill level.

(From left to right and top to bottom)

A person voting at a voting machine

Members of a political party at their convention (The photograph shows the Republican National Convention in 2008 with presidential candidate John McCain.)

Campaign workers helping with a political campaign (The photograph shows campaign workers for Democratic presidential candidate Barack Obama during the 2008 campaign.)

People/Children who are in a group that is doing cleanup in their neighborhood (The photograph shows a civic group in Los Angeles.)

A public official talking on the telephone (The photograph shows Congressman Charles Rangel, a member of the U.S. House of Representatives, who represents New York's 15th District.)

Citizens meeting with a public official (The photograph shows Congresswoman Loretta Sanchez, a member of the U.S. House of Representatives, who represents California's 47th District.)

A person running for office in an election campaign (The photograph shows a candidate for the City Council in Syracuse, New York.)

A letter to the editor in a newspaper

People demonstrating about a housing issue (The photograph shows a demonstration by senior citizens afraid of losing their public housing in Massachusetts.)

READING THE PASSAGE

Note: The captions under the photographs are part of the passage.

1. Have students read the passage silently. (If you wish, you may read the passage aloud or play the audio program as students read along silently.)

2. **Check Reading Comprehension:** Ask students a question about each line of the passage (except the first). For beginning-level students, ask these questions in the order below, so that the questions follow the sequence of the passage. For higher-level students, ask the questions in random order.

> You can participate in our democracy in many ways.
> What can you do on Election Day?* (* In some cities and towns, non-citizens can vote in local elections.)
> What kind of party can you join?
> What can you help with?
> What kind of group can you join that helps in your community?
> Who can you call?
> What can you give to an elected official?
> What can you run for?
> What can you write?
> What can you publicly support or oppose?

3. Ask students if they have any questions about the passage; check understanding of vocabulary.

4. **Choral Repetition:** Read aloud each line of the passage and have students repeat.

5. **Class Circle Reading:** Have students read the passage aloud as a class, with different students reading each line. (You can assign each line to a particular student or by seating patterns, or by letting students take turns spontaneously. In large classes, have a different group or row of students read each line or caption.)

6. **Pair Practice:** Have students work in pairs, reading the passage to each other. Circulate around the room and check students' reading and pronunciation, focusing more attention on students who need more assistance.

CHECK-UP

VOCABULARY CHECK

1. opinion
2. oppose
3. write
4. campaign
5. run

CIVICS CHECK

Note: Since this question has multiple acceptable answers, encourage low beginners to consistently practice a single answer, while higher-level students can practice the multiple answers.

1. **Listening:** Have students read along silently as they listen to the question and answers—presented by you, by a pair of students, or on the audio program.
2. **Choral Repetition:** Model the question and answers and have the whole class repeat in unison.
3. **Choral Conversation Practice:** Divide the class in half. Have Group 1 ask the question and Group 2 give the answers; then reverse. (Or: You ask the question and have the whole class answer in unison; then reverse.)
4. **Pair Practice:** Have students practice the question and answers in pairs.
5. **Presentation:** Call on one or two pairs of students to present the question and answers to the class.

DISCUSSION

Have students discuss these questions in pairs or small groups and then share as a class.

Note: The information about the Oath of Allegiance on text page 206 is required for the USCIS civics test. The Oath of Allegiance itself on text page 207 is not required for the test since its language is very difficult, but students should study it now for two important reasons:

1) During the USCIS interview, officers commonly ask applicants if they understand the full Oath of Allegiance to the United States and if they are willing to take the Oath.

2) During the naturalization ceremony, students will recite the Oath in order to become citizens.

FOCUS

TOPIC
The Oath of Allegiance
GRAMMAR
Will
You **will** recite an oath of allegiance.

KEY VOCABULARY

PAGE 206:

citizen	naturalization ceremony
country	Oath of Allegiance
defend the Constitution and laws	obey the laws
	promise (v.)
do important work	promises (n.)
give up loyalty	recite
if needed	serve in the U.S.
loyal	military
member	serve the nation
nation	U.S. military

PAGE 207 (OATH OF ALLEGIANCE):

abjure	evasion	purpose
absolutely	fidelity	renounce
all	foreign	required by the
allegiance	freely	law
Armed Forces	hereby	same
of the United	heretofore	so help me God
States	laws	sovereignty
bear (v.)	mental	state
bear arms	reservation	subject
citizen	noncombatant	support
civilian direction	service	take this
Constitution	obligation	obligation
declare	on behalf of	freely
defend against	on oath	true faith
domestic	perform	without
enemies	potentate	work of national
entirely	prince	importance

PREVIEWING THE READING

Have students talk about what they see in the photographs:

In both photographs, what hand is each person holding up? (The right hand.)
What are they doing? (They're taking an oath. / They're making a promise. / They're becoming citizens. / They're at a ceremony.)
Where are the people in the photograph on the left? (They're at Monticello, the home of President Thomas Jefferson, in Virginia.)
Who are the people in the photograph on the right? (They're soldiers. / They're in the Army. / They're members of the military / Armed Forces.)
Where are they? (In Iraq.)

READING THE PASSAGE

Note: Practice page 206 first. (Don't practice the Oath of Allegiance on the next page yet.)

1. Have students read the passage silently. (If you wish, you may read the passage aloud or play the audio program as students read along silently.)

2. Check Reading Comprehension: Ask students a question about each line of the passage. For beginning-level students, ask these questions in the order below, so that the questions follow the sequence of the passage. For higher-level students, ask the questions in random order.

Where will you become a citizen?
What will you recite during the ceremony?
What will you do when you recite the oath?

What do you promise to give up loyalty to?
What do you promise to defend?
What do you promise to obey?
What do you promise to do for the U.S. military if needed?
What do you promise to do for the nation if needed?
Who do you promise to do important work for if needed?
What do you promise to be loyal to?

3. Ask students if they have any questions about the passage; check understanding of vocabulary.

4. **Choral Repetition:** Read aloud each line of the passage and have students repeat.

5. **Class Circle Reading:** Have students read the passage aloud as a class, with different students reading each line. (You can assign each line to a particular student or by seating patterns, or by letting students take turns spontaneously. In large classes, have a different group or row of students read each line or caption.)

6. **Pair Practice:** Have students work in pairs, reading the passage to each other. Circulate around the room and check students' reading and pronunciation, focusing more attention on students who need more assistance.

PRACTICING THE OATH OF ALLEGIANCE

1. **Listening:** Have students read along silently as you recite the oath or play the audio.

2. **Choral Repetition (phrase by phrase):** Separate the oath into the following phrases, read them aloud, and have students repeat in unison:

> I hereby declare, on oath,
>
> that I absolutely and entirely
>
> renounce and abjure
>
> all allegiance and fidelity
>
> to any foreign prince, potentate, state, or sovereignty,
>
> of whom or which I have heretofore
>
> been a subject or citizen;
>
> that I will support and defend
>
> the Constitution and laws of the United States of America
>
> against all enemies, foreign and domestic;
>
> that I will bear true faith and allegiance to the same;
>
> that I will bear arms on behalf of the United States
>
> when required by the law;
>
> that I will perform noncombatant service
>
> in the Armed Forces of the United States
>
> when required by the law;
>
> that I will perform work of national importance
>
> under civilian direction
>
> when required by the law;
>
> and that I take this obligation freely
>
> without any mental reservation
>
> or purpose of evasion;
>
> so help me God.

3. **Reading:** Have students practice reading aloud the oath as a class, in small groups, or on their own.

4. Ask students if they understand the general meaning of the oath. Point out that the lines connecting pages 206 and 207 show the general meaning of the lines of the oath. Explain to students that many of the words in the oath are very old and not commonly used.

5. **Public Speaking Practice:** Have individual students present the oath to the class. If you feel it is appropriate to do so, help students with their diction and projection to improve their public speaking skills in English.

CIVICS CHECK

Note: Since this question has multiple acceptable answers, encourage low beginners to consistently practice a single answer, while higher-level students can practice the multiple answers.

1. **Listening:** Have students read along silently as they listen to the question and answers—presented by you, by a pair of students, or on the audio program.

2. **Choral Repetition:** Model the question and answers and have the whole class repeat in unison.

3. **Choral Conversation Practice:** Divide the class in half. Have Group 1 ask the question and Group 2 give the answers; then reverse. (Or: You ask the question and have the whole class answer in unison; then reverse.)

4. **Pair Practice:** Have students practice the question and answers in pairs.

5. **Presentation:** Call on one or two pairs of students to present the question and answers to the class.

EXPANSION

Oratorical Contest

Have interested students memorize the oath and recite it for the class. Have class members vote on the best rendition, and award a prize to the winner.

FOCUS

TOPICS

Civic Rights and Responsibilities
Participating in Our Democracy

GRAMMAR

WH-Questions

What are two rights of everyone living in the United
States?

FUNCTIONAL INTERVIEW SKILLS

Asking for clarification
Hesitating
Asking for repetition

KEY VOCABULARY

Could you please repeat the question?
Did you say . . . ?
Did you say _____ or _____?
I'm sorry.
I see.
. . . let me see . . .
. . . let me think for a moment . . .
Sure.
Tell me . . .

GETTING READY

**1. Practicing how to ask for clarification when
different civics questions sound very similar.**

Point out that the first two dialogs contain an
important strategy that students can use when they
need to confirm part of what they think they heard
in a question. Confirming the precise information
needed can be more helpful than asking the officer
to repeat the entire question because it focuses on
the specific thing the student needs to clarify. This
is especially important because several USCIS civics
questions are very similar to other civics questions.

As a class, have students look at the first two
dialogs and identify how the applicant confirms part
of a question.

1st dialog: The officer asks about the rights
of *everyone* in the United States, but there
is a similar civics question that asks about
the rights of *United States citizens only*. The
applicant therefore wants to confirm the
question and asks: "Did you say *everyone*?"
The officer confirms "everyone" and also
explains the question further by adding
"citizens and non-citizens."

2nd dialog: The officer asks about one
responsibility of citizens, but there is a similar
civics question that asks about one *right* of
citizens. The applicant therefore wants to
confirm the question and asks: "I'm sorry. Did
you say one *right* or one *responsibility*?"

2. Practicing how to hesitate to fill time.

Point out that the first and third dialogs contain an
important strategy (hesitating) that students can use
when they need time to think of an answer. Explain
to students that it is much better to fill the thinking
time with words than to be silent.

1st dialog: The applicant needs to name two
rights of everyone living in the United States.
The applicant is able to name one right very
quickly but needs a moment to think of a
second right. The applicant fills the thinking
time by saying, "let me see . . .". Then the
applicant gives the answer.

3rd dialog: The applicant needs to give two
ways that Americans can participate in their
democracy. The applicant is able to give
one way very quickly but needs some time to
think of a second way. The applicant fills the
thinking time by saying, "let me think for a
moment . . .".

**3. Practicing how to ask for repetition and respond to
a paraphrased question.**

Point out that in the third dialog, the applicant asks
the officer to repeat the question:

"Could you please repeat the question?"

As a result, the officer paraphrases—the officer
changes the long question into two sentences (a
statement and a command).

1st Line A: What are two ways that Americans
can participate in their democracy?

2nd Line A: Americans can participate in their
democracy in many ways. Tell me two ways.

Explain to students that the officer is rephrasing the
question (saying the question a different way) to make
it more understandable. When students ask the officer
to repeat a question, they should know that the officer
might or might not repeat the question exactly word-for-
word. If the sentence sounds different, it is because
the officer is trying to be helpful.

PRACTICING THE DIALOG

Notes:
- There are three short dialogs. Lower-level
students should practice each dialog separately.
Higher-level students can practice the dialogs
either separately or together.

- The dialogs have answer-choice boxes with multiple acceptable answers. The first and third dialogs require two answers; the second dialog requires one answer. Encourage low beginners to consistently practice the same answer(s) to a question. Higher-level students can practice the multiple answers. (The audio contains the first answer, or the first two answers for the questions requiring two.)

1. **Setting the Scene:** Establish the context: "The USCIS officer is asking a citizenship applicant some civics questions."

2. **Listening:** With books closed, have students listen to the dialog—presented by you, by a pair of students, or on the audio program.

3. **Choral Repetition:** With books still closed, model each line and have the whole class repeat in unison.

4. **Reading:** With books open, have students follow along as two students present the dialog. Ask students if they have any questions and check understanding of vocabulary.

5. **Choral Conversation Practice:** Divide the class in half. Have Group 1 ask the questions and Group 2 give the answers; then reverse. (Or: You ask the questions and have the whole class answer in unison; then reverse.)

6. **Pair Practice:** Have students practice the dialog in pairs, taking turns being the USCIS officer and the applicant.

7. **Presentations:** Call on pairs of students to present the dialog to the class.

TEXT PAGES 209–211 UNIT TEST

The end-of-unit assessment evaluates student achievement of the unit's learning objectives while developing the specific test-taking skills required for success during the USCIS English and civics exam. Students can practice and complete the tests in class or at home.

A. CIVICS: *Rights and Responsibilities*

B. CIVICS: *Principles of American Democracy Review*

These sections contain the official USCIS questions that appear in the unit and additional questions for review. Students can practice the questions and answers outside of class on their own or with a study partner. (Since many questions have multiple acceptable answers, encourage low beginners to consistently practice a single answer to a question, while higher-level students can practice the multiple answers.) For in-class assessment, call on students to answer different questions, or observe students as they test each other through pair practice.

C. KEY VOCABULARY

1. pay
2. right
3. United States
4. taxes
5. free
6. flag
7. Senator

D. READING AND WRITING

This section contains the types of reading and writing questions on the USCIS test. You can assess students' reading skills by their ability to read aloud the questions. You can assess their writing skills by their ability to write the sentences from dictation. (The dictation sentences appear below, in the text on page 239, and on the audio program. Each dictation sentence is on a separate audio track so that the audio can be paused while students write.)

1. People in the United States pay taxes.
2. Citizens have the right to vote.
3. Citizens can vote for President and Congress.
4. Citizens of the United States elect the President.
5. People in the United States have to pay taxes.

TEXT PAGE 212

CIVICS ENRICHMENT

These civics enrichment activities are designed to promote students' active participation in class and in the civic life of the community—through projects, issues discussions, community tasks, field trips, and Internet activities. Reproducible performance-based assessment forms for use in evaluating and documenting student participation in these activities are included in the Appendix.

CIVIC PARTICIPATION

Have students discuss election practices in their community, including which local government positions are filled by elected officials, what happens at polling places, the types of voting machines, and how people register to vote.

COMMUNITY ISSUES

Have students discuss the rights and responsibilities of all people in their communities and in the nation, and how some of these may differ for citizens and non-citizens.

DEBATE ACTIVITY

Have students participate in a classroom debate about the voting age. Divide the class into two teams, or have students choose their teams based on the position they want to take. Each team should take one of these positions:

a) Non-citizens should have the right to vote in local elections.

b) Non-citizens shouldn't have the right to vote in local elections.

TECHNOLOGY ENRICHMENT

See Appendix page 312 for Internet enrichment activities related to this unit.

UNIT SUMMARY

KEY VOCABULARY

Have students review the lists of words and phrases they have learned in this unit. Encourage students to get a small notebook where they can write down vocabulary that is new for them.

GRAMMAR

Have students review the sentence-examples of grammar in this unit and then write new sentences using this grammar.

FUNCTIONAL EXPRESSIONS

Have students review the functional expressions and find where they occur in the unit. For enrichment, have students practice new conversations using these different expressions.

UNIT REVIEW WORKSHEETS

Unit 12 Writing Practice
Unit 12 Reading Practice
Unit 12 Civics Practice

FOCUS

TOPIC

Answering Form N-400 "Part 10" questions during
the USCIS interview

FUNCTIONAL INTERVIEW SKILL

Reporting information

KEY VOCABULARY

application file	only
bear arms	perform noncombatant
because of	services
beliefs	perform work of national
believe in	importance under civilian
civilian direction	direction
community	promise
Constitution	ready
country	religion
do work	require
during	serve
emergency	state
explain	support the Constitution
fight	supreme law of the land
form of government	take the full Oath of Allegiance
full	understand
help	United States
if needed	use a weapon
law	U.S. Armed Forces
letter	U.S. laws
loyal	U.S. military
military	willing
Oath of Allegiance	work
on behalf of	

ROLE PLAY: Questions 34–39

Have students work in pairs and role-play interviews
using questions 34–39. Have them use in their
conversations some of the expressions that appear in
the blue boxes on pages 216, 220, and 222 to practice
asking for repetition and clarification. Have students
take turns being the USCIS officer and the applicant.
Then have pairs of students present their role plays to
the class.

WORKSHEETS

Interview Practice Worksheets 44–46

APPENDIX

ON THE DAY OF YOUR USCIS INTERVIEW
THE ENGLISH TEST: SPEAKING
THE READING TEST
THE WRITING TEST
100 CIVICS TEST QUESTIONS

Note: The Appendix of the student text contains essential information and preparation students need for success in the USCIS interview and civics and English tests. This material is provided in a comprehensive Appendix section for students' convenience as they review and prepare for their USCIS appointment. However, it is preferable to introduce the material progressively during the entire course rather than at the end. Each unit therefore includes an interview preparation lesson that covers some of the Appendix content. You may choose to cover this content in a different sequence or at a different pace based on the needs of your students and the timing of their USCIS interviews. This chart indicates the Teacher's Guide pages on which teaching instructions for the Appendix lessons are located. Reproducible Interview Practice worksheets accompany these lessons.

LESSONS (UNIT CORRELATIONS)	OBJECTIVES	STUDENT TEXT	TEACHER'S GUIDE
On the Day of Your USCIS Interview (Unit A)	Identifying what to bring to the USCIS interview; Arriving at the USCIS office; Checking in	213	14
The English Test: Speaking (Unit A)	Greeting the USCIS officer; Walking to the office; Swearing in; Presenting your identification	214–215	15
The English Test: Speaking (Unit B)	Identifying requirements of the English Speaking Test; Asking for repetition; Showing confidence and pride during the interview; Giving information about name, other names used, or the desire to change name; Giving information about eligibility for citizenship	216–217	25
The English Test: Speaking (Unit 1)	Giving information about yourself; Giving information about address and telephone numbers; Asking for clarification; Saying you don't understand	218–219	37
The English Test: Speaking (Unit 2)	Giving information for criminal records search: height, weight, race, hair color, eye color	219	45
The English Test: Speaking (Unit 3)	Asking the officer to paraphrase a question; Giving information about residence and employment; Talking about time outside the United States	220–221	54–55
The English Test: Speaking (Unit 4)	Recognizing how the USCIS officer might check the applicant's understanding; Asking for an explanation or paraphrasing; Giving information about marital history and children	222	73
The English Test: Speaking (Unit 5)	Answering Form N-400 "Part 10" questions during the USCIS interview	223	87
The English Test: Speaking (Unit 6)	Answering Form N-400 "Part 10" questions during the USCIS interview	223–224	99
The English Test: Speaking (Unit 7)	Answering Form N-400 "Part 10" questions during the USCIS interview	224	115
The English Test: Speaking (Unit 8)	Answering Form N-400 "Part 10" questions during the USCIS interview	224	133
The English Test: Speaking (Unit 9)	Answering Form N-400 "Part 10" questions during the USCIS interview	224	149
The English Test: Speaking (Unit 10)	Answering Form N-400 "Part 10" questions during the USCIS interview	224–225	165
The English Test: Speaking (Unit 11)	Answering Form N-400 "Part 10" questions during the USCIS interview	225	175
The English Test: Speaking (Unit 12)	Answering Form N-400 "Part 10" questions during the USCIS interview	225	189
The Reading Test*	Word list; Sample sentences	226	—
The Writing Test*	Word list; Sample sentences	227	—
100 Civics Test Questions*	Official civics questions and answers (English and Spanish)	228–237	—

* For end-of-course review and test preparation.

Voices of Freedom
WORKSHEETS

Writing Practice	193
Reading Practice	207
Civics Practice	221
Interview Practice	233
Worksheets Answer Key	279

These worksheets are fully coordinated with the units in the student book and with the English Test practice sections in the appendix. They are designed to offer valuable supplemental practice in class or at home. These materials may be reproduced for use only in conjunction with the *Voices of Freedom* instructional program.

WRITING PRACTICE

The Writing Practice worksheets offer students fundamental practice tracing and copying letters, numbers, words, and sentences. The worksheets for preparatory Units A and B provide students with practice writing the alphabet, numbers, months, and dates. The worksheets for Units 1–12 include all the words on the official USCIS writing vocabulary list. Even if students already have basic writing skills, they may benefit from this practice in order to assure that their formation of letters and their writing of words and sentences is legible and accurate. Lower-level students will find it helpful to complete a unit's tracing and copying practice before taking the unit test in the student book, which requires students to write sentences from dictation as on the USCIS exam.

READING PRACTICE

The Reading Practice worksheets provide a unique combination of reading and writing practice that prepares students for the reading portion of the USCIS exam. The first section of each worksheet contains columns of words that appear on the official USCIS reading vocabulary list. Students should practice reading these words aloud. The second section of each worksheet consists of sentences with blanks, which students complete by filling in the correct words from a choice-box. All the words students write are included on the official USCIS writing vocabulary list. And all the sentences that students complete in the worksheets for Units 1–12 are plausible sentences that might occur in the reading portion of the USCIS exam. Therefore, after students fill in the sentences, they should practice reading the sentences aloud.

CIVICS PRACTICE

The Civics Practice worksheets offer practice with all the USCIS civics test content, including principles of American democracy, the system of government, rights and responsibilities, U.S. history, geography, national symbols, and holidays.

INTERVIEW PRACTICE

The Interview Practice worksheets include a variety of resources that support the English Test practice sections on pages 213–225 of the student book. The specific pages and sections are indicated at the bottom of each worksheet.

FLASH CARDS: The *Voices of Freedom* Flash Card reproducibles provide 100 picture cards and accompanying word/sentence cards that highlight key vocabulary related to the USCIS interview. These include the actions involved in arriving at the office, checking in, being sworn in, and presenting identification. They also include the most important words and concepts related to the officer's questions concerning the applicant's Form N-400, including eligibility for citizenship, residence, family, employment, time outside the United States, and the very challenging "Part 10" questions—the "Have you ever . . . " questions that contain particularly difficult vocabulary about criminal offenses, beliefs, attachment to the Constitution, and other topics.

Some Flash Card sheets contain two columns with pairs of matching pictures and words/sentences. Other sheets contain three columns with trios of matching pictures, questions, and answers. The sheets can be reproduced for each student, cut up, and used in a variety of ways:

- With Flash Card sheets containing two columns, you or the student can glue each picture card and its accompanying word/ sentence card back-to-back to create a set of flash cards for vocabulary practice. With Flash Card sheets containing three columns, you can glue each picture card and its accompanying question card back-to-back, allowing students to practice the meaning of the questions and then answer them; or you can glue each question card and answer card back-to-back to create a set of flash cards with text only.

- With all Flash Card sheets (containing two or three columns), the cards with pictures and text can be cut up in order to play various memory and matching games.

Students can play individual games such as concentration by placing a set of cards face down and then turning over two (or three) cards at a time to try to match the cards.

Students can play a classroom matching game, in which you distribute the cards randomly to different students who then walk around the classroom to find the classmate(s) with their matching card(s).

MATCHING ACTIVITY WORKSHEETS: Matching activities offer students practice matching pictures and words/sentences, practice matching questions that have the same meaning (in order to recognize different ways the USCIS officer might ask a question), and practice matching questions and answers.

Name _____

Date _____

Trace and copy the alphabet.

Aa _____   Bb _____   Cc _____   Dd _____

Ee _____   Ff _____   Gg _____   Hh _____

Ii _____   Jj _____   Kk _____   Ll _____

Mm _____   Nn _____   Oo _____   Pp _____

Qq _____   Rr _____   Ss _____   Tt _____

Uu _____   Vv _____   Ww _____

Xx _____   Yy _____   Zz _____

Trace and copy the numbers.

0 _____   1 _____   2 _____   3 _____   4 _____

5 _____   6 _____   7 _____   8 _____   9 _____

10 _____   11 _____   12 _____   13 _____   14 _____

15 _____   16 _____   17 _____   18 _____   19 _____

© 2010 Pearson Education, Inc.
Duplication for classroom use is permitted.

Trace and copy the months.

January _____   July _____

February _____   August _____

March _____   September _____

April _____   October _____

May _____   November _____

June _____   December _____

Trace and copy the dates.

May 25, 2011 _____   05/25/2011 _____

June 3, 1987 _____   06/03/1987 _____

October 1, 2007 _____   10/01/2007 _____

July 4, 1776 _____   07/04/1776 _____

© 2010 Pearson Education, Inc.
Duplication for classroom use is permitted.

Voices of Freedom
Unit 1 Writing Practice

Name _____

Date _____

Trace and copy the words.

has _____   Alaska _____

is _____   Canada _____

largest _____   capital _____

Mexico _____   New York City _____

most _____   people _____

north _____   south _____

of _____   United States _____

the _____   Washington, D.C. _____

Trace and copy the sentences.

Canada is north of the United States.

_____

Alaska is the largest state in the United States.

_____

The capital of the United States is Washington, D.C.

_____

© 2010 Pearson Education, Inc.
Duplication for classroom use is permitted.

Name _____

Date _____

Trace and copy the words.

and _____   Alaska _____

blue _____   California _____

flag _____   capital _____

has _____   fifty _____

is _____   50 _____

most _____   largest _____

of _____   people _____

red _____   United States _____

state _____   Washington, D.C. _____

the _____   white _____

Trace and copy the sentences.

The United States has fifty states.

_____

The flag is red, white, and blue.

_____

The state of California has the most people.

© 2010 Pearson Education, Inc.
Duplication for classroom use is permitted.

Voices of Freedom
Unit 3 Writing Practice

Trace and copy the words.

in _____   Congress _____

is _____   President _____

lives _____   Senators _____

meet _____   United States _____

meets _____   Washington, D.C. _____

of _____   White House _____

the _____

Trace and copy the sentences.

The President lives in the White House.

_____

The Congress meets in Washington, D.C.

_____

United States Senators meet in Washington, D.C.

_____

© 2010 Pearson Education, Inc.
Duplication for classroom use is permitted.

VOICES of FREEDOM
Unit 4 Writing Practice

Name _____

Date _____

Trace and copy the words.

can _____   citizens _____

elect _____   Congress _____

fifty _____   November _____

50 _____   one hundred _____

for _____   100 _____

has _____   people _____

in _____   President _____

of _____   Senators _____

the _____   states _____

vote _____   United States _____

Trace and copy the sentences.

Citizens vote in November.

_____

The Congress has 100 Senators.

_____

People vote for President in November.

_____

© 2010 Pearson Education, Inc.
Duplication for classroom use is permitted.

Voices of Freedom
Unit 5 Writing Practice

Name _____

Date _____

Trace and copy the words.

we _____   elect _____

for _____   citizens _____

have _____   Congress _____

in _____   November _____

lives _____   people _____

of _____   President _____

the _____   United States _____

vote _____   White House _____

freedom of speech _____

Trace and copy the sentences.

We vote for the President in November.

_____

Citizens of the United States elect the Congress.

_____

People in the United States have freedom of speech.

_____

© 2010 Pearson Education, Inc.
Duplication for classroom use is permitted.

Name _____

Date _____

Trace and copy the words.

be _____   want _____

first _____   was _____

free _____   October _____

here _____   November _____

in _____   people _____

is _____   Thanksgiving _____

lived _____   Columbus Day _____

the _____   American Indians _____

to _____

Trace and copy the sentences.

Thanksgiving is in November.

_____

Columbus Day is in October.

_____

American Indians lived here first.

_____

© 2010 Pearson Education, Inc.
Duplication for classroom use is permitted.

Name _____

Date _____

Trace and copy the words.

be _____   first _____

free _____   capital _____

have _____   people _____

in _____   President _____

is _____   right _____

July _____   United States _____

of _____   Washington _____

the _____   Washington, D.C. _____

to _____   Independence Day _____

was _____

Trace and copy the sentences.

Independence Day is in July.

_____

People have the right to be free.

_____

Washington was the first President of the United States.

_____

© 2010 Pearson Education, Inc.
Duplication for classroom use is permitted.

Name _____

Date _____

Trace and copy the words.

first _____   capital _____

is _____   Delaware _____

of _____   dollar bill _____

on _____   President _____

state _____   Washington _____

the _____   United States _____

was _____   New York City _____

Father of Our Country _____

Trace and copy the sentences.

Delaware was the first state.

_____

The President on the dollar bill is Washington.

_____

The first United States capital was New York City.

_____

© 2010 Pearson Education, Inc.
Duplication for classroom use is permitted.

Name _____

Date _____

Trace and copy the words.

can _____   during _____

have _____   citizens _____

one _____   Civil War _____

was _____   February _____

vote _____   largest _____

right _____   President _____

state _____   Presidents' Day _____

people _____   United States _____

Alaska _____   Abraham Lincoln _____

freedom of speech _____

Trace and copy the sentences.

Presidents' Day is in February.

_____

Alaska is the largest state in the United States.

_____

Abraham Lincoln was President during the Civil War.

© 2010 Pearson Education, Inc.
Duplication for classroom use is permitted.

Voices of Freedom
Unit 10 Writing Practice

Name _____

Date _____

Trace and copy the words.

and _____

be _____

can _____

come _____

for _____

free _____

to _____

of _____

the _____

freedom of speech _____

have _____

vote _____

citizens _____

Labor Day _____

people _____

President _____

Senators _____

September _____

United States _____

Trace and copy the sentences.

Labor Day is in September.

_____

People in the United States have freedom of speech.

_____

Citizens can vote for the President of the United States.

_____

© 2010 Pearson Education, Inc.
Duplication for classroom use is permitted.

Name _____

Date _____

Trace and copy the words.

February _____   Presidents' Day _____

May _____   Memorial Day _____

June _____   Flag Day _____

July _____   Independence Day _____

September _____   Labor Day _____

October _____   Columbus Day _____

November _____   Thanksgiving _____

Trace and copy the sentences.

Flag Day is in June.

_____

Memorial Day is in May.

_____

Columbus Day is in October.

_____

Thanksgiving is in November.

_____

Independence Day is in July.

_____

© 2010 Pearson Education, Inc.
Duplication for classroom use is permitted.

Voices of Freedom
Unit 12 Writing Practice

Trace and copy the words.

and _____   citizens _____

can _____   Congress _____

for _____   elect _____

have _____   people _____

in _____   President _____

of _____   right _____

pay _____   taxes _____

the _____   United States _____

to _____   vote _____

Trace and copy the sentences.

People in the United States have to pay taxes.

_____

Citizens of the United States elect the President.

_____

Citizens can vote for the President and the Congress.

_____

© 2010 Pearson Education, Inc.
Duplication for classroom use is permitted.

A. Read these words.

a	the	what
is	for	last
in	name	first
of	city	state
be	want	citizen

B. Write the correct word. Then read the sentence.

be	for	first	is	United States

1. My name _____ Carlos Rivera.

2. My _____ name is Carlos.

3. I want to _____ a citizen.

4. I'm applying _____ citizenship.

5. California is in the _____ .

citizen	first	is	of	state

6. What _____ do you live in?

7. Where _____ Los Angeles?

8. What's your _____ name?

9. What's the name _____ your city?

10. Do you want to be a _____ ?

© 2010 Pearson Education, Inc.
Duplication for classroom use is permitted.

Voices of Freedom
Unit B Reading Practice

Name _____

Date _____

A. Read these words.

a	was	what
is	are	where
in	the	state
be	city	citizen
of	name	country

B. Write the correct word. Then read the sentence.

citizens	city	country	name	state

1. My _____ is Maria Lopez.

2. Houston is a _____ in Texas.

3. Texas is a _____.

4. My native _____ is Mexico.

5. My mother and father are _____.

are	citizens	country	first	is

6. What's your _____ name?

7. Where _____ you from?

8. What _____ your address?

9. What _____ are you from?

10. Are your mother and father _____ of the United States?

© 2010 Pearson Education, Inc.
Duplication for classroom use is permitted.

Voices of Freedom
Unit 1 Reading Practice

A. Read these words.

is	most	capital
of	what	country
has	north	largest
the	south	United States
city	people	

B. Write the correct word. Then read the sentence.

capital	has	largest	south	the

1. What country is _____ of the United States?

2. What is the _____ of the United States?

3. What is the _____ state in the United States?

4. What city _____ the most people?

5. What country is north of _____ United States?

is	north	of	people	state

6. What city in the United States has the most _____?

7. What is the capital _____ the United States?

8. What country _____ south of the United States?

9. What is the largest _____ in the United States?

10. What country is _____ of the United States?

© 2010 Pearson Education, Inc.
Duplication for classroom use is permitted.

VOICES of FREEDOM
Unit 2 Reading Practice

A. Read these words.

in	has	state	how many
is	have	colors	American flag
on	does	people	United States
are	most	country	Washington, D.C.
the	what	largest	

B. Write the correct word. Then read the sentence.

capital	flag	largest	people	states

1. What are the colors on the American _____?

2. How many _____ does the United States have?

3. What is the _____ state in the United States?

4. What is the _____ of the United States?

5. What state has the most _____ in the United States?

American	have	is	state	United States

6. What _____ Washington, D.C.?

7. What are the colors on the _____ flag?

8. How many states does the United States _____?

9. What _____ has the most people?

10. Where is the capital of the _____?

210

© 2010 Pearson Education, Inc.
Duplication for classroom use is permitted.

Voices of Freedom
Unit 3 Reading Practice

A. Read these words.

do	who	Congress
in	does	Senators
is	meet	President
of	lives	White House
the	where	United States

B. Write the correct word. Then read the sentence.

capital	President	Senators	United States	White House

1. Who is the President of the _____?

2. Where do United States _____ meet?

3. Where does the _____ live?

4. Who lives in the _____?

5. What is the _____ of the United States?

lives	meet	of	the	Washington, D.C.

6. Who _____ in the White House?

7. Where does the Congress _____?

8. What is _____?

9. Who is _____ President of the United States?

10. What is the capital _____ the United States?

© 2010 Pearson Education, Inc.
Duplication for classroom use is permitted.

Name _____

Date _____

A. Read these words.

do	the	vote	Senators
in	who	elects	President
of	when	people	government
can	does	citizens	how many
for	have	Congress	United States

B. Write the correct word. Then read the sentence.

citizens	elects	Senators	United States	vote

1. Who elects the _____ Senators?

2. When do people in the United States _____ for the President?

3. How many _____ does the Congress have?

4. When do _____ vote for the government?

5. Who _____ the President?

Congress	elects	people	the	vote

6. Who can _____ for the President of the United States?

7. When do _____ in the United States vote for Congress?

8. How many Senators does the _____ have?

9. Who _____ the Congress of the United States?

10. When do citizens vote for _____ President?

212

© 2010 Pearson Education, Inc.
Duplication for classroom use is permitted.

Voices of Freedom
Unit 5 Reading Practice

Name _____

Date _____

A. Read these words.

do	the	what	people
in	who	when	Congress
is	does	where	President
of	live	right	United States
for	vote	elects	Bill of Rights
one			

B. Write the correct word. Then read the sentence.

elects	one	people	President	votes

1. When do _____ in the United States vote for the Congress?

2. Where does the _____ of the United States live?

3. Who _____ the President?

4. What is _____ right in the Bill of Rights?

5. Who _____ for the Congress?

citizens	Congress	in	of	votes	White House

6. Who _____ for the President of the United States?

7. How many Senators are in the _____?

8. When do _____ elect the Congress?

9. Who lives in the _____?

10. What is one right _____ the Bill _____ Rights?

© 2010 Pearson Education, Inc.
Duplication for classroom use is permitted.

Voices of Freedom
Unit 6 Reading Practice

A. Read these words.

do	the	when	people
in	was	come	America
is	who	first	Columbus Day
to	why	lived	Thanksgiving

B. Write the correct word. Then read the sentence.

come	first	is	people	Thanksgiving

1. When is _____?

2. Why do _____ come to America?

3. Who lived in America _____?

4. When _____ Columbus Day?

5. When did you _____ to the United States?

Columbus Day	come	lived	want	was

6. When _____ the first Thanksgiving?

7. Why do people want to _____ here?

8. Who _____ in America first?

9. When is _____?

10. Do you _____ to be a citizen?

© 2010 Pearson Education, Inc.
Duplication for classroom use is permitted.

Name _____

Date _____

A. Read these words.

do	was	right	President
in	who	first	United States
is	what	people	Independence Day
of	when	capital	George Washington
the	have		

B. Write the correct word. Then read the sentence.

George Washington	is	President	right	United States

1. When _____ Independence Day?

2. Who was the first _____ of the United States?

3. What _____ do people in the United States have?

4. Who was _____?

5. What is the capital of the _____?

capital	have	Independence Day	President	was

6. Where does the _____ live?

7. Who _____ George Washington?

8. When is _____?

9. What right do people _____ in America?

10. What is the _____ of the United States?

215
© 2010 Pearson Education, Inc.
Duplication for classroom use is permitted.

A. Read these words.

in	was	city	dollar bill
is	who	first	United States
of	why	state	George Washington
on	what	capital	Father of Our Country
the			

B. Write the correct word. Then read the sentence.

Father of Our Country	first	state	United States	was

1. What _____ one of the first states?

2. Who was the first President of the _____?

3. What city was the _____ capital of the country?

4. Who is the _____?

5. What was the first _____ in the United States?

capital	city	dollar bill	George Washington	President

6. Who was the first _____ of the United States?

7. What _____ was the first capital of the United States?

8. Who was _____?

9. Who is on the _____?

10. What is the _____ of the United States?

216

© 2010 Pearson Education, Inc.
Duplication for classroom use is permitted.

Name _____

Date _____

A. Read these words.

in	the	vote	Bill of Rights
is	was	right	United States
can	who	state	Presidents' Day
for	what	largest	Abraham Lincoln
one	when	President	

B. Write the correct word. Then read the sentence.

is	President	right	state	vote

1. When _____ Presidents' Day?

2. What is one _____ people have?

3. When was Abraham Lincoln the _____?

4. What is the largest _____ in the country?

5. Who can citizens _____ for?

Abraham Lincoln	citizen	have	largest	Presidents' Day

6. What is the _____ state in the United States?

7. What right do people in the United States _____?

8. When is _____?

9. When can a _____ vote for President?

10. When was _____ the President?

217

© 2010 Pearson Education, Inc.
Duplication for classroom use is permitted.

Name _____

Date _____

A. Read these words.

do	for	when	right
in	one	come	people
is	the	have	citizens
of	who	name	Labor Day
to	why	vote	United States
can	what		

B. Write the correct word. Then read the sentence.

citizens	come	is	right	vote

1. When _____ Labor Day?

2. Why do people _____ to the United States?

3. Who can _____ of the United States vote for?

4. Name one _____ people have in the United States.

5. When do we _____ for the Congress?

Labor Day	Name	people	United States	vote

6. What is one right _____ have?

7. Who can _____ for President?

8. _____ the first President of the United States.

9. When is _____?

10. What can citizens of the _____ do?

218

© 2010 Pearson Education, Inc.
Duplication for classroom use is permitted.

A. Read these words.

in	July	September	Memorial Day
is	October	Flag Day	Columbus Day
when	November	Labor Day	Presidents' Day
May	February	Thanksgiving	Independence Day
June			

B. Write the correct word. Then read the sentence.

is	Labor Day	lives	Memorial	President

1. When _____ Thanksgiving?

2. When is _____ Day?

3. When is _____?

4. Who was the first _____ of the United States?

5. Who _____ in the White House?

Independence	is	of	Presidents' Day	Washington

6. When _____ Flag Day?

7. When is _____ Day?

8. When is _____?

9. Who is the Father _____ Our Country?

10. Who was George _____?

© 2010 Pearson Education, Inc.
Duplication for classroom use is permitted.

Name _____

Date _____

A. Read these words.

do	for	what	people
in	one	have	citizens
is	pay	vote	President
of	the	right	government
to	who	elects	United States
can			

B. Write the correct word. Then read the sentence.

citizens	pay	President	right	vote

1. When do we _____ for the Congress?

2. Who can _____ vote for?

3. Who elects the _____ of the United States?

4. Who has the _____ to vote?

5. Why do people in the United States have to _____ taxes?

can	elect	have	taxes	vote

6. When do citizens _____ the President?

7. Who _____ vote for the President?

8. Who has to pay _____?

9. When do citizens _____ for the Congress?

10. What do people _____ to pay to the government?

220

© 2010 Pearson Education, Inc.
Duplication for classroom use is permitted.

Name _____

Date _____

A. Match the question and the correct answer.

____ 1. What is the capital of the United States?

____ 2. Where is the Statue of Liberty?

____ 3. What ocean is on the East Coast of the United States?

____ 4. What ocean is on the West Coast of the United States?

____ 5. Name one state that borders Mexico.

____ 6. Name one state that borders Canada.

____ 7. Name one U.S. territory.

____ 8. Name one of the two longest rivers in the United States.

a. The Atlantic Ocean

b. Puerto Rico

c. Ohio

d. The Missouri River

e. Washington, D.C.

f. The Pacific Ocean

g. Texas

h. New York Harbor

B. Match the words.

____ 1. The Mississippi   a. Islands

____ 2. The Pacific   b. River

____ 3. The U.S. Virgin   c. Harbor

____ 4. New York   d. Ocean

© 2010 Pearson Education, Inc.
Duplication for classroom use is permitted.

Name _____

Date _____

A. Match the question and the correct answer.

____ 1. What are the colors on the American flag?

____ 2. Why does the flag have fifty stars?

____ 3. Why does the flag have thirteen stripes?

____ 4. What do we show loyalty to when we say the Pledge of Allegiance?

a. The flag

b. Red, white, and blue

c. Because there are fifty states

d. Because there were thirteen original colonies

B. Write the correct words. Then read the Pledge of Allegiance.

and	flag	for	one	to	United States

I pledge allegiance to the _____ [1]

of the _____ [2] of America,

and _____ [3] the republic

_____ [4] which it stands,

_____ [5] nation, under God,

indivisible, with liberty _____ [6] justice for all.

© 2010 Pearson Education, Inc.
Duplication for classroom use is permitted.

A. Match the people and the correct branch of the government.

_____ 1. The Supreme Court justices   **a.** The executive branch

_____ 2. The President and the Vice President   **b.** The legislative branch

_____ 3. Senators and representatives   **c.** The judicial branch

B. Write the correct word to complete the sentence.

checks	executive	judicial	legislative	President

1. The _____ branch makes the laws.

2. The _____ branch explains the laws.

3. The _____ branch enforces the laws.

4. A system of _____ and balances stops one branch of government from becoming too powerful.

5. The _____ is in charge of the executive branch.

C. Match the question and the correct answer.

_____ 1. Name one branch of the government.   **a.** Separation of powers

_____ 2. Who is in charge of the executive branch?   **b.** The legislative branch

_____ 3. What stops one branch of government from becoming too powerful?   **c.** The President

© 2010 Pearson Education, Inc.
Duplication for classroom use is permitted.

Voices of Freedom
Unit 4 Civics Practice

A. Match the question and the correct answer.

_____ 1. What are the two parts of the U.S. Congress?

_____ 2. Who does a U.S. Senator represent?

_____ 3. Why do some states have more representatives than other states?

_____ 4. Who signs bills to become laws?

_____ 5. If the President can no longer serve, who becomes President?

_____ 6. What are two Cabinet-level positions?

a. All the people of the state

b. Attorney General and Secretary of Labor

c. The Vice President

d. Because of the state's population

e. The Senate and House

f. The President

B. Match the question and the correct answer.

_____ 1. Who makes federal laws?

_____ 2. Who is the Commander-in-Chief of the military?

_____ 3. What is the highest court in the United States?

_____ 4. In what month do we vote for President?

_____ 5. What does the President's Cabinet do?

_____ 6. What does the judicial branch do?

a. It advises the President.

b. The Supreme Court

c. It explains laws.

d. Congress

e. November

f. The President

C. Write the correct number to answer the question.

1. The House of Representatives has how many voting members? _____

2. We elect a U.S. representative for how many years? _____

3. We elect a President for how many years? _____

4. How many U.S. Senators are there? _____

5. We elect a U.S. Senator for how many years? _____

© 2010 Pearson Education, Inc.
Duplication for classroom use is permitted.

Voices of Freedom
Unit 5 Civics Practice

Match the question and the correct answer.

_____ 1. What is the supreme law of the land?

_____ 2. What does the Constitution do?

_____ 3. What is the economic system in the United States?

_____ 4. What is an amendment?

_____ 5. What is one right or freedom from the First Amendment?

_____ 6. What is the "rule of law"?

_____ 7. What do we call the first ten amendments to the Constitution?

_____ 8. What is freedom of religion?

_____ 9. What is one power of the federal government?

_____ 10. What is one power of the states?

_____ 11. How many amendments does the Constitution have?

_____ 12. The idea of self-government is in the first three words of the Constitution. What are these words?

a. A capitalist economy

b. To print money

c. Everyone must follow the law.

d. It means you can practice any religion, or not practice a religion.

e. The Constitution

f. Twenty-seven

g. Freedom of speech

h. We the People

i. It sets up the government.

j. The Bill of Rights

k. To give a driver's license

l. A change to the Constitution

© 2010 Pearson Education, Inc.
Duplication for classroom use is permitted.

Voices of Freedom
Unit 6 Civics Practice

A. Match the question and the correct answer.

_____ 1. What is one reason colonists came to America?

_____ 2. Who lived in America before the Europeans arrived?

_____ 3. Name one American Indian tribe in the United States.

_____ 4. When is Thanksgiving?

_____ 5. When is Columbus Day?

a. October

b. November

c. American Indians

d. Religious freedom

e. Cherokee

B. Match the question and the correct answer.

_____ 1. Name one American Indian tribe in the United States.

_____ 2. What is one reason colonists came to America?

_____ 3. Who lived in America before the Europeans arrived?

a. Freedom

b. Native Americans

c. Navajo

C. Match the words that have the same meaning.

_____ 1. colonies

_____ 2. American Indians

_____ 3. colonists

a. People who came to live in America

b. Original thirteen states

c. Native Americans

D. Match the words to complete the reasons people came to America.

_____ 1. Practice their

_____ 2. Economic

_____ 3. Escape

_____ 4. Political

a. opportunity

b. persecution

c. liberty

d. religion

© 2010 Pearson Education, Inc.
Duplication for classroom use is permitted.

A. Match the question and the correct answer.

_____ 1. Who wrote the Declaration of Independence?

_____ 2. When was the Declaration of Independence adopted?

_____ 3. Why did the colonists fight the British?

_____ 4. What did the Declaration of Independence do?

_____ 5. When do we celebrate Independence Day?

_____ 6. What are two rights in the Declaration of Independence?

a. Life and liberty

b. Thomas Jefferson

c. It announced our independence from Great Britain.

d. Because of high taxes

e. July 4

f. July 4, 1776

B. Match to complete the reasons the colonists fought the British.

_____ 1. Because they didn't have

_____ 2. Because of high

_____ 3. Because of boarding and quartering

_____ 4. Because of taxation without

_____ 5. Because the British army stayed in their

a. houses

b. the British army

c. taxes

d. self-government

e. representation

© 2010 Pearson Education, Inc.
Duplication for classroom use is permitted.

Voices of Freedom
Unit 8 Civics Practice

Match the question and the correct answer.

_____ 1. Who is the *Father of Our Country?*

_____ 2. What is the supreme law of the land?

_____ 3. When was the Constitution written?

_____ 4. What is an amendment?

_____ 5. How many amendments does the Constitution have?

_____ 6. There were thirteen original states. Name three.

_____ 7. What happened at the Constitutional Convention?

_____ 8. What does the Constitution do?

_____ 9. What do we call the first ten amendments to the Constitution?

_____ 10. The Federalist Papers supported the passage of the U.S. Constitution. Name one of the writers.

_____ 11. What is one thing Benjamin Franklin is famous for?

_____ 12. What is one right or freedom from the First Amendment?

a. The Bill of Rights

b. 1787

c. New York, New Jersey, and Pennsylvania

d. George Washington

e. It defines the government.

f. He was a U.S. diplomat.

g. The Constitution

h. James Madison

i. 27

j. Freedom of the press

k. The Constitution was written.

l. A change to the Constitution

© 2010 Pearson Education, Inc.
Duplication for classroom use is permitted.

Voices of Freedom

Unit 9 Civics Practice

Match the question and the correct answer.

_____ 1. What is an amendment?

_____ 2. How many amendments does the Constitution have?

_____ 3. How old do citizens have to be to vote for President?

_____ 4. What is the name of the national anthem?

_____ 5. What group of people was taken to America and sold as slaves?

_____ 6. Name the U.S. war between the North and the South.

_____ 7. What do we call the first ten amendments to the Constitution?

_____ 8. Name one problem that led to the Civil War.

_____ 9. What territory did the United States buy from France in 1803?

_____ 10. What did the Emancipation Proclamation do?

_____ 11. What was one important thing that Abraham Lincoln did?

_____ 12. What is one right or freedom from the First Amendment?

_____ 13. What did Susan B. Anthony do?

_____ 14. There are four amendments to the Constitution about who can vote. Describe one of them.

a. The Bill of Rights

b. 18 and older

c. The Louisiana Territory

d. She fought for women's rights.

e. He saved the Union.

f. People from Africa

g. It freed the slaves.

h. An addition to the Constitution

i. Freedom of assembly

j. Any citizen can vote.

k. The Civil War

l. The *Star-Spangled Banner*

m. States' rights

n. 27

© 2010 Pearson Education, Inc.
Duplication for classroom use is permitted.

Voices of Freedom
Unit 10 Civics Practice

A. Match the question and the correct answer.

____ 1. Who was President during the Great Depression?

____ 2. What did Martin Luther King, Jr., do?

____ 3. Name one war fought by the United States in the 1900s.

____ 4. During the Cold War, what was the main concern of the United States?

____ 5. Who was President during World War I?

____ 6. Who did the United States fight in World War II?

a. Communism

b. The Vietnam War

c. Japan, Germany, and Italy

d. He fought for civil rights.

e. Woodrow Wilson

f. Franklin Roosevelt

B. Match the question and the correct answer.

____ 1. Before he was President, Eisenhower was a general. What war was he in?

____ 2. What movement tried to end racial discrimination?

____ 3. Who was President during World War II?

____ 4. What did Martin Luther King, Jr., do?

____ 5. What major event happened on September 11, 2001, in the United States?

a. The civil rights movement

b. He worked for equality for all Americans.

c. World War II

d. Terrorists attacked the United States.

e. Franklin Roosevelt

© 2010 Pearson Education, Inc.
Duplication for classroom use is permitted.

Name _____

Date _____

Match the question and the correct answer.

_____ 1. Who was the first President?

_____ 2. What are the two major political parties in the United States?

_____ 3. When do we celebrate Independence Day?

_____ 4. Who wrote the Declaration of Independence?

_____ 5. The Federalist Papers supported the passage of the U.S. Constitution. Name one of the writers.

_____ 6. Who was President during World War I?

_____ 7. Before he was President, Eisenhower was a general. What war was he in?

_____ 8. What did the Emancipation Proclamation do?

_____ 9. What was one important thing that Abraham Lincoln did?

_____ 10. Name two national U.S. holidays.

_____ 11. What territory did the United States buy from France in 1803?

_____ 12. What major event happened on September 11, 2001, in the United States?

_____ 13. Who was President during World War II?

a. Alexander Hamilton

b. It freed slaves in most Southern states.

c. World War II

d. George Washington

e. Louisiana

f. Memorial Day and Veterans Day

g. Franklin Roosevelt

h. Terrorists attacked the United States.

i. Democratic and Republican

j. Woodrow Wilson

k. Thomas Jefferson

l. He preserved the Union.

m. July 4

© 2010 Pearson Education, Inc.
Duplication for classroom use is permitted.

A. Match the question and the correct answer.

____ 1. How old do citizens have to be to vote for President?

____ 2. What are two rights of everyone living in the United States?

____ 3. What are the two major political parties in the United States?

____ 4. Name one right only for United States citizens.

____ 5. What is one responsibility that is only for United States citizens?

____ 6. What are two ways that Americans can participate in their democracy?

a. Democratic and Republican

b. Join a civic group and give an elected official your opinion on an issue.

c. Serve on a jury.

d. 18 and older

e. Freedom of expression and the right to bear arms

f. The right to vote in a federal election

B. Match the question and the correct answer.

____ 1. Name one right only for United States citizens.

____ 2. When is the last day you can send in federal income tax forms?

____ 3. When must all men register for the Selective Service?

____ 4. What is one promise you make when you become a United States citizen?

____ 5. What are two rights of everyone living in the United States?

a. April 15

b. Freedom of speech and freedom of worship

c. The right to run for federal office

d. At age 18

e. Give up loyalty to other countries.

© 2010 Pearson Education, Inc.
Duplication for classroom use is permitted.

Show your appointment letter to the security guard.

Put your bag on the conveyor belt.

Put any metal objects in the tray.

Step through the metal detector.

Check in at the reception counter.

Take a seat in the waiting area.

© 2010 Pearson Education, Inc.
Duplication for classroom use is permitted.

Voices of Freedom
Interview Practice 2: Matching

Match the picture and the correct sentence.

_____ 1.

a. Put any metal objects in the tray.

_____ 2.

b. Take a seat in the waiting area.

_____ 3.

c. Check in at the reception counter.

_____ 4.

d. Step through the metal detector.

_____ 5.

e. Show your appointment letter to the security guard.

_____ 6.

f. Put your bag on the conveyor belt.

© 2010 Pearson Education, Inc.
Duplication for classroom use is permitted.

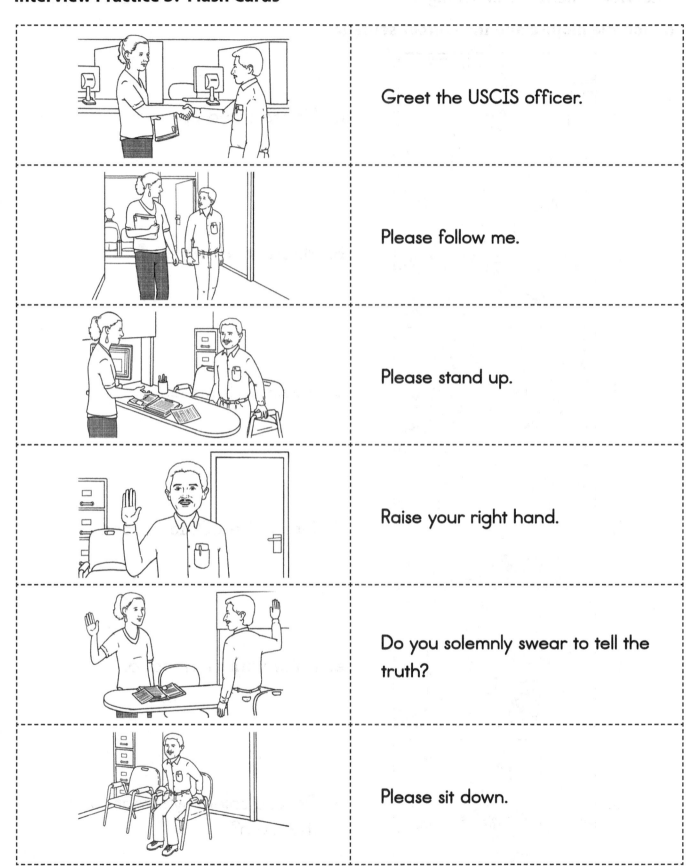

Greet the USCIS officer.

Please follow me.

Please stand up.

Raise your right hand.

Do you solemnly swear to tell the truth?

Please sit down.

© 2010 Pearson Education, Inc.
Duplication for classroom use is permitted.

Voices of Freedom
Interview Practice 4: Matching

Name _____

Date _____

Match the picture and the correct sentence.

_____ 1.

a. Please stand up.

_____ 2.

b. Please sit down.

_____ 3.

c. Please follow me.

_____ 4.

d. Greet the USCIS officer.

_____ 5.

e. Raise your right hand.

_____ 6.

f. Do you solemnly swear to tell the truth?

© 2010 Pearson Education, Inc.
Duplication for classroom use is permitted.

Please show me your permanent resident card.

Please show me your passport.

Please show me your driver's license.

Please show me your state identification card.

Do you have two passport-size photographs?

© 2010 Pearson Education, Inc.
Duplication for classroom use is permitted.

Name _____

Date _____

Match the picture and the correct sentence.

_____ 1.

a. Please show me your passport.

_____ 2.

b. Do you have two passport-size photographs?

_____ 3.

c. Please show me your permanent resident card.

_____ 4.

d. Please show me your state identification card.

_____ 5.

e. Please show me your driver's license.

© 2010 Pearson Education, Inc.
Duplication for classroom use is permitted.

Carlos Manuel **Rivera**	What's your family name?* (*last name / surname)
Carlos Manuel Rivera	What's your first name?* (*given name)
Carlos **Manuel** Rivera	What's your middle name?
Carlos Manuel Rivera	What's your full name?
Carlos Manuel Rivera	Print your name.
Carlos M. Rivera SIGNATURE	Sign your name.

© 2010 Pearson Education, Inc.
Duplication for classroom use is permitted.

Voices of Freedom
Interview Practice 8: Matching

Name _____

Date _____

Match the picture and the correct sentence.

_____ 1. | Carlos Manuel Rivera |

a. What's your family name?

_____ 2. | Carlos *Manuel Rivera* |

b. Sign your name.

_____ 3. | *Carlos Manuel* Rivera |

c. What's your full name?

_____ 4. | Carlos Manuel Rivera |

d. What's your middle name?

_____ 5. | Carlos **Manuel** *Rivera* |

e. What's your first name?

_____ 6. | *Carlos M. Rivera*
SIGNATURE |

f. Print your name.

© 2010 Pearson Education, Inc.
Duplication for classroom use is permitted.

	husband
	wife
	father
	mother
	son
	daughter

© 2010 Pearson Education, Inc.
Duplication for classroom use is permitted.

Name _____

Date _____

Match the picture and the correct word.

_____ 1.

a. son

_____ 2.

b. mother

_____ 3.

c. husband

_____ 4.

d. daughter

_____ 5.

e. father

_____ 6.

f. wife

© 2010 Pearson Education, Inc.
Duplication for classroom use is permitted.

Voices *of* Freedom
Interview Practice 11: Flash Cards

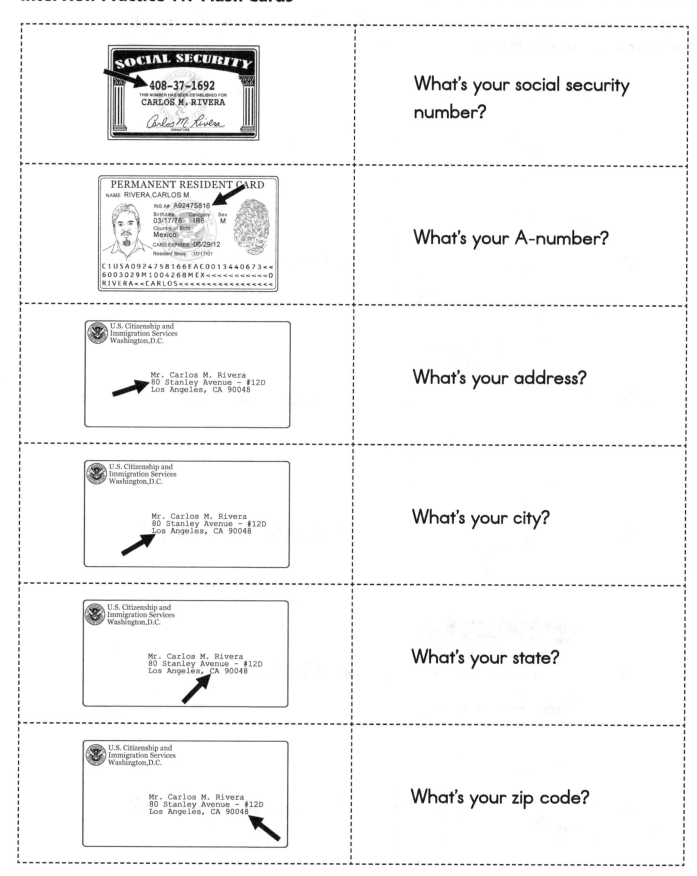

SOCIAL SECURITY
408-37-1692
THIS NUMBER HAS BEEN ESTABLISHED FOR
CARLOS M. RIVERA
Carlos M. Rivera
SIGNATURE

What's your social security number?

PERMANENT RESIDENT CARD
NAME RIVERA,CARLOS M.
INS A# A92475816
Birthdate Category Sex
03/17/76   IR6   M
Country of Birth
Mexico
CARD EXPIRES 06/29/12
Resident Since 11/17/01
C1USA0924758166EAC0013440673<<
6003029M1004268MEX<<<<<<<<<<0
RIVERA<<CARLOS<<<<<<<<<<<<<<<

What's your A-number?

U.S. Citizenship and
Immigration Services
Washington,D.C.

Mr. Carlos M. Rivera
80 Stanley Avenue - #12D
Los Angeles, CA 90048

What's your address?

U.S. Citizenship and
Immigration Services
Washington,D.C.

Mr. Carlos M. Rivera
80 Stanley Avenue - #12D
Los Angeles, CA 90048

What's your city?

U.S. Citizenship and
Immigration Services
Washington,D.C.

Mr. Carlos M. Rivera
80 Stanley Avenue - #12D
Los Angeles, CA 90048

What's your state?

U.S. Citizenship and
Immigration Services
Washington,D.C.

Mr. Carlos M. Rivera
80 Stanley Avenue - #12D
Los Angeles, CA 90048

What's your zip code?

© 2010 Pearson Education, Inc.
Duplication for classroom use is permitted.

Name _____

Date _____

Match the picture and the correct question. Then answer the question with your own information.

_____ 1.
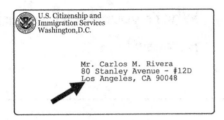

a. What's your social security number?

_____ 2.
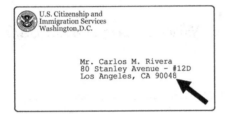

b. What's your A-number?

_____ 3.

c. What's your city?

_____ 4.

d. What's your address?

_____ 5.

e. What's your state?

_____ 6.
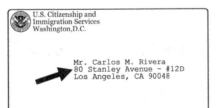

f. What's your zip code?

© 2010 Pearson Education, Inc.
Duplication for classroom use is permitted.

RIVERA Carlos M   80 Stanley Av
Los Angeles 213 257-9108

What's your phone number?

From: ascis@dhs.gov
Date: Tuesday, June 16, 2009
To: cmrivera1976@ail.com
Subject: Application

What's your email address?

05/ 04 /1979

What's your date of birth?*

(*birth date)

May

05/ 04 /1979

In what month were you born?

1979

05/ 04 /1979

In what year were you born?

© 2010 Pearson Education, Inc.
Duplication for classroom use is permitted.

Voices of Freedom
Interview Practice 14: Matching

Match the picture and the correct question. Then answer the question with your own information.

_____ 1. | 05 / 04 / 1979 | **a.** In what year were you born?

_____ 2.   **b.** What's your email address?

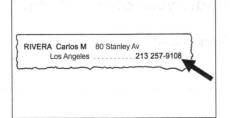

_____ 3.   **c.** In what month were you born?

_____ 4.   **d.** What's your date of birth?

_____ 5.   **e.** What's your phone number?

© 2010 Pearson Education, Inc.
Duplication for classroom use is permitted.

Mexico	**What's your country of birth?*** (*Where were you born?)
Mexican	**What's your nationality?*** (*What's your country of nationality?)
	Are you single?
	Are you married?
	Are you divorced?
	Are you widowed?

© 2010 Pearson Education, Inc.
Duplication for classroom use is permitted.

Voices of Freedom

Interview Practice 16: Matching

Match the picture and the correct question. Then answer the question with your own information.

_____ 1.

a. Are you divorced?

_____ 2.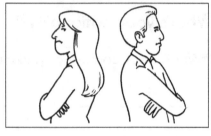

b. Are you widowed?

_____ 3.
Mexican

c. Are you married?

_____ 4.

d. Are you single?

_____ 5.
Mexico

e. What's your nationality?

_____ 6.

f. What's your country of birth?

© 2010 Pearson Education, Inc.
Duplication for classroom use is permitted.

Voices of Freedom

Interview Practice 17: Flash Cards

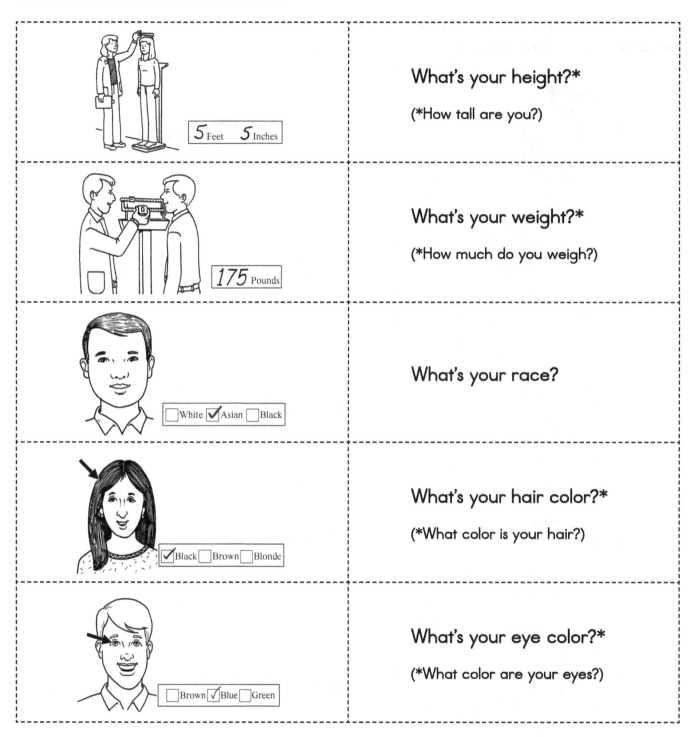

5 Feet 5 Inches	**What's your height?*** (*How tall are you?)
175 Pounds	**What's your weight?*** (*How much do you weigh?)
☐ White ☑ Asian ☐ Black	**What's your race?**
☑ Black ☐ Brown ☐ Blonde	**What's your hair color?*** (*What color is your hair?)
☐ Brown ☑ Blue ☐ Green	**What's your eye color?*** (*What color are your eyes?)

© 2010 Pearson Education, Inc.
Duplication for classroom use is permitted.

Voices of Freedom
Interview Practice 18: Matching

Name _____

Date _____

Match the picture and the correct question. Then answer the question with your own information.

_____ 1.

    a. What's your race?

_____ 2.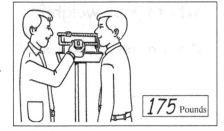

    b. What color are your eyes?

_____ 3.

    c. What's your weight?

_____ 4.

    d. How tall are you?

_____ 5.

    e. What's your hair color?

© 2010 Pearson Education, Inc.
Duplication for classroom use is permitted.

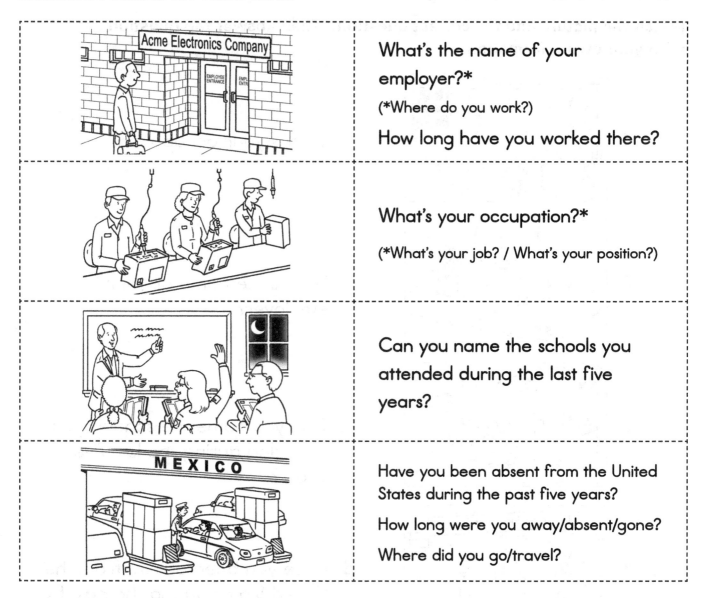

What's the name of your employer?*

(*Where do you work?)

How long have you worked there?

What's your occupation?*

(*What's your job? / What's your position?)

Can you name the schools you attended during the last five years?

Have you been absent from the United States during the past five years?

How long were you away/absent/gone?

Where did you go/travel?

© 2010 Pearson Education, Inc.
Duplication for classroom use is permitted.

Name _____

Date _____

Match the picture and the correct question. Then answer the question with your own information.

_____ 1.

a. What's your occupation?

_____ 2.

b. What's the name of your employer?

_____ 3.

c. Can you name the schools you attended during the last five years?

_____ 4.

d. Have you been absent from the United States during the past five years?

© 2010 Pearson Education, Inc.
Duplication for classroom use is permitted.

Match the questions that have the same meaning. Then answer the questions.

_____ 1. Are you employed?

_____ 2. What's your position?

_____ 3. What was your previous address?

_____ 4. When was your most recent trip outside the United States?

_____ 5. Have you been absent from the United States during the past five years?

_____ 6. What was the reason for the trip?

_____ 7. How long were you away?

a. Why did you travel?

b. What's your occupation?

c. Where did you live before where you live now?

d. Have you spent time outside the United States during the past five years?

e. When did you last leave the country?

f. How long were you absent?

g. Do you work now?

© 2010 Pearson Education, Inc.
Duplication for classroom use is permitted.

Voices of Freedom
Interview Practice 22: Matching

Name _____

Date _____

Match the questions that have the same meaning.

_____ 1. Do you understand?

_____ 2. Are you currently married?

_____ 3. When were you married?

_____ 4. Where do you live?

_____ 5. Could you please say the question another way?

_____ 6. Would you like me to explain that?

_____ 7. How many children do you have?

_____ 8. When were they born?

a. How many children have you had?

b. What's your current address?

c. Could you please ask that again using different words?

d. Should I explain that for you?

e. Do you have a spouse?

f. What are their dates of birth?

g. Do you know what that means?

h. What's the date of your marriage?

© 2010 Pearson Education, Inc.
Duplication for classroom use is permitted.

	Have you ever claimed to be a U.S. citizen?	No. I've never told anyone I am a U.S. citizen.
	Have you ever registered to vote in any federal, state, or local election in the United States?	No. I've never registered to vote in this country. I want to be a citizen so I can vote in the future.
	Have you ever voted in any federal, state, or local election in the United States?	No. I've never voted in an election. I want to be a citizen so I can vote in the future.
	Since becoming a lawful permanent resident, have you ever failed to file a required federal, state, or local tax return?	No. I always send in all the required tax forms.
	Do you owe any federal, state, or local taxes that are overdue?	No. I always pay my taxes on time.
	Do you have any title of nobility in any foreign country?	No. I was just a regular person in my country—not a prince/princess or anything like that.

© 2010 Pearson Education, Inc.
Duplication for classroom use is permitted.

Voices of Freedom
Interview Practice 24: Matching

Match the question and the correct answer.

_____ 1. Have you ever voted in any federal, state, or local election in the United States?

a. No. I always pay my taxes on time.

_____ 2. Do you owe any federal, state, or local taxes that are overdue?

b. No. I've never registered to vote in this country. I want to be a citizen so I can vote in the future.

_____ 3. Do you have any title of nobility in any foreign country?

c. No. I always send in all the required tax forms.

_____ 4. Have you ever registered to vote in any federal, state, or local election in the United States?

d. No. I've never told anyone I am a U.S. citizen.

_____ 5. Have you ever claimed to be a U.S. citizen?

e. No. I've never voted in an election. I want to be a citizen so I can vote in the future.

_____ 6. Since becoming a lawful permanent resident, have you ever failed to file a required federal, state, or local tax return?

f. No. I was just a regular person in my country—not a prince / princess or anything like that.

© 2010 Pearson Education, Inc.
Duplication for classroom use is permitted.

Voices of Freedom
Interview Practice 25: Matching

Name _____

Date _____

Match the picture and the correct question. Then answer the question with your own information.

_____ 1.

a. Have you ever registered to vote in any federal, state, or local election in the United States?

_____ 2.

b. Have you ever claimed to be a U.S. citizen?

_____ 3.

c. Do you have any title of nobility in any foreign country?

_____ 4.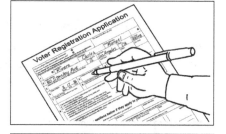

d. Do you owe any federal, state, or local taxes that are overdue?

_____ 5.

e. Have you ever voted in any federal, state, or local election in the United States?

_____ 6.

f. Since becoming a lawful permanent resident, have you ever failed to file a required federal, state, or local tax return?

© 2010 Pearson Education, Inc.
Duplication for classroom use is permitted.

	Have you ever been declared legally incompetent or been confined to a mental institution within the last five years?	No. I've never had mental health problems.
	Have you ever been a member of or associated with any organization, association, fund, foundation, party, club, society, or similar group in the United States or in any other place?	Yes. I'm a member of the parents' association in my children's school.
	Have you ever been a member of or in any way associated with the Communist Party?	No. I am not a Communist, and I never was a Communist. I don't believe in Communism.
	Have you ever been a member of or in any way associated with any other totalitarian party?	No. I believe that dictators are bad and that people in all countries should have rights and freedoms.
	Have you ever been a member of or in any way associated with a terrorist organization?	No. I believe that terrorism is very bad.
	Have you ever advocated the overthrow of any government by force or violence?	No. I think violence is bad. I believe that government should change peacefully through elections.

© 2010 Pearson Education, Inc.
Duplication for classroom use is permitted.

Voices of Freedom

Interview Practice 27: Matching

Match the question and the correct answer.

_____ 1. Have you ever been a member of or in any way associated with the Communist Party?

_____ 2. Have you ever been declared legally incompetent or been confined to a mental institution within the last five years?

_____ 3. Have you ever been a member of or in any way associated with a terrorist organization?

_____ 4. Have you ever advocated the overthrow of any government by force or violence?

_____ 5. Have you ever been a member of or in any way associated with any other totalitarian party?

_____ 6. Have you ever been a member of or associated with any organization, association, fund, foundation, party, club, society, or similar group in the United States or in any other place?

a. No. I believe that terrorism is very bad.

b. No. I believe that dictators are bad and that people in all countries should have rights and freedoms.

c. Yes. I'm a member of the parents' association in my children's school.

d. No. I've never had mental health problems.

e. No. I am not a Communist, and I never was a Communist. I don't believe in Communism.

f. No. I think violence is bad. I believe that government should change peacefully through elections.

© 2010 Pearson Education, Inc.
Duplication for classroom use is permitted.

Name _____

Date _____

**Match the picture and the correct question. Then answer the question
with your own information.**

 ____ 1.

 ____ 2.

 ____ 3.

 ____ 4.

 ____ 5.

 ____ 6.

a. Have you ever been declared legally incompetent or been confined to a mental institution within the last five years?

b. Have you ever been a member of or associated with any organization, association, fund, foundation, party, club, society, or similar group in the United States or in any other place?

c. Have you ever been a member of or in any way associated with a terrorist organization?

d. Have you ever been a member of or in any way associated with any other totalitarian party?

e. Have you ever been a member of or in any way associated with the Communist Party?

f. Have you ever advocated the overthrow of any government by force or violence?

© 2010 Pearson Education, Inc.
Duplication for classroom use is permitted.

	Have you ever persecuted any person because of race, religion, national origin, membership in a particular social group, or political opinion?	No. I've never hurt any person in this way. I believe that people of all races, religions, and groups should have the same rights.
	Between March 23, 1933, and May 8, 1945, did you work for or associate in any way with the Nazi government of Germany?	No. I was never a Nazi. I had no connection with that government.
	Have you ever called yourself a "nonresident" on a federal, state, or local tax return?	No. When I file my tax returns, I file as a resident.
	Have you ever failed to file a federal, state, or local tax return because you considered yourself to be a nonresident?	No. I have always sent in all required tax forms.
	Have you ever committed a crime or offense for which you were not arrested?	No. I've never done anything that is against the law.
	Have you ever been arrested, cited, or detained by any law enforcement officer for any reason?	No. I've never had a problem with a police officer or other officer. Yes. _____* (*A police officer game me a ticket for _____. / I was arrested for _____.)

© 2010 Pearson Education, Inc.
Duplication for classroom use is permitted.

Voices of Freedom
Interview Practice 30: Matching

Match the question and the correct answer.

_____ 1. Have you ever called yourself a "nonresident" on a federal, state, or local tax return?

a. No. I was never a Nazi. I had no connection with that government.

_____ 2. Have you ever committed a crime or offense for which you were not arrested?

b. No. I've never hurt any person in this way. I believe that people of all races, religions, and groups should have the same rights.

_____ 3. Between March 23, 1933, and May 8, 1945, did you work for or associate in any way with the Nazi government of Germany?

c. Yes. A police officer gave me a ticket for not wearing my seat belt while driving.

_____ 4. Have you ever failed to file a federal, state, or local tax return because you considered yourself to be a nonresident?

d. No. When I file my tax returns, I file as a resident.

_____ 5. Have you ever been arrested, cited, or detained by any law enforcement officer for any reason?

e. No. I have always sent in all required tax forms.

_____ 6. Have you ever persecuted any person because of race, religion, national origin, membership in a particular social group, or political opinion?

f. No. I've never done anything that is against the law.

© 2010 Pearson Education, Inc.
Duplication for classroom use is permitted.

Match the picture and the correct question. Then answer the question with your own information.

_____ 1.

_____ 2.

_____ 3.

_____ 4.

_____ 5.

_____ 6.

a. Between March 23, 1933, and May 8, 1945, did you work for or associate in any way with the Nazi government of Germany?

b. Have you ever failed to file a federal, state, or local tax return because you considered yourself to be a nonresident?

c. Have you ever called yourself a "nonresident" on a federal, state, or local tax return?

d. Have you ever persecuted any person because of race, religion, national origin, membership in a particular social group, or political opinion?

e. Have you ever been arrested, cited, or detained by any law enforcement officer for any reason?

f. Have you ever committed a crime or offense for which you were not arrested?

© 2010 Pearson Education, Inc.
Duplication for classroom use is permitted.

	Have you ever been charged with committing any crime or offense?	No. I've never been accused of doing anything against the law.
	Have you ever been convicted of a crime or offense?	No. I've never been found guilty of doing anything against the law.
	Have you ever been placed in an alternative sentencing or a rehabilitative program?	No. I've never done anything against the law, so I've never been placed in a program like this.
	Have you ever received a suspended sentence?	No. I've never done anything against the law, so I've never received a suspended sentence.
	Have you ever been placed on probation?	No. I've never done anything against the law, so I've never been placed on probation.
	Have you ever been paroled?	No. I've never done anything against the law, so I've never been paroled.

© 2010 Pearson Education, Inc.
Duplication for classroom use is permitted.

Name _____

Date _____

Match the question and the correct answer.

_____ 1. Have you ever been charged with committing any crime or offense?

a. No. I've never done anything against the law, so I've never received a suspended sentence.

_____ 2. Have you ever been convicted of a crime or offense?

b. No. I've never done anything against the law, so I've never been placed in a program like this.

_____ 3. Have you ever received a suspended sentence?

c. No. I've never done anything against the law, so I've never been paroled.

_____ 4. Have you ever been placed on probation?

d. No. I've never been found guilty of doing anything against the law.

_____ 5. Have you ever been paroled?

e. No. I've never been accused of doing anything against the law.

_____ 6. Have you ever been placed in an alternative sentencing or a rehabilitative program?

f. No. I've never done anything against the law, so I've never been placed on probation.

© 2010 Pearson Education, Inc.
Duplication for classroom use is permitted.

Voices of Freedom
Interview Practice 34: Matching

Name _____

Date _____

Match the picture and the correct question. Then answer the question with your own information.

_____ 1.

a. Have you ever been charged with committing any crime or offense?

_____ 2.

b. Have you ever been convicted of a crime or offense?

_____ 3.

c. Have you ever been placed on probation?

_____ 4.

d. Have you ever been placed in an alternative sentencing or a rehabilitative program?

_____ 5.

e. Have you ever been paroled?

_____ 6.

f. Have you ever received a suspended sentence?

© 2010 Pearson Education, Inc.
Duplication for classroom use is permitted.

	Have you ever been in jail or prison?	No. I've never been found guilty of anything, so I've never been in jail or prison.
	Have you ever been a habitual drunkard?	No. I don't drink alcohol. No. I rarely drink alcohol.
	Have you ever been a prostitute, or procured anyone for prostitution?	No. I've never sold my body or paid for sex.
	Have you ever sold or smuggled controlled substances, illegal drugs, or narcotics?	No. I've never sold any illegal drugs or brought them into the country.
	Have you ever been married to more than one person at the same time?	No. I've never had more than one wife/husband at a time. No. I've never been married to anyone.
	Have you ever helped anyone enter or try to enter the United States illegally?	No. I've never helped anyone come into the country without permission.

© 2010 Pearson Education, Inc.
Duplication for classroom use is permitted.

Voices of Freedom

Interview Practice 36: Matching

Name _____

Date _____

Match the question and the correct answer.

_____ 1. Have you ever been a habitual drunkard?

    a. No. I've never been found guilty of anything, so I've never been in jail or prison.

_____ 2. Have you ever helped anyone enter or try to enter the United States illegally?

    b. No. I've never had more than one wife/husband at a time.

_____ 3. Have you ever been in jail or prison?

    c. No. I don't drink alcohol.

_____ 4. Have you ever sold or smuggled controlled substances, illegal drugs, or narcotics?

    d. No. I've never sold my body or paid for sex.

_____ 5. Have you ever been married to more than one person at the same time?

    e. No. I've never helped anyone come into the country without permission.

_____ 6. Have you ever been a prostitute, or procured anyone for prostitution?

    f. No. I've never sold any illegal drugs or brought them into the country.

© 2010 Pearson Education, Inc.
Duplication for classroom use is permitted.

Match the picture and the correct question. Then answer the question with your own information.

_____ 1.

a. Have you ever helped anyone enter or try to enter the United States illegally?

_____ 2.

b. Have you ever been in jail or prison?

_____ 3.

c. Have you ever been a habitual drunkard?

_____ 4.

d. Have you ever been married to more than one person at the same time?

_____ 5.

e. Have you ever sold or smuggled controlled substances, illegal drugs, or narcotics?

_____ 6.

f. Have you ever been a prostitute, or procured anyone for prostitution?

© 2010 Pearson Education, Inc.
Duplication for classroom use is permitted.

	Have you ever gambled illegally or received income from illegal gambling?	No. I've never gambled money in a way that's against the law.
	Have you ever failed to support your dependents or pay alimony?	No. I always provide money to my children and former wife.
	Have you ever given false or misleading information to any U.S. government official while applying for any immigration benefit or to prevent deportation, exclusion, or removal?	No. I have never lied while applying for any immigration benefit or to prevent being ordered to leave the United States.
	Have you ever lied to any U.S. government official to gain entry or admission into the United States?	No. I have always told the truth when entering the United States.
	Have you ever been removed, excluded, or deported from the United States?	No. I have never been ordered to leave the United States.

© 2010 Pearson Education, Inc.
Duplication for classroom use is permitted.

Name _____

Date _____

Match the question and the correct answer.

_____ 1. Have you ever failed to support your dependents or pay alimony?

a. No. I've never gambled money in a way that's against the law.

_____ 2. Have you ever lied to any U.S. government official to gain entry or admission into the United States?

b. No. I have never been ordered to leave the United States.

_____ 3. Have you ever gambled illegally or received income from illegal gambling?

c. No. I always provide money to my children and former wife.

_____ 4. Have you ever been removed, excluded, or deported from the United States?

d. No. I have never lied while applying for any immigration benefit or to prevent being ordered to leave the United States.

_____ 5. Have you ever given false or misleading information to any U.S. government official while applying for any immigration benefit or to prevent deportation, exclusion, or removal?

e. No. I have always told the truth when entering the United States.

© 2010 Pearson Education, Inc.
Duplication for classroom use is permitted.

Match the picture and the correct question. Then answer the question with your own information.

_____ 1.

a. Have you ever lied to any U.S. government official to gain entry or admission into the United States?

_____ 2.

b. Have you ever gambled illegally or received income from illegal gambling?

_____ 3.

c. Have you ever been removed, excluded, or deported from the United States?

_____ 4.

d. Have you ever given false or misleading information to any U.S. government official while applying for any immigration benefit or to prevent deportation, exclusion, or removal?

_____ 5.

e. Have you ever failed to support your dependents or pay alimony?

© 2010 Pearson Education, Inc.
Duplication for classroom use is permitted.

	Have you ever served in the U.S. Armed Forces?	Yes. I have served in the U.S. military. No. I haven't served in the U.S. military.
	Have you ever left the United States to avoid being drafted into the U.S. Armed Forces?	No. I have never left the country to avoid military service.
	Have you ever applied for any kind of exemption from military service in the U.S. Armed Forces?	No. I have never asked to be excused from military service.
	Have you ever deserted from the U.S. Armed Forces?	No. I never ran away during my military service.
	Have you registered with the Selective Service System?	Yes. I registered for military service _____.* (*online / at the post office / at my high school) No. I wasn't a resident of the United States when I was between the ages of 18 and 26.

© 2010 Pearson Education, Inc.
Duplication for classroom use is permitted.

Voices of Freedom

Interview Practice 42: Matching

Match the question and the correct answer.

_____ 1. Have you registered with the Selective Service System?

_____ 2. Have you ever served in the U.S. Armed Forces?

_____ 3. Have you ever applied for any kind of exemption from military service in the U.S. Armed Forces?

_____ 4. Have you ever deserted from the U.S. Armed Forces?

_____ 5. Have you ever left the United States to avoid being drafted into the U.S. Armed Forces?

a. No. I have never asked to be excused from military service.

b. No. I have never left the country to avoid military service.

c. Yes. I have served in the U.S. military.

d. Yes. I registered for military service at the post office.

e. No. I never ran away during my military service.

© 2010 Pearson Education, Inc.
Duplication for classroom use is permitted.

Voices of Freedom

Interview Practice 43: Matching

Name _____

Date _____

Match the picture and the correct question. Then answer the question with your own information.

_____ 1.

a. Have you ever deserted from the U.S. Armed Forces?

_____ 2.

b. Have you ever left the United States to avoid being drafted into the U.S. Armed Forces?

_____ 3.

c. Have you ever applied for any kind of exemption from military service in the U.S. Armed Forces?

_____ 4.

d. Have you ever served in the U.S. Armed Forces?

_____ 5.

e. Have you registered with the Selective Service System?

© 2010 Pearson Education, Inc.
Duplication for classroom use is permitted.

VOICES of FREEDOM
Interview Practice 44: Flash Cards

	Do you support the Constitution and form of government of the United States?	Yes. I believe in the Constitution as the supreme law of the land, and I believe in our form of government.
"I hereby declare ..."	Are you willing to take the full Oath of Allegiance to the United States?	Yes. I am ready to promise to be loyal only to the United States, to support the Constitution and U.S. laws, and to fight or work for the United States if needed.
	If the law requires it, are you willing to bear arms on behalf of the United States?	Yes. I am willing to serve in the U.S. military and use a weapon.
	If the law requires it, are you willing to perform noncombatant services in the U.S. Armed Forces?	Yes. I am willing to serve in the U.S. military and not use a weapon.
	If the law requires it, are you willing to perform work of national importance under civilian direction?	Yes. I am willing to do work to help my community, my state, or the country during an emergency.

© 2010 Pearson Education, Inc.
Duplication for classroom use is permitted.

Name _____

Date _____

Match the question and the correct answer.

_____ 1. Do you understand the full Oath of Allegiance to the United States?

a. Yes. I am willing to serve in the U.S. military and use a weapon.

_____ 2. If the law requires it, are you willing to bear arms on behalf of the United States?

b. Yes. I am ready to promise to be loyal only to the United States, to support the Constitution and U.S. laws, and to fight or work for the United States if needed.

_____ 3. Do you support the Constitution and form of government of the United States?

c. Yes. I understand that I promise to be loyal only to the United States, to support the Constitution and U.S. laws, and to fight or work for the United States if needed.

_____ 4. Are you willing to take the full Oath of Allegiance to the United States?

d. Yes. I am willing to serve in the U.S. military and not use a weapon.

_____ 5. If the law requires it, are you willing to perform work of national importance under civilian direction?

e. Yes. I believe in the Constitution as the supreme law of the land, and I believe in our form of government.

_____ 6. If the law requires it, are you willing to perform noncombatant services in the U.S. Armed Forces?

f. Yes. I am willing to do work to help my community, my state, or the country during an emergency.

© 2010 Pearson Education, Inc.
Duplication for classroom use is permitted.

Voices *of* FREEDOM
Interview Practice 46: Matching

Name _____

Date _____

Match the picture and the correct question. Then answer the question with your own information.

_____ 1.

a. If the law requires it, are you willing to perform noncombatant services in the U.S. Armed Forces?

_____ 2.

b. Do you support the Constitution and form of government of the United States?

_____ 3

c. If the law requires it, are you willing to perform work of national importance under civilian direction?

_____ 4.

d. Are you willing to take the full Oath of Allegiance to the United States?

_____ 5.

e. If the law requires it, are you willing to bear arms on behalf of the United States?

© 2010 Pearson Education, Inc.
Duplication for classroom use is permitted.

Voices of Freedom

WORKSHEETS ANSWER KEY

READING PRACTICE

Unit A

B.
1. is
2. first
3. be
4. for
5. United States
6. state
7. is
8. first
9. of
10. citizen

Unit B

B.
1. name
2. city
3. state
4. country
5. citizens
6. first
7. are
8. is
9. country
10. citizens

Unit 1

B.
1. south
2. capital
3. largest
4. has
5. the
6. people
7. of
8. is
9. state
10. north

Unit 2

B.
1. flag
2. states
3. largest
4. capital
5. people
6. is
7. American
8. have
9. state
10. United States

Unit 3

B.
1. United States
2. Senators
3. President
4. White House
5. capital
6. lives
7. meet
8. Washington, D.C.
9. the
10. of

Unit 4

B.
1. United States
2. vote
3. Senators
4. citizens
5. elects
6. vote
7. people
8. Congress
9. elects
10. the

Unit 5

B.
1. people
2. President
3. elects
4. one
5. votes
6. votes
7. Congress
8. citizens
9. White House
10. in, of

Unit 6

B.
1. Thanksgiving
2. people
3. first
4. is
5. come
6. was
7. come
8. lived
9. Columbus Day
10. want

Unit 7

B.
1. is
2. President
3. right
4. George Washington
5. United States
6. President
7. was
8. Independence Day
9. have
10. capital

Unit 8

B.
1. was
2. United States
3. first
4. Father of Our Country
5. state
6. President
7. city
8. George Washington
9. dollar bill
10. capital

Unit 9

B.
1. is
2. right
3. President
4. state
5. vote
6. largest
7. have
8. Presidents' Day
9. citizen
10. Abraham Lincoln

Unit 10

B.
1. is
2. come
3. citizens
4. right
5. vote
6. people
7. vote
8. Name
9. Labor Day
10. United States

© 2010 Pearson Education, Inc.
Duplication for classroom use is permitted.

Unit 11

B. 1. is
2. Memorial
3. Labor Day
4. President
5. lives
6. is
7. Independence
8. Presidents' Day
9. of
10. Washington

Unit 12

B. 1. vote
2. citizens
3. President
4. right
5. pay
6. elect
7. can
8. taxes
9. vote
10. have

CIVICS PRACTICE

Unit 1

A. 1. e
2. h
3. a
4. f
5. g
6. c
7. b
8. d

B. 1. b
2. d
3. a
4. c

Unit 2

A. 1. b
2. c
3. d
4. a

B. 1. flag
2. United States
3. to
4. for
5. one
6. and

Unit 3

A. 1. c
2. a
3. b

B. 1. legislative
2. judicial
3. executive
4. checks
5. President

C. 1. b
2. c
3. a

Unit 4

A. 1. e
2. a
3. d
4. f
5. c
6. b

B. 1. d
2. f
3. b
4. e
5. a
6. c

C. 1. 435
2. 2
3. 4
4. 100
5. 6

Unit 5

1. e
2. i
3. a
4. l
5. g
6. c
7. j
8. d
9. b
10. k
11. f
12. h

Unit 6

A. 1. d
2. c
3. e
4. b
5. a

B. 1. c
2. a
3. b

C. 1. b
2. c
3. a

D. 1. d
2. a
3. b
4. c

Unit 7

A. 1. b
2. f
3. d
4. c
5. e
6. a

B. 1. d
2. c
3. b
4. e
5. a

Unit 8

1. d
2. g
3. b
4. l
5. i
6. c
7. k
8. e
9. a
10. h
11. f
12. j

© 2010 Pearson Education, Inc.
Duplication for classroom use is permitted.

Unit 9

1. h
2. n
3. b
4. l
5. f
6. k
7. a
8. m
9. c
10. g
11. e
12. i
13. d
14. j

Unit 10

A.
1. f
2. d
3. b
4. a
5. e
6. c

B.
1. c
2. a
3. e
4. b
5. d

Unit 11

1. d
2. i
3. m
4. k
5. a
6. j
7. c
8. b
9. l
10. f
11. e
12. h
13. g

Unit 12

A.
1. d
2. e
3. a
4. f
5. c
6. b

B.
1. c
2. a
3. d
4. e
5. b

INTERVIEW PRACTICE

Interview Practice 2

1. b
2. d
3. e
4. a
5. f
6. c

Interview Practice 4

1. e
2. d
3. a
4. f
5. c
6. b

Interview Practice 6

1. e
2. c
3. a
4. b
5. d

Interview Practice 8

1. c
2. e
3. a
4. f
5. d
6. b

Interview Practice 10

1. b
2. d
3. f
4. a
5. c
6. e

Interview Practice 12

1. c
2. f
3. b
4. e
5. a
6. d

Interview Practice 14

1. d
2. a
3. e
4. c
5. b

Interview Practice 16

1. d
2. a
3. e
4. b
5. f
6. c

Interview Practice 18

1. e
2. c
3. a
4. b
5. d

Interview Practice 20

1. c
2. a
3. d
4. b

Interview Practice 21

1. g
2. b
3. c
4. e
5. d
6. a
7. f

© 2010 Pearson Education, Inc.
Duplication for classroom use is permitted.

Interview Practice 22

1. g
2. e
3. h
4. b
5. c
6. d
7. a
8. f

Interview Practice 24

1. e
2. a
3. f
4. b
5. d
6. c

Interview Practice 25

1. d
2. e
3. b
4. a
5. c
6. f

Interview Practice 27

1. e
2. d
3. a
4. f
5. b
6. c

Interview Practice 28

1. f
2. d
3. a
4. c
5. e
6. b

Interview Practice 30

1. d
2. f
3. a
4. e
5. c
6. b

Interview Practice 31

1. c
2. f
3. a
4. e
5. b
6. d

Interview Practice 33

1. e
2. d
3. a
4. f
5. c
6. b

Interview Practice 34

1. b
2. e
3. a
4. c
5. f
6. d

Interview Practice 36

1. c
2. e
3. a
4. f
5. b
6. d

Interview Practice 37

1. d
2. c
3. a
4. f
5. b
6. e

Interview Practice 39

1. c
2. e
3. a
4. b
5. d

Interview Practice 40

1. c
2. e
3. a
4. b
5. d

Interview Practice 42

1. d
2. c
3. a
4. e
5. b

Interview Practice 43

1. b
2. e
3. d
4. a
5. c

Interview Practice 45

1. c
2. a
3. e
4. b
5. f
6. d

Interview Practice 46

1. e
2. d
3. a
4. b
5. c

© 2010 Pearson Education, Inc.
Duplication for classroom use is permitted.

Voices of Freedom
TEACHER'S RESOURCES

Needs Assessment—Pictorial Version	285
Needs Assessment—Checklist Version	287
Pre/Post Assessment Form A	289
Pre/Post Assessment Form B	291
Pre/Post Assessment Answer Key	293
Student Name List Mask	295
Project Activity Observation Checklist	296
Performance-Based Assessment Records	297
Technology Enrichment: Websites for Internet Activities	311

The resources in this section are designed as tools for effective instruction, assessment, and documentation of student progress. These materials may be reproduced for classroom use only in conjunction with the *Voices of Freedom* instructional program.

NEEDS ASSESSMENT

The two Needs Assessment forms are designed to help programs and teachers gather input from students about their needs and interests in order to guide the development of instruction. A Pictorial Version provides a simple illustrated format for low-beginning-level students. Students can check the pictures and draw their own to indicate their curriculum preferences. A Checklist Version offers a more detailed list of topics for high-beginning-level and intermediate-level students with some reading ability.

PRE/POST ASSESSMENT

The two Pre/Post Assessments can be used to evaluate students' prior knowledge and skills before instruction as well as to assess their achievement of learning objectives and readiness for the USCIS exam at the end of the course. In each assessment, Part A contains sixteen of the 100 official USCIS civics questions. Part B contains questions about the student's Form N-400 information that typically occur during the USCIS interview and serve as the basis for the officer's evaluation of English verbal skills. If time and resources allow for one-to-one administration of the assessment, evaluate each student individually as the student answers the questions in Parts A and B orally. Alternatively, students can write answers to the questions. Part C requires a brief one-to-one administration to evaluate the student's ability to read the sentences aloud. Part D can be a whole-class dictation.

Each test question is worth four points. Score each question according to the following guidelines:

Civics Questions: Score as correct each answer that is acceptable according to the official USCIS civics questions and answers. (An Answer Key is provided.)

Interview Questions: Score as correct each answer that is a meaningful response to the question that may occur during the USCIS interview.

Reading: Score as correct each sentence the student reads without extended pauses and without pronunciation or intonation errors that would interfere with meaning. Score as incorrect any sentence the student does not read, or if the student omits or substitutes a content word, pauses for extended periods of time, or makes pronunciation or intonation errors that interfere with meaning.

Writing: Score as correct each sentence the student writes completely with only minor errors that wouldn't interfere with meaning, such as grammar, spelling, punctuation, or capitalization errors or the omission of short function words. Score as incorrect any sentence the student does not write, or if the student omits a content word, writes illegibly, writes a different sentence or word, or does not communicate the meaning of the dictated sentence.

(Note: To assure that students are prepared for the USCIS reading and writing tests, you may want to score the reading and writing portions of these pre/post assessments more strictly and only give students credit for answers that are complete and error-free. Analyze students' errors in order to plan lessons that focus on the particular reading and writing skills that students need to improve.)

PERFORMANCE-BASED ASSESSMENT RECORDS

Performance-Based Assessment Records are tools for evaluating and documenting student participation and performance in each unit's Civics Enrichment activities, which are designed to promote students' active participation in class and in the civic life of the community. Scoring rubrics guide the alternative assessment of these projects, issues discussions, community tasks, field trips, and Internet activities.

The Student Name List Mask provides a convenient way to make a list of students' names and then affix it to each of the Assessment Record forms.

The Project Activity Observation Checklist provides an assessment tool for evaluating students as they participate in all phases of a project and develop skills in leadership, teamwork, and communicating information—key workplace skills identified by the Secretary's Commission on Achieving Necessary Skills (SCANS).

TECHNOLOGY ENRICHMENT

A Technology Enrichment section provides a list of websites for additional Internet activities that expand upon the topics in each unit.

Student's Name _____	I.D. Number _____
Course _____ Teacher _____	Date _____

I want to use English at the _____.

___ bank

___ bus station

___ clinic

___ clothing store

___ drug store

___ library

___ post office

___ shopping mall

___ supermarket

_____

_____

_____

© 2010 Pearson Education, Inc.
Duplication for classroom use is permitted.

Student's Name _____

I want to learn English to _____.

___ talk with people

___ find an apartment

___ get a job

___ read English books

___ read the newspaper

___ write in English

___ use money

___ use a computer

_____

- -

I want to learn about _____.

___ the government of
the United States

___ the history of
the United States

_____

© 2010 Pearson Education, Inc.
Duplication for classroom use is permitted.

Student's Name _____ I.D. Number _____

Course _____ Teacher _____ Date _____

I want to use English at the _____.

____ bank

____ supermarket

____ post office

____ library

____ bus or train station

____ clothing store

____ department store

____ shopping mall

____ clinic

____ drug store

____ hospital

____ USCIS office

____ social security office

____ welfare office

____ _____

____ _____

- -

I want to learn English to _____.

____ talk to my neighbors

____ talk to people at my children's school

____ talk to people at my church/temple/ mosque

____ talk to my building manager

____ talk to the police

____ use the telephone

____ report emergencies (call 911)

____ become a citizen

____ use money

____ find an apartment

____ get job training

____ get a job

____ get a better job

____ use a computer

____ use a checkbook

____ get a loan

____ get a driver's license

____ report housing repair problems

____ use local government services

____ understand and speak at school meetings

____ understand and speak at local government meetings

____ _____

- -

I want to learn to read _____ in English.

____ books

____ newspapers

____ magazines

____ advertisements (ads)

____ safety signs

____ road signs

____ bills

____ labels

____ schedules

____ maps

____ letters from school

____ report cards from school

____ stories to my children

____ the driver's manual

____ want ads

____ business letters

____ pay checks and pay stubs

____ E-mail

____ online information (on the Internet)

____ warranties (guarantees) on things I buy

____ insurance policies

____ contracts and rental agreements/leases

____ _____

____ _____

© 2010 Pearson Education, Inc.
Duplication for classroom use is permitted.

Student's Name _____

I want to learn to write in English to _____.

____ fill out forms

____ write letters

____ write E-mail messages

____ write notes to my children's teachers

____ pay taxes

____ _____

____ _____

____ _____

I want to learn about _____.

____ the government of the United States

____ the history of the United States

____ holidays in the United States

____ culture and attitudes in the United States

____ career options

____ education options

____ _____

____ _____

I want to talk about and solve problems about _____.

____ my neighborhood

____ transportation

____ crime

____ alcohol or drugs

____ domestic violence

____ children or teenagers

____ discrimination/prejudice

____ my workplace/job

____ housing

____ _____

____ _____

____ _____

What else do you want to learn?

_____

_____

_____

_____

_____

_____

_____

_____

Voices of Freedom

Student's Name _____ I.D. Number _____

Course _____ Teacher _____ Date _____

A. CIVICS QUESTIONS

1. What is the supreme law of the land?

   _____

2. What did the Declaration of Independence do?

   _____

3. What are the two parts of the U.S. Congress?

   _____

4. What are two Cabinet-level positions?

   _____

5. The House of Representatives has how many voting members?

   _____

6. We elect a U.S. Representative for how many years?

   _____

7. Under our Constitution, some powers belong to the federal government. What is one power of the federal government?

   _____

8. What are two ways that Americans can participate in their democracy?

   _____

9. When must all men register for the Selective Service?

   _____

10. Why did the colonists fight the British?

    _____

11. What is one thing Benjamin Franklin is famous for?

    _____

12. Name one problem that led to the Civil War.

    _____

© 2010 Pearson Education, Inc.
Duplication for classroom use is permitted.

13. Who was President during the Great Depression and World War II?

_____

14. During the Cold War, what was the main concern of the United States?

_____

15. Name one state that borders Canada.

_____

16. Why does the flag have fifty stars?

_____

B. INTERVIEW QUESTIONS

Answer the questions.

1. How long have you been a lawful permanent resident?

_____

2. What's your marital status?

_____

3. When was your most recent trip outside the United States? How long were you away?

_____

C. READING

Say the questions.

1. What is the capital of the United States?

2. What city in the United States has the most people?

3. What is one right in the Bill of Rights?

D. WRITING

Listen and write the sentence you hear.

1. _____

2. _____

3. _____

Score: _____ correct x **4** points = _____

© 2010 Pearson Education, Inc.
Duplication for classroom use is permitted.

Voices of Freedom

Student's Name _____	I.D. Number _____
Course _____ Teacher _____	Date _____

A. CIVICS QUESTIONS

1. What do we call the first ten amendments to the Constitution?

   _____

2. What are two rights in the Declaration of Independence?

   _____

3. What does the judicial branch do?

   _____

4. What are two Cabinet-level positions?

   _____

5. How many U.S. Senators are there?

   _____

6. We elect a U.S. Senator for how many years?

   _____

7. Under our Constitution, some powers belong to the states. What is one power of the states?

   _____

8. What is one promise you make when you become a United States citizen?

   _____

9. When is the last day you can send in federal tax forms?

   _____

10. What is one reason colonists came to America?

    _____

11. The Federalist Papers supported the passage of the U.S. Constitution. Name one of the writers.

    _____

12. What territory did the United States buy from France in 1803?

    _____

© 2010 Pearson Education, Inc.
Duplication for classroom use is permitted.

13. Who was President during World War I?

    _____

14. Who did the United States fight in World War II?

    _____

15. Name one U.S. territory.

    _____

16. Why does the flag have 13 stripes?

    _____

B. INTERVIEW QUESTIONS

Answer the questions.

1. When did you become a permanent resident?

   _____

2. Are you currently employed? What's your position?

   _____

3. When was the last time you left the United States? Where did you travel?
   What was the reason for the trip?

   _____

C. READING

Say the questions.

1. What country is south of the United States?
2. When do people in the United States vote for Senators?
3. Who was the first President of the United States?

D. WRITING

Listen and write the sentence you hear.

1. _____

2. _____

3. _____

Score: _____ correct x **4** points = _____

© 2010 Pearson Education, Inc.
Duplication for classroom use is permitted.

Voices of Freedom
PRE/POST ASSESSMENT FORM A ANSWER KEY

A. CIVICS QUESTIONS

1. The Constitution
2. It announced our independence (from Great Britain). / It declared our independence (from Great Britain). / It said that the United States is free (from Great Britain).
3. The Senate and House (of Representatives)
4. Two of the following: Secretary of Agriculture / Secretary of Commerce / Secretary of Defense / Secretary of Education / Secretary of Energy / Secretary of Health and Human Services / Secretary of Homeland Security / Secretary of Housing and Urban Development / Secretary of the Interior / Secretary of Labor / Secretary of State / Secretary of Transportation / Secretary of the Treasury / Secretary of Veterans Affairs / Attorney General / Vice President
5. Four hundred thirty-five (435)
6. Two (2)
7. To print money / To declare war / To create an army / To make treaties
8. Two of the following: Vote. / Join a political party. / Help with a campaign. / Join a civic group. / Join a community group. / Give an elected official your opinion on an issue. / Call Senators and Representatives. / Publicly support or oppose an issue or policy. / Run for office. / Write to a newspaper.
9. At age eighteen (18) / Between eighteen (18) and twenty-six (26)
10. Because of high taxes (taxation without representation) / Because the British army stayed in their houses (boarding, quartering) / Because they didn't have self-government
11. U.S. diplomat / Oldest member of the Constitutional Convention / First Postmaster General of the United States / Writer of "Poor Richard's Almanack" / Started the first free libraries
12. Slavery / Economic reasons / States' rights
13. (Franklin) Roosevelt
14. Communism
15. Maine / New Hampshire / Vermont / New York / North Dakota / Pennsylvania / Ohio / Michigan / Minnesota / Montana / Idaho / Washington / Alaska
16. Because there is one star for each state / Because each star represents a state / Because there are 50 states

B. INTERVIEW QUESTIONS

Answers will vary.

C. READING

Students read the sentences aloud.

D. WRITING

Read each sentence twice and have students write what they hear.
1. Washington, D.C. is the capital of the United States.
2. Independence Day is in July.
3. Abraham Lincoln was the President during the Civil War.

© 2010 Pearson Education, Inc.
Duplication for classroom use is permitted.

Voices of Freedom
PRE/POST ASSESSMENT FORM B ANSWER KEY

A. CIVICS QUESTIONS

1. The Bill of Rights
2. Two of the following: Life / Liberty / The pursuit of happiness
3. Reviews laws / Explains laws / Resolves disputes (disagreements) / Decides if a law goes against the Constitution
4. Two of the following: Secretary of Agriculture / Secretary of Commerce / Secretary of Defense / Secretary of Education / Secretary of Energy / Secretary of Health and Human Services / Secretary of Homeland Security / Secretary of Housing and Urban Development / Secretary of the Interior / Secretary of Labor / Secretary of State / Secretary of Transportation / Secretary of the Treasury / Secretary of Veterans Affairs / Attorney General / Vice President
5. One hundred (100)
6. Six (6)
7. Provide schooling and education / Provide protection (police) / Provide safety (fire departments) / Give a driver's license / Approve zoning and land use
8. Give up loyalty to other countries / Defend the Constitution and laws of the United States / Obey the laws of the United States / Serve in the U.S. military (if needed) / Serve (do important work for) the nation (if needed) / Be loyal to the United States
9. April 15
10. Freedom / Political liberty / Religious freedom / Economic opportunity / Practice their religion / Escape persecution
11. (James) Madison / (Alexander) Hamilton / (John) Jay / Publius
12. The Louisiana Territory / Louisiana
13. (Woodrow) Wilson
14. Japan, Germany, and Italy
15. Puerto Rico / U.S. Virgin Islands / American Samoa / Northern Mariana Islands / Guam
16. Because there were 13 original colonies / Because the stripes represent the original colonies

B. INTERVIEW QUESTIONS

Answers will vary.

C. READING

Students read the sentences aloud.

D. WRITING

Read each sentence twice and have students write what they hear.

1. Washington was the Father of Our Country.
2. Memorial Day is in May.
3. People in the United States have freedom of speech.

© 2010 Pearson Education, Inc.
Duplication for classroom use is permitted.

Student Name
1.
2.
3.
4.
5.
6.
7.
8.
9.
10.
11.
12.
13.
14.
15.
16.
17.
18.
19.
20.

Instructions: Fill in student names on the list mask and affix to Assessment Record sheets.

© 2010 Pearson Education, Inc.
Duplication for classroom use is permitted.

Project Activity Observation Checklist Activity _____ Date _____

Student Name	Identifying/ Assigning Tasks	Accomplishing Assigned Task(s)	Leadership	Teamwork	Quality of Final Product	TOTAL SCORE
1.						
2.						
3.						
4.						
5.						
6.						
7.						
8.						
9.						
10.						
11.						
12.						
13.						
14.						
15.						
16.						
17.						
18.						
19.						
20.						

Scoring Rubrics:

Voices of Freedom project activities build students' skills in leadership, teamwork, and communicating information—key workplace skills identified by the Secretary's Commission on Achieving Necessary Skills (SCANS). Students should take responsibility for all aspects of the project. Have them identify the particular tasks involved in the project, assign the tasks to different students, gather needed resources, work as a team, and complete the finished product. Use this Project Activity Observation Checklist to evaluate students as you observe them participating in all phases of the project.

Score **1** (Satisfactory) or **0** (Unsatisfactory) for each student's performance in each of the following: Identifying/Assigning Tasks; Accomplishing Assigned Task(s); Leadership; Teamwork; Quality of Final Product.

© 2010 Pearson Education, Inc.
Duplication for classroom use is permitted.

Voices of Freedom
Unit A

Student Name	Civic Participation	Project	Community Issues
1.			
2.			
3.			
4.			
5.			
6.			
7.			
8.			
9.			
10.			
11.			
12.			
13.			
14.			
15.			
16.			
17.			
18.			
19.			
20.			

Scoring Rubrics:

CIVIC PARTICIPATION Score the student's participation in the discussion:
   5 (Excellent), 4 (Good), 3 (Fair), 2 (Poor), or 1 (Unsatisfactory)

PROJECT Score 1 (Satisfactory) or 0 (Unsatisfactory) for the student's performance in each of the following:
   Identifying/Assigning Tasks; Accomplishing Assigned Task(s); Leadership; Teamwork; Quality of Final Product.
   (The Project Activity Observation Checklist can be used for scoring this activity.)

COMMUNITY ISSUES Score the student's participation in the discussion:
   5 (Excellent), 4 (Good), 3 (Fair), 2 (Poor), or 1 (Unsatisfactory)

© 2010 Pearson Education, Inc.
Duplication for classroom use is permitted.

VOICES of FREEDOM
Unit B

Performance-Based Assessment Record

Student Name	Civic Participation	Bulletin Brd. Project	Calendar Project
1.			
2.			
3.			
4.			
5.			
6.			
7.			
8.			
9.			
10.			
11.			
12.			
13.			
14.			
15.			
16.			
17.			
18.			
19.			
20.			

Scoring Rubrics:

CIVIC PARTICIPATION Score the student's participation in the activity as the class circulates around the school and students introduce themselves to school personnel: **5** (Excellent), **4** (Good), **3** (Fair), **2** (Poor), or **1** (Unsatisfactory)

BULLETIN BOARD PROJECT Score **1** (Satisfactory) or **0** (Unsatisfactory) for the student's performance in each of the following: Identifying/Assigning Tasks; Accomplishing Assigned Task(s); Leadership; Teamwork; Quality of Final Product. (The Project Activity Observation Checklist can be used for scoring this activity.)

CALENDAR PROJECT Score **1** (Satisfactory) or **0** (Unsatisfactory) for the student's performance in each of the following: Identifying/Assigning Tasks; Accomplishing Assigned Task(s); Leadership; Teamwork; Quality of Final Product. (The Project Activity Observation Checklist can be used for scoring this activity.)

© 2010 Pearson Education, Inc.
Duplication for classroom use is permitted.

Student Name	Civic Participation	Project	Internet Activity
1.			
2.			
3.			
4.			
5.			
6.			
7.			
8.			
9.			
10.			
11.			
12.			
13.			
14.			
15.			
16.			
17.			
18.			
19.			
20.			

Scoring Rubrics:

CIVIC PARTICIPATION Score the student's participation in the map activity:
   5 (Excellent), **4** (Good), **3** (Fair), **2** (Poor), or **1** (Unsatisfactory)

PROJECT Score **1** (Satisfactory) or **0** (Unsatisfactory) for the student's performance in each of the following:
   Identifying/Assigning Tasks; Accomplishing Assigned Task(s); Leadership; Teamwork; Quality of Final Product.
   (The Project Activity Observation Checklist can be used for scoring this activity.)

INTERNET ACTIVITY Score the student's ability to access and navigate the website and the student's ability to answer
   the questions correctly:
   5 (Excellent), **4** (Good), **3** (Fair), **2** (Poor), or **1** (Unsatisfactory)

© 2010 Pearson Education, Inc.
Duplication for classroom use is permitted.

Student Name	Civic Participation	Project	Internet Activity
1.			
2.			
3.			
4.			
5.			
6.			
7.			
8.			
9.			
10.			
11.			
12.			
13.			
14.			
15.			
16.			
17.			
18.			
19.			
20.			

Scoring Rubrics:

CIVIC PARTICIPATION Score the student's participation in the discussion:
   5 (Excellent), **4** (Good), **3** (Fair), **2** (Poor), or **1** (Unsatisfactory)

PROJECT Score **1** (Satisfactory) or **0** (Unsatisfactory) for the student's performance in each of the following:
   Identifying/Assigning Tasks; Accomplishing Assigned Task(s); Leadership; Teamwork; Quality of Final Product.
   (The Project Activity Observation Checklist can be used for scoring this activity.)

INTERNET ACTIVITY Score the student's ability to access and navigate the search engine and the student's ability
   to answer the questions correctly:
   5 (Excellent), **4** (Good), **3** (Fair), **2** (Poor), or **1** (Unsatisfactory)

© 2010 Pearson Education, Inc.
Duplication for classroom use is permitted.

Voices of Freedom
Unit 3

Student Name	Civic Participation	Community Issues	Internet Activity
1.			
2.			
3.			
4.			
5.			
6.			
7.			
8.			
9.			
10.			
11.			
12.			
13.			
14.			
15.			
16.			
17.			
18.			
19.			
20.			

Scoring Rubrics:

CIVIC PARTICIPATION Score the student's participation in the conversation practice in preparation for the field trip:
5 (Excellent), 4 (Good), 3 (Fair), 2 (Poor), or 1 (Unsatisfactory)

COMMUNITY ISSUES Score the student's participation in the discussion:
5 (Excellent), 4 (Good), 3 (Fair), 2 (Poor), or 1 (Unsatisfactory)

INTERNET ACTIVITY Score the student's ability to access and navigate the website and to describe the kind of information it has:
5 (Excellent), 4 (Good), 3 (Fair), 2 (Poor), or 1 (Unsatisfactory)

© 2010 Pearson Education, Inc.
Duplication for classroom use is permitted.

Student Name	Civic Participation	Internet Activity 1	Internet Activity 2
1.			
2.			
3.			
4.			
5.			
6.			
7.			
8.			
9.			
10.			
11.			
12.			
13.			
14.			
15.			
16.			
17.			
18.			
19.			
20.			

Scoring Rubrics:

CIVIC PARTICIPATION Score the student's participation during the visit with the U.S. representative:
  5 (Excellent), **4** (Good), **3** (Fair), **2** (Poor), or **1** (Unsatisfactory)

INTERNET ACTIVITY 1 Score the student's ability to access and navigate the website and to describe the information provided about the U.S. Capitol:
  5 (Excellent), **4** (Good), **3** (Fair), **2** (Poor), or **1** (Unsatisfactory)

INTERNET ACTIVITY 2 Score the student's ability to access and navigate the website and to describe the information provided about the President, the Vice President, and the Cabinet:
  5 (Excellent), **4** (Good), **3** (Fair), **2** (Poor), or **1** (Unsatisfactory)

© 2010 Pearson Education, Inc.
Duplication for classroom use is permitted.

Voices of Freedom
Unit 5

Performance-Based Assessment Record

Student Name	Civic Participation	Project	Internet Activity
1.			
2.			
3.			
4.			
5.			
6.			
7.			
8.			
9.			
10.			
11.			
12.			
13.			
14.			
15.			
16.			
17.			
18.			
19.			
20.			

Scoring Rubrics:

CIVIC PARTICIPATION Score the student's participation during the field trip:
5 (Excellent), 4 (Good), 3 (Fair), 2 (Poor), or 1 (Unsatisfactory)

PROJECT Score 1 (Satisfactory) or 0 (Unsatisfactory) for the student's performance in each of the following:
Identifying/Assigning Tasks; Accomplishing Assigned Task(s); Leadership; Teamwork; Quality of Final Product.
(The Project Activity Observation Checklist can be used for scoring this activity.)

INTERNET ACTIVITY Score the student's ability to access and navigate the state's official website and the student's ability to describe the information provided:
5 (Excellent), 4 (Good), 3 (Fair), 2 (Poor), or 1 (Unsatisfactory)

© 2010 Pearson Education, Inc.
Duplication for classroom use is permitted.

Voices of Freedom
Unit 6

Student Name	Civic Participation	Project	Internet Activity
1.			
2.			
3.			
4.			
5.			
6.			
7.			
8.			
9.			
10.			
11.			
12.			
13.			
14.			
15.			
16.			
17.			
18.			
19.			
20.			

Scoring Rubrics:

CIVIC PARTICIPATION Score the student's participation during the field trip:
5 (Excellent), 4 (Good), 3 (Fair), 2 (Poor), or 1 (Unsatisfactory)

PROJECT Score 1 (Satisfactory) or 0 (Unsatisfactory) for the student's performance in each of the following: Identifying/Assigning Tasks; Accomplishing Assigned Task(s); Leadership; Teamwork; Ability to Share Recipe Instructions with the class. (The Project Activity Observation Checklist can be used for scoring this activity.)

INTERNET ACTIVITY Score the student's ability to access and navigate the website and to describe the information provided about Plimoth Plantation:
5 (Excellent), 4 (Good), 3 (Fair), 2 (Poor), or 1 (Unsatisfactory)

© 2010 Pearson Education, Inc.
Duplication for classroom use is permitted.

Voices of Freedom

Unit 7

Student Name	Civic Participation	Project	Internet Activity
1.			
2.			
3.			
4.			
5.			
6.			
7.			
8.			
9.			
10.			
11.			
12.			
13.			
14.			
15.			
16.			
17.			
18.			
19.			
20.			

Scoring Rubrics:

CIVIC PARTICIPATION Score the student's participation in gathering the requested information and making the class chart about local government services: **5** (Excellent), **4** (Good), **3** (Fair), **2** (Poor), or **1** (Unsatisfactory)

PROJECT Score **1** (Satisfactory) or **0** (Unsatisfactory) for the student's performance in each of the following: Identifying/Assigning Tasks; Accomplishing Assigned Task(s); Leadership; Teamwork; Quality of Final Product. (The Project Activity Observation Checklist can be used for scoring this activity.)

INTERNET ACTIVITY Score the student's ability to access and navigate the website and to locate and describe the information provided about historic places in Philadelphia: **5** (Excellent), **4** (Good), **3** (Fair), **2** (Poor), or **1** (Unsatisfactory)

© 2010 Pearson Education, Inc.
Duplication for classroom use is permitted.

Performance-Based Assessment Record

Student Name	Civic Participation	Project	Community Issues
1.			
2.			
3.			
4.			
5.			
6.			
7.			
8.			
9.			
10.			
11.			
12.			
13.			
14.			
15.			
16.			
17.			
18.			
19.			
20.			

Scoring Rubrics:

CIVIC PARTICIPATION Score the student's participation in the discussion about rights guaranteed by the 1st Amendment:
   5 (Excellent), **4** (Good), **3** (Fair), **2** (Poor), or **1** (Unsatisfactory)

PROJECT Score **1** (Satisfactory) or **0** (Unsatisfactory) for the student's performance in each of the following:
   Identifying/Assigning Tasks; Accomplishing Assigned Task(s); Leadership; Teamwork; Quality of Final Product.
   (The Project Activity Observation Checklist can be used for scoring this activity.)

COMMUNITY ISSUES Score the student's participation in the discussion:
   5 (Excellent), **4** (Good), **3** (Fair), **2** (Poor), or **1** (Unsatisfactory)

© 2010 Pearson Education, Inc.
Duplication for classroom use is permitted.

Student Name	Civic Participation	Debate Activity	Internet Activity
1.			
2.			
3.			
4.			
5.			
6.			
7.			
8.			
9.			
10.			
11.			
12.			
13.			
14.			
15.			
16.			
17.			
18.			
19.			
20.			

Scoring Rubrics:

CIVIC PARTICIPATION Score the student's participation in the small group activity about amendments to the U.S. Constitution, including the group's presentation to the class about a new amendment:
5 (Excellent), 4 (Good), 3 (Fair), 2 (Poor), or 1 (Unsatisfactory)

DEBATE ACTIVITY Score the student's participation in the debate:
5 (Excellent), 4 (Good), 3 (Fair), 2 (Poor), or 1 (Unsatisfactory)

INTERNET ACTIVITY Score the student's ability to access and navigate the websites and to describe the information provided:
5 (Excellent), 4 (Good), 3 (Fair), 2 (Poor), or 1 (Unsatisfactory)

© 2010 Pearson Education, Inc.
Duplication for classroom use is permitted.

Voices of Freedom

Unit 10

Performance-Based Assessment Record

Student Name	Internet Activity 1	Internet Activity 2	Debate Activity
1.			
2.			
3.			
4.			
5.			
6.			
7.			
8.			
9.			
10.			
11.			
12.			
13.			
14.			
15.			
16.			
17.			
18.			
19.			
20.			

Scoring Rubrics:

INTERNET ACTIVITY 1 Score the student's ability to access and navigate the websites and to describe the information provided about the famous inventors:
5 (Excellent), 4 (Good), 3 (Fair), 2 (Poor), or 1 (Unsatisfactory)

INTERNET ACTIVITY 2 Score the student's ability to access and navigate the website and to describe the information provided about the Ellis Island immigration station:
5 (Excellent), 4 (Good), 3 (Fair), 2 (Poor), or 1 (Unsatisfactory)

DEBATE ACTIVITY Score the student's participation in the debate:
5 (Excellent), 4 (Good), 3 (Fair), 2 (Poor), or 1 (Unsatisfactory)

© 2010 Pearson Education, Inc.
Duplication for classroom use is permitted.

Student Name	Civic Participation	Internet Activity	Biography Project
1.			
2.			
3.			
4.			
5.			
6.			
7.			
8.			
9.			
10.			
11.			
12.			
13.			
14.			
15.			
16.			
17.			
18.			
19.			
20.			

Scoring Rubrics:

CIVIC PARTICIPATION Score the student's participation in the discussion about favorite national holidays:
5 (Excellent), 4 (Good), 3 (Fair), 2 (Poor), or 1 (Unsatisfactory)

INTERNET ACTIVITY Score the student's ability to access and navigate the website and to describe the information provided about the Presidents:
5 (Excellent), 4 (Good), 3 (Fair), 2 (Poor), or 1 (Unsatisfactory)

BIOGRAPHY PROJECT Score the student's short written biography and presentation about a President:
5 (Excellent), 4 (Good), 3 (Fair), 2 (Poor), or 1 (Unsatisfactory)

© 2010 Pearson Education, Inc.
Duplication for classroom use is permitted.

Student Name	Civic Participation	Community Issues	Debate Activity
1.			
2.			
3.			
4.			
5.			
6.			
7.			
8.			
9.			
10.			
11.			
12.			
13.			
14.			
15.			
16.			
17.			
18.			
19.			
20.			

Scoring Rubrics:

CIVIC PARTICIPATION Score the student's participation in the gathering and sharing of information about local elections:
  5 (Excellent), **4** (Good), **3** (Fair), **2** (Poor), or **1** (Unsatisfactory)

COMMUNITY ISSUES Score the student's participation in the discussion:
  5 (Excellent), **4** (Good), **3** (Fair), **2** (Poor), or **1** (Unsatisfactory)

DEBATE ACTIVITY Score the student's participation in the debate:
  5 (Excellent), **4** (Good), **3** (Fair), **2** (Poor), or **1** (Unsatisfactory)

© 2010 Pearson Education, Inc.
Duplication for classroom use is permitted.

TECHNOLOGY ENRICHMENT: Websites for Internet Activities

Links to these websites are provided at: http://www.pearsonlongman.com/ae/voices_of_freedom/index.html

UNIT 1

http://www.sheppardsoftware.com/web_games.htm
This website offers a variety of U.S. geography games about states, state capitals, postal abbreviations for states, and geographic regions.

http://kids.niehs.nih.gov/lyrics/america.htm
This website offers the lyrics and music of *America the Beautiful*. Students can read the lyrics and sing along.

http://bensguide.gpo.gov/3-5/index.html
Click on "Our Nation" for geographic facts about the United States. Click on "Symbols of U.S. Government" for information about U.S. landmarks. Click on "Games and Activities," then click on "Interactive Games," then select "Place the State" for an entertaining game in which students drag states or state names to complete a map of the United States.

UNIT 2

http://www.ushistory.org/betsy/index.html
The Betsy Ross Homepage gives information about the woman who sewed the first American flag. It also gives instructions on how to display the flag, and it includes drawings to show how the flag appeared at different times in U.S. history. You can use this website to create an online scavenger hunt for students. Browse the site, find pieces of information in different locations, and write a list of questions for students to answer by locating the information.

http://www.ushistory.org/documents/pledge.htm
Students can read the words to the original Pledge of Allegiance written by Francis Bellamy in 1892, and they can learn about the changes to the Pledge of Allegiance over the years.

http://www.link4u.com/pledge.htm
This presentation in words and music describes the meaning of the Pledge of Allegiance.

UNIT 3

http://www.senate.gov/
Students can visit their state senators online at this official website of the U.S. Senate. (Students visit their representative's website in the Civics Enrichment activity on text page 56.) Have students describe the information they find.

UNIT 4

http://bensguide.gpo.gov/3-5/index.html
Click on "How Laws Are Made" for easy-to-read lessons about how national laws are written and voted on in the U.S. Congress.

http://www.supremecourtus.gov/about/photos.html
The official website of the U.S. Supreme Court includes photographs of the Supreme Court building. Ask students the following questions, which they can answer by locating information at this website: What are the names of the two statues at the entrance of the Supreme Court building? Where do the Supreme Court justices meet to discuss cases? Where did the Supreme Court sit (meet) from 1860 to 1935?

UNIT 5

http://bensguide.gpo.gov/3-5/index.html
Have students click on "National versus State Government" for information about the division of powers between the national and state governments.

UNIT 6

http://www.historyisfun.org/jyf1/js.html
This website describes the Jamestown Settlement in Virginia, which is featured on page 105. Ask students the following questions, which they can answer by locating information at this website: What was the name of the native people who lived there? What were the names of the three ships that the colonists sailed to Jamestown? How many colonists arrived on those ships in 1607?

http://www.thanksgivingrecipe.com/default.asp
This website provides Thanksgiving recipes. Have students browse the site, choose interesting recipes, and perhaps prepare them for the classroom Thanksgiving celebration suggested on page 108.

UNIT 7

http://chnm.gmu.edu/declaration/
This website provides translations of the Declaration of Independence in Spanish and several other languages. Students can read the document in the native language in order to better understand its meaning and significance in the history of the United States.

UNIT 8

http://www.archives.gov/exhibits/charters/constitution_transcript.html
This website offers the complete transcript of the U.S. Constitution. Have students notice how the Constitution is organized into articles and sections. Ask them why the following articles and sections are important:

    Article 1 Section 2 (established the House of Representatives)
    Article 1 Section 3 (established the Senate)
    Article 2 Section 1 (established the office of President)
    Article 3 Section 1 (established the Supreme Court)

http://www.infoplease.com/states.html
This website features information about each state, including the state capital, population, history, flag, economy, and places of interest. Students can use the information as they complete their report on one of the states—the social studies enrichment activity on page 129.

http://www.fi.edu/franklin/index.html
This website of the Franklin Institute in Philadelphia offers a brief biography of Benjamin Franklin and links to descriptions of his work as an inventor, a statesman, a printer, and his many other roles.

http://www.archives.gov/exhibits/charters/bill_of_rights_transcript.html
This website presents the entire Bill of Rights. Have students work in pairs or groups and try to understand the meaning of the 2nd through 10th amendments. Then discuss these amendments as a class.

UNIT 9

http://www.contemplator.com/america/ssbanner.html
This website offers the lyrics and music of the *Star-Spangled Banner*. Students can read the lyrics and sing along.

http://xroads.virginia.edu/~MAP/terr_hp.html
Maps show the expansion of the United States during the period 1775 to 1920. Students can click on the different years and see how the United States grew through expansion.

http://bensguide.gpo.gov/3-5/documents/gettysburg/index.html
This website offers the complete text of Abraham Lincoln's Gettysburg Address. For enrichment, higher-level students can practice the entire speech and present it to the class.

http://www.nps.gov/liho/index.htm
This National Park Service website offers information about Abraham Lincoln's home in Springfield, Illinois. Students can explore the neighborhood where Lincoln grew up and take a virtual tour of his home.

UNIT 10

http://smithsonianeducation.org/spotlight/inventors1.html
This Smithsonian Institution website provides information about famous American inventors not already covered in Unit 10, including Robert Fulton, Samuel F. B. Morse, and Wilbur Wright. Students can choose any inventor, use the links to go to other sites about the topic, and then report what they learn to the class.

UNIT 11

http://www.whitehouse.gov/history/presidents/
This official White House website provides information about all past presidents of the United States. Students can browse the information, choose a president that interests them, and report about the president to the class.

UNIT 12

http://bensguide.gpo.gov/3-5/index.html
Have students click on "Citizenship" for information about becoming a U.S. citizen and the rights and responsibilities of citizenship.

**San Diego
County Library**

5560 Overland Ave.
Suite 110
San Diego, CA 92123

www.sdcl.org